From Snowdon to the sea : stirring stories of north and south Wales

Marie Trevelyan

FROM SNOWDON TO THE SEA

FROM SNOWDON TO THE SEA

STIRRING STORIES OF
NORTH AND SOUTH WALES

BY

MARIE TREVELYAN

AUTHOR OF

"GLIMPSES OF WELSH LIFE AND CHARACTER," "BRAVE LITTLE WOMEN,"
ETC.

LONDON
JOHN HOGG, 13 PATERNOSTER ROW

Dedicated

BY KIND PERMISSION

TO

THE RIGHT HONOURABLE LORD WINDSOR,

LORD LIEUTENANT OF GLAMORGANSHIRE.

PREFACE

FAIR WALES, the region of thrilling song and witching romance, of gloomy tragedy and quaint comedy, is again my theme, and the English who have had glimpses of my native land and its people are invited to accompany me in spirit to the lofty summit of Snowdon and the solitary *traeth* of the sea.

To the heights of Snowdon, Vortigern retreated after the treachery of the Long Knives, and there Merlin the magician assisted the king to build the wonderful castle, supposed to be impregnable, but ultimately destroyed by the enemy,—after which, in a lonely valley near the sea, the unfortunate monarch was buried in all his bravery of green armour.

Through the passes of Snowdon, Llewellyn, the last native prince of Wales, descended to his doom on the banks of the Irvon ; and, from the rocky fastnesses of the same mountain range, Prince David was dragged to his barbarous death at Rhuddlan.

After privation, loneliness, and cold, Owen Glendower and his men went from the celebrated mountain to meet the troops of King Henry the Fourth, and, later on, retired to the sea cave known as Ogof Owain, where, according to tradition, the great leader of rebellion with his soldiers wait, ready to rush forth at the command of Wales, should an enemy assail the dear old land.

From the crest of Snowdon to the verge of the restless sea waters that wash the Northern, Western, and Southern boundaries of Wales, the Awen or Muse has descended to the sons and daughters of the bards who revered Eryri as the Parnassus of the Principality.

Among the grand and impressive highlands of the North, and the pastoral and beautiful lowlands of the South, the traditions, folk-lore, and romances that are woven into these stories, have been collected.

To itinerant preachers, to the humble and primitive peasantry, to the grand-sire who holds the place of honour in the fireside corner of the settle, and to grand-dames, who, while knitting, croon at eventide over the long ago, I am indebted for the threads that form the warp and woof of my mental weavings, which I hope will aid in bringing England and Wales into still closer communion, under the good old Welsh motto, " Calon Wrth Galon "—" Heart to Heart."

My publisher, Mr. John Hogg, once more entering into the spirit of the Celtic subject, as in the case of my former work, " Glimpses of Welsh Life and Character," suggested a national emblem for the cover design of this book. In preparing the sketch of the arms supplied by the Heralds' College, most valuable assistance has been kindly and courteously rendered by Mr. Everard Green (" Rouge Dragon "), who thus certifies the design :—

" I hereby certify that the arms on the other side are those of Llewellyn, Prince of North Wales, and of Rhys ap Tewdwr, the last King of South Wales, who bore the arms of Howell Dda his ancestor, as did the subsequent Princes of South Wales.

" EVERARD GREEN "

(" Rouge Dragon ").

The shields of Prince Llewellyn and of Rhys

ap Tewdwr, united above the motto of the Bardic Chair of Dyfed (Dimetia), which is also frequently called the Chair of South Wales (Deheubarth), are most appropriate symbols for a volume of stories founded upon Welsh traditions and folk-lore.

MARIE TREVELYAN.

1894.

CONTENTS

The Master of Llantysilio

A STORY OF THE DEE SIDE

IT was a midsummer hush.

Not a sound could be heard save the ceaseless murmuring of the sacred Dee, as it rushed over the Horse Shoe Weir, or the occasional chaunting of missel thrushes in the elm trees fringing the foaming torrent.

The cloudless sky, gleaming like sapphire, was clearly reflected upon the river, where tree-shadows fell brokenly as the sun-kissed waters glided serenely onward to the verge of the Weir.

Noontide splendour filled the beautiful Vale of Llantysilio with golden glory.

Through woven branches and wild rose sprays, the sunlight slanted downward into peaceful pasture lands, where sweet meadow grasses mingled with red and purple clover bloom, and delicate ferns fringed the luxuriant hedge-rows.

13

Blackbirds nestled closely in their leafy retreats, the yellow hammer moved more lazily than usual, water ouzels darted to and fro beside the Dee waters, and water wagtails and linnets vied with each other in idly dipping their heads and wings in the river, then scattering silvery showers like dewdrops on the mossy sward.

So sultry and still was the noontide, that the sheep and cattle were gathered together under the shady trees which here and there were grouped about the fields, while even the ever restless Welsh mountain ponies, known as "merlyns," were obliged to lie down in cool shadows.

Where now the pretty church of Llantysilio stands, an older edifice stood in the latter half of the last century, and, on the site of the modern hall, an ancient residence was then to be found.

The old ivy-covered church crumbling to decay, stood as a monument of the far past, when cowled monk and girdled friar moved leisurely to and fro the beautiful valleys of Wales, and the sound of the Angelus penetrated the narrow ravines or floated like a mystic melody downward with the Dee waters.

The ancient Hall looked grand and stately in the midsummer glow.

Not a shadow flecked the flood of sunshine that filled the mossy lawns and terraces, where the hoary sundial recorded the fleeting hours,

and, above and beyond it, the gilded weather-
vane stood motionless upon the ivy-covered out-
buildings.

In the cool and shady study, looking on to
the terrace, the Master of the Hall was busily
engaged in writing. His swift and impatient pen
hurried over page after page, and, when that work
was completed, he began summing up various
accounts. The occupation of casting and balanc-
ing was by no means congenial to the Squire of
Llantysilio, whose expenditure was always greater
than his income. Presently he dashed his pen
upon the table, leaned back in his comfortable
chair, and began running his fingers through the
heavy masses of his dark hair, where silvery
threads already appeared.

The Squire—or Master, as he was generally
called—of Llantysilio, was a handsome man
above the average height of modern Welshmen.
He was sprightly, somewhat proud, reticent, but
extremely good-natured. In his dark eyes a
fiery light lurked, ready to flash forth lightnings
when matters went wrong, and his keen-cut
mouth curved with scorn when anything affected
his dignity. He was a Welshman of the old
school—a typical gentleman of the period, when
to be deeply in debt was the rule, and to be
fairly sober was the exception.

The Master of Llantysilio was the youngest

survivor of three brothers, all of whom had been brought up by their only half-sister, k. own in her age as Madam.   She was about six.v-eight and the Master was forty-five.   Not one ` the brothers ever married or thought of marriage, and the Master was, to the world of Llantysilio, a bachelor, though it was rumoured that he had a wife and children in England, where he spent most part of the year.

Madam said she was married to Duty, but she believed the Master had "some kind of tie somewhere."   Else how could the money go so *fast? She* had been a "saving woman" all her lifetime, but all her economy failed to bring the Master's expenditure within the limits of his income.

Thoughts like these kept running in her mind, while she replenished the pot-pourri and harvested the lavender on that sultry midsummer morning.

"Is Robin Ddu coming to-morrow?" asked the Master, breaking in on Madam's reverie.

"That is more than I can tell," replied Madam. "Robin is flighty.   If he wills it to come, he will come."

Robert Lloyd, the tailor of Llangollen, was popularly known by the soubriquet of Robin Ddu —pronounced Thé—or Black, because some said he was acquainted with the *black art*.

Even as the Master and Madam were speaking,

Robin Ddu appeared coming up the drive, like a long thin shadow fleeting across the sunshine. He was a tall shadowy man, with a wan and ghost-like face, hollow eyes, hollow cheeks, and high cheek-bones. His whole frame was painfully attenuated, and his long, thin arms and bony hands looked more like angular appendages of a wooden doll than limbs of real flesh and blood.

"The more you do feed him, the thinner he do look," said the farmer folk; and the villagers added, "Robin Ddu is tormented by a ghost."

Strange stories were told about him, all of which were discredited by both the Master and Madam. But country people from Llangollen to Llantysilio declared that the tailor heard unearthly noises, and saw strange sights, and went through gruesome midnight experiences, all of which caused his poor wretched body to waste away, even though, wherever he worked, "the best of food" was put before him.

He was the best tailor "for forty miles round," and it was regarded as quite a favour to be able to obtain Robin Ddu's services. Robin booked engagements twelve months in advance, and, as a rule, regularly as clockwork fulfilled them.

In those days as now, in many parts of Wales, the tailors went from house to house, working for weeks in one family, just as dressmakers in country places do in these times.

B

Robin Ddu was announced, the servant letting him into the morning-room, where the Master and Madam stood beside the harvested lavender.

"Sirr!" said Robin with a strong double r, and bowing respectfully to the Master, "I did think to finish at the parson's to-day, but I kent till to-morrow night, an' if you'd be so kind as to wait till then for me, I shall be thankful. The parson's boys——"

"What have the parson's boys to do with me?" said the Master, impatiently stamping his foot.

"Nothin', sirr—nothin' whatever. But now an' then we *do* like to 'blige a neighbour, an'——"

"Neighbour, indeed!" exclaimed the Master. "The parson's no neighbour of mine! I say you must begin to work here to-morrow morning."

"Why will you be so unreasonable?" remarked Madam. "A day makes little difference to you. I should think to-morrow night, or Thursday morning, would do well enough. You're in no immediate hurry."

"Much you know about it," exclaimed the Master. "Six months ago, Robin promised to begin work on Midsummer Day, and begin on that day he shall!"

"Very good, sirr; very good," said Robin. "I'll put the work by, and come here by eight o'clock to-morrow mornin'."

With that, Robin Ddu bowed himself out of the room, and Madam followed.

"You'll take a crust of bread and cheese and a tankard of *cwrw da,*" said Madam to the tailor.

"Thank you kindly," replied Robin, following Madam to the servants' hall.

"The Master is getting more impatient and irritable than ever," remarked Madam confidentially to Robin, while he took the offered refreshment.

"It's his way, Madam," replied Robin. "'Twas the natur of all the gentlemen of the Hall. There was Master Griffith — he worrited hisself to death."

"Yes ; but he had a cause after Gwen Hughes jilted him."

"Well, Master David was jest the same," added Robin. "He was always a troublin' his mind 'bout somethin' or another."

"*He* was never well," pleaded Madam. "But my brother Owen has no *cause* for impatience and irritability."

"How do we know, Madam ? Perhaps he's got his worries in Llundain (London), or them other places he do go to."

"But what worries or cares can he have there ?" curiously asked Madam.

"How do I know. But they do say," said

Robin, cautiously lowering his voice, "the Master spends a sight o' money in Llundain."

"I think so too," said Madam. "But the extravagance and irritability of Owen, and Griffith, and David come from their mother's side. My mother was most amiable, but——"

"So I've heerd my father tell," interrupted Robin.

"But their mother—my stepmother, you know —was always fretful, though she died when Owen was only a year old."

"I've heerd them say so," said Robin, looking up with a start when the cuckoo clock struck the hour of one.

"How Madam ken talk to Robin Ddu as much as she do, I don't know," commented one servant to another in the butler's pantry.

"I'm afeard of him," said the housemaid.

"An' I wouldn't meet him in the dark for the life of me," added the cook.

Five minutes later Robin Ddu fleeted like a shadow through the sunshine, his attenuated form looking cold and ghost-like even in the splendour of midsummer.

Robin Ddu toiled hard and fast through the burning hours of that afternoon. It was after eight o'clock when he put his work aside and went to his lodgings. He was, as a rule, very reticent, talking freely only to those with whom

he had been thoroughly familiar all his lifetime.
To his few chosen friends he admitted that both
he and "his father before him" were haunted.
It was said that Robin's grandfather had robbed
an aged aunt of a large sum of money which she
had saved for her only daughter. The old woman
on her deathbed begged for restitution, which
was promised ; but the daughter eventually
died of starvation, while her heartless cousin
prospered.

Soon after the death of the injured woman,
her cousin became an altered man. People said
that the aged aunt and her daughter haunted
him. At last he declared he could not get any
rest between midnight and sunrise, and very
often in the day he was pinched, struck, and tormented by unseen assailants.

In a few years his business went to its lowest
ebb, then he died.

The heritage of ghostly annoyance fell to his
son, who became a soldier, and sought in change
of scene and active life, respite from the angered
ghosts. He returned home to Wales, and was
worried almost to death by the obnoxious ghosts,
who would not give him peace by night or day.
The worst part of it all was that Robin, even as
a child, looked ghost-ridden. He was apprenticed
to a tailor, and then became a soldier, but from
his youth upward he was very delicate. Soon

after his father's death the ghosts began to worry him, and continued to do so from manhood to middle age.

"They do never give me an hour's peace," lamented Robin to his friend Timothy, with whom he always lodged when working in the neighbourhood of Llantysilio. "I be better when I'm away from home. But wherever I do go they do find me out, if 'tis only for a little spell."

"Did you never try to get somebody to lay the ghosts?" asked his friend.

"Lay these here ghosts!" exclaimed Robin. "There'll be no layin' to them till I be in my grave!"

Robin sighed deeply.

Later on he went out for a stroll. It was a glorious night—that Eve of St. John and midsummer. Moonbeams fell in silvery radiance upon the waters of the Dee as the river poured ceaselessly over the Horse Shoe Weir, and the dark trees looked like grim sentinels standing out clear against the moonlight.

Robin Ddu walked on like one in a dream. To him it was a pleasure to find peace and rest of body and brain. In his reverie he thought of the Eve of St. John, of the many associations and superstitions connected therewith; then feeling more peaceful than he had felt for many months, he returned to his lodgings and went to bed.

Robin Ddu slept well for the first three hours that night, even though the moonlight, streaming in through the curtained window, almost forbade sleep.

Just as the clock struck 1 A.M., Robin awoke, and fancied he felt a breath of cold air in the room. The moon was setting, and the light in the window had become dim and shadowy, when suddenly he heard the latch of the door clicking. Robin Ddu turned in his bed. He expected his usual ghostly visitants, instead of which he saw a mysterious and stately lady, robed in grey, coming towards him from the doorway. She went to Robin, touched him on the lips with an icy finger, and whispered, " Follow me."

Robin hesitated, but the lady moved to the doorway, and therefrom earnestly beckoned him with her forefinger and whispered, " Come ! Come !"

Robin Ddu, fearful of incurring the displeasure of the apparition, dressed himself immediately.

The ghostly visitor, in a calm and dignified manner, preceded Robin downstairs, and out on to the road. She went on a little ahead of her companion, and led the way to Llantysilio church.

To Robin's surprise pale tapers shed ghostly light through the church windows. The church door was open, and the spectral lady, followed by Robin, entered. Then the apparition led him to the chancel, and vanished.

Alone, before the altar steps stood Robin Ddu. The pale glimmering radiance of lighted tapers illuminated the altar, and shed a dim and unearthly light upon all the surrounding objects.

Robin Ddu's teeth chattered, and he chafed his long thin hands to get warmth into them. The night, or rather, the morning air was keenly cold, quite unlike the atmosphere of midsummer, and a sudden gust of wind threw open the chancel door, through which, in the dawn-light, a spectral figure entered. It was that of a tall man, clothed in a swallow-tailed coat, with dark plush knee-breeches, white stockings, and low shoes with bows on the insteps. His white wig was tied at the base with black ribbons. He was soon followed by two other men dressed after the same fashion. The trio entered within the altar rails, and turned their faces towards the stone cross above the communion table. In hollow sepulchral tones the three spectral figures denounced the Master of the Hall.

"Woe be to him walking!" said one in a hoarse, unearthly voice.

"Woe be to him standing!" almost groaned the second figure.

"Woe be to him sitting!" wailed the third person.

"Woe-be-to-him-wherever-he-goes!" chanted the trio as in one voice.

The first speaker then turned round face towards the nave.

Robin Ddu shuddered.

The speaker's face was white as with passion, and from his eyes a strange and lurid light flashed, as he said—"Let him think what he may, the Master of the Hall shall not die a natural death. He shall go to his grave un-mourned and forgotten. When he dies, the Hall shall be seized by one without legal right to it. Strangers shall dwell therein, and, in course of time, the Hall shall crumble to the ground. Thereon shall rank and noxious weeds grow, and when the mouldering wall can no longer stand, a new Hall shall be built to cover the ruins of the old habitation!"

The spectral figures then vanished, and, a moment later, a tall gentleman of military ap-pearance strode into the chancel, entered the Hall-pew, looked around, then passed down the nave, and went out through the west door of the church.

Robin Ddu, trembling from head to foot, and

shivering with cold, stood as one tran-fixed with amazement. He rubbed his eyes. Was it a dream, or real?

At that moment the altar lights went out, and the golden radiance of sunrise streamed in through the stained-glass window of the chancel, already gorgeous with prismatic colours.

Robin Ddu walked slowly to the western door, which he found open as when he entered. He returned to his lodgings, where his friend Timothy's wife greeted him with a pleasant " Good morning ; " adding, " You've been out for a walk betimes, Robin."

" Ay ! " he replied, drawing near the newly-lighted fire.

" Art cold ? " asked Timothy, coming in later on from his work.

"That I be," replied Robin.

"Seen ghosts agen, I s'pose," remarked Timothy.

" Ay ! Ay ! " said Robin.

" Well, well ! Thee'rt an odd one," said Timothy. " I do b'lieve thee wast born at mid-night of a Nos dydd Calan. Thee'rt a man of second sight sure—ly ! But come to breakfast."

Robin broke his fast in almost complete silence, and afterwards went to the Hall, where he soon commenced working away upon the Master's clothes.

At nine o'clock Madam put in an appearance, and at ten o'clock the Master strode into the room.

"So you've come," said the Master.

"Yes, sirr," replied Robin. "An how may you please to find yourself, sirr?"

"Pretty fair, pretty fair," said the Master, sinking into the depths of a big arm-chair near Robin's low deal work-table.

The Master of Llantysilio ran his fingers through his hair, then he got up and restlessly paced the room.

"I know you believe in ghosts," said the Master suddenly.

"Ay, ay, sirr!" chimed in Robin.

"But do you believe in dreams?" asked the Master, curiously scanning the tailor's face.

"I do believe in some dreams," said Robin. "But it isn't everybody as has dreams what do come true."

"Mine never come true," continued the Master impetuously. "But I had an odd dream last night."

The Master crossed the room, shut the door, then sank again into the arm-chair, and told his dream.

"I dreamt that three bad men came and dragged me from my bed, and took me to the church. There, before the high altar, they blasphemously denounced me, and one of them said the cause of my death should be unnatural. I felt miserable, and returned home. As soon as I entered the Hall, a military-looking man ordered me out. I refused to go, whereupon he took me by the shoulders and turned me out. He bolted and barred the doors, and I found myself left to the mercy of the world, or to die on the roadside."

The Master shivered as though cold, yet great beads of burning sweat moistened his forehead, followed by fevered heat, then by icy coldness.

Rousing himself, he imperiously asked, " What is the meaning of my dream ? Tell the truth ; screen nothing, Robin Ddu."

Robin set aside his needle

" It is a dream of warnin', I should say, sirr," said the tailor.

" Warning ? warning to me ? What have I done, what do I do, that I should need a warning from anybody ?" asked the Master almost angrily.

" You did tell me to give you the truth an' screen nothin'," said Robin, who had descended from his table and stood upon the floor.

Robin Ddu drew himself up to his full height, his long attenuated figure looking shadowy in the sunlight, his hollow eyes and high cheek bones appearing ghostly even in the warm daytime. Dark rings were under his eyes, his fingers trembled, his brain whirled with the memory of the last night's scene and present thoughts of the Master's dreams.

"Beware!" exclaimed Robin Ddu, in a husky voice, as he raised the forefinger of his right hand at the Master; "beware of three bad men, who will tempt thee to do evil; and beware of the military man, who means to work out thy destruction!"

"My destruction!" shouted the Master, stamping his foot until the room rang with the sound.

"My destruction!" reiterated the Master. "Thy warning shall be *thy* destruction for a very certainty!" he continued. "Give up thy work, thou ghost-ridden skeleton; I can find another tailor!"

"So be it," said Robin Ddu. "When I've done this work I'll go. There's a plenty waitin' for me for forty miles round."

The Master was in a rage, and strode out of the room, while, through another door, Madam came in.

"What's all this hubbub about?" asked Madam.

Robin told her all, screening nothing of that which had passed between him and the Master; but to Madam he related his experiences of the previous night.

He dared not have told so much to the Master.

Madam was surprised, and to some extent alarmed.

"The Master ought to take warnin'," said Robin Ddu. "I kent say I do like that dream, coming after what I did see with my own eyes."

"But warning in what way?" asked Madam.

"I do believe that the Master do gamble," said Robin firmly; "an' I do believe he do lose money thereby."

"Never!" exclaimed Madam, testily adding, "Not one of *our* boys or *our* family was ever given to gaming!"

"'Tisn't for me to speak on the Master's private affairs, Madam; but as I do live he's given to gamin'."

"I know he has expensive tastes," said Madam quietly, "and he uses a lot of money. There's always more going out than coming in. But where the Master takes the money is more than I can tell."

"He do take the money to the gamblin' table as safe as I'm a living man, Madam," said the tailor.

"I'll find out if there's any truth in what you say," said Madam, "and, if possible, put a stop to his gaming. That any one of *our* family should be given to such evil ways is more than I can at present believe. But time will tell."

Madam quitted the room, and soon was busily engaged in turning the sun-dried lavender and adding to the pot-pourri.

"Robin Ddu!" shouted the Master from the Hall.

Robin quickly responded.

"Come here," said the Master, flourishing his hunting-crop above his head.

Robin went towards the Master.

"Thee dost deserve a sound thrashing," said the Master. "But I'll let thee off this time with only a—a—warning!"

The Master brought his hunting-crop with a crack upon the great oaken table in the Hall.

"Robin Ddu!" shouted the Master.

"Yes, sirr," replied the tailor.

"If thee dost repeat the offence, look out for thy head," said the Master.

Robin smiled.

"'Tis no smiling work," continued the Master, whose irascibility was always impetuous, but soon over. "Only remember this, take—warning in time. Now, go to work."

"I leave to-night," said Robin.

"No, no, Robin Ddu," said the Master. "Let bygones be bygones. Go to work for the time I've hired thee. There, go and have a tankard of beer. It'll put flesh upon thy skeleton."

With that the Master strode away, and Robin Ddu repaired to the servants' hall, where Madam served him with her own hands.

Robin fulfilled his term of engagement at Llantysilio, and, in due course, returned home to Llangollen.

The news of the tailor's night visit to Llantysilio church was soon whispered abroad, but people kept it from the Master.

Henceforth, wherever Robin went, the memory of that Eve of St. John and midsummer kept beside him like a grim shadow which would not be shaken off.

.   .   .   .

Several years passed.

The waters of the Dee still ran over the Horse Shoe Weir, and, as of old, the Master of the Hall went to and fro, now fiercely scolding, and now immoderately praising those around him.

Robin Ddu still plied his needle, paid his periodical visits to Llantysilio, and as usual went to the Hall.

One day in the autumn of a year that had been very rainy, the Master went to the cellar to decant some wine. By some mischance he missed his footing, slipped and fell on some of the bottles, and severely cut his hand with the broken glass.

For several hours the bleeding could not be

staunched, and afterwards a wound formed which became obstinate, and would not heal.

The Master went to London, and remained there for more than a year, much to Madam's vexation. The hand grew worse, and the Master returned home. Madam tenderly nursed him, but all her care was of no avail. Worse and worse became the wound, and at length the Master died of what doctors to-day call "blood-poisoning."

On the morning of the funeral Robin Ddu, with others, came to take a last look at the Master, whose face had a peaceful expression, though the features were worn almost to a shadow with suffering.

At the hour named for the funeral a gentleman, of military appearance, arrived at the Hall in order to take part, he said, in the ceremony. He was not known—not even to Madam.

But Robin Ddu, standing far back among the shadows of the entrance-hall, recognised in the stranger the man of St. John's Eve and the Master's dream.

The funeral procession set out, and the keen eyes of the tailor noticed that the stranger did not follow the mourners, nor mingle with the tenantry and general public.

Robin remarked this to his friend Timothy, who walked with him in the procession.

c

"P'rhaps he's behind us," whispered Timothy.

"I don't think so," said Robin.   "I do think he do mean no good."

It happened as the tailor prophesied.

When the mourners—chief of whom was Madam—returned to the Hall, they could not re-enter. Every door was bolted and barred—every window was securely fastened. The military man had taken possession of the place.

From the top of the porch to which he had gained access by means of the French window, the stranger informed Madam, and those of the Master's next-of-kin who were present, that he claimed the Hall as a stake he had won when gambling with the late proprietor. He further stated that as soon as his solicitors arrived from London, Madam should come in and take out all her own possessions in the shape of goods and chattels.

Madam, broken down with grief for the loss of her brother, found herself suddenly and un-expectedly, in her age, turned out of house and home.

All the people of Llantysilio, and many miles around, offered shelter to Madam, but the rector and his wife took her to the Rectory, where she was to remain until her rightful property was restored.

But Madam died of a broken heart in six

months after the Master, and was buried in the same grave as her brothers.

The estate was thrown into Chancery, and remained there for long years, and when it came at last into the possession of the Master's next-of-kin, the walls had crumbled away and the Hall was almost a ruin. The owners—remote relatives of the Master and Madam—being too poor to rebuild the Hall, sold the ground on which it stood, and the estate that surrounded it.

On the site of the old mansion a new Hall was built, and strangers paced the mossy lawns and flower gardens, where the Master of Llantysilio once loved to wander, and where silvery-haired Madam replenished her pot-pourri, and harvested her sweet lavender in the midsummers of long ago.

Roger Meyrick's Ride

A FOLK-STORY OF CASTELL CARREG

LONG stretches of purple heather fringed the brown moorland pools, around which yellow marsh marigolds bloom in profusion in the spring, and tall golden irises hold their heads aloft in the early summer.

It was a glorious evening. The mellow radiance of the autumnal sunset glowed in the western sky, lighting up for a brief time the darkest corners, and gilding the tarnished livery of the woodlands.

To the south, the Severn Sea was almost lost in the golden haze, through which the Steep Holm loomed like a fairy fortress or a lonely dream island, where one could forget the bitter past, and conjure up a mystical future that should atone for the uncertain present.

Here and there, on the sea, the ships looked like phantoms gliding to or from unknown havens, and the little skiffs sailed lazily along like a fairy flotilla bound for the islands of the Hesperides.

To the west, embowered in woodlands, is the Vale of Worship, dotted here and there by hoary and moss-grown druidical stones, beyond which stands the largest cromlech in all Britain.

Looking from the high moorland, the surrounding country appeared like a fairy realm stretching towards the region of the setting sun.

On the outskirts of the moorland a few straggling cottages remained in the days of which I write, and in one of these lived an old woman known by the sobriquet of "Mary the Downs."

Waste common land, moorland, and unenclosed heaths are frequently called "the downs" in Wales.

Mary lived on St. Lythan's Down, near St. Nicholas, in the Vale of Glamorgan. She retained a bright intellect, and could thread her needle without the aid of glasses at the age of ninety-three, and even then remembered all the old folk-stories that were told in her childhood. In her quaint Anglo-Cymric *patois* she would tell the tales of her grandmother, and all the traditions, and nursery stories, handed orally down from one generation to another. She remembered ministers and pious men coming long distances to lay ghosts, and she was per-

fectly certain her great-grandmother was a friend
of the "little people," as the fairies are sometimes called in Wales. The Tylwyth Têg and
the Bendith-y-Mamau had visited Cogan Pill in
her own childhood, and she had been fairy-led
in a field near Wenvoe Castle when quite a
grown woman! She had also found strange
small silver in her own new tin money-box before anybody had placed a contribution therein.
Mary would not have it that her mother had
possibly put some small silver in the box "for
luck's sake."

Seated in her arm-chair beside the glowing
fire, Mary would tell her stories as long as anybody cared to listen, and many pleasant hours
could be wiled away in the old woman's company.
Her language was not polished, and sometimes
it became confused; but she was one of the last
of the old Welsh story-tellers, the last of a
generation that has seen its day, and is lost in
the peaceful past.

"Did you ever hear the story of Castell Carreg?"
asked Mary.

I told her I had heard much about the celebrated cromlech, and others of its kind in the
neighbourhood.

"Oh, 'tis nothin' 'bout the Druids an' Bards,"
said she. "'Tis a story my great-grandfather
used to tell my grandfather."

Mary related the story in her own old fashion. I have woven it thus :—

Although nearly five years had passed since the terrible battle of St. Fagan's was fought, the conflict was still cruelly fresh in the people's memory, and many lamented the loss of relatives and friends as if they had only just been severed from them.

In the lowest end of the druidical Vale of Worship, a small farm-house called Northcliffe nestles under the trees in a veritable sleepy hollow. Away beyond it, broad meadow lands stretch from the mill of Duffryn to that of Lidmoor, both in full working order in the days of Cromwell. On the heights above Northcliffe stood Sutton, then a quaint old Tudor-built house, now it is an ordinary farm. Even in the present days of toil and traffic, Northcliffe is secluded ; still, in the stream that flows through the mill-meadows, otters are to be seen, and still in the orchards the nightingales sing, as though the world was in its youth.

Roger Meyrick of Northcliffe was a rich man before Cromwell scoured the country, but afterwards he found it difficult to make ends meet. He had lost two sons in the battle of St. Fagan's, and one of them had left a widow and children, the care of whom fell to Roger's lot. Another son, named Cyril, was taken prisoner, and still remained in exile.

Late in the autumn of 1649, Roger Meyrick took the path through the fields in the Vale of Worship, and passed Castell Carreg on his way to the village of St. Nicholas. He had many calls to make, and twilight was deepening into night, when he started to walk home again, this time by way of the road.

Autumn leaves fluttered silently downward into one of the most beautiful roadways in South Wales. Broad margins of grass are on each side of the thoroughfare, and, under stately and ancient oaks and elms, a sparkling brook glides onward to the valley below. Hoary oaks, that have stood the storms of centuries, crown each upland, and groves of the same venerable trees still remain where once the Druids worshipped.

As Roger Meyrick went past the Manor House, St. Nicholas, where chestnut trees form a dense canopy even in the daytime, and make the road-way as dark as night, early in the evening a man accosted him.

" It is dark hereabouts," said the man.

" That it is," replied Roger; " but who may you be?"

" You know my voice, don't you?" asked the stranger.

" I can't say that I do," replied Roger.

" Don't you remember Miles Button of Sheep-cote?" asked the stranger.

"I do. He was taken prisoner at the battle of St. Fagan's."

"Yes, and he had a son named Morgan," said the stranger.

"I remember," said Roger, sighing deeply. "Poor fellow! He was killed in the great battle."

"Was he?" curiously asked the stranger.

"To be sure he was," said Roger sorrowfully.

"No, no," said the man decidedly.

"Well, if he wasn't killed, why didn't he come home when 'twas safe for him to come? 'Tis goin' on five years since that terrible battle."

Roger sighed deeply, and tears filled his eyes.

"Morgan Button escaped," said the stranger hurriedly; "he went abroad and returned."

"When did he come back?" asked Roger.

"The last week in October," replied the man.

"I've not heard a word about it," said Roger, somewhat tartly.

Roger Meyrick was always one of the earliest to know the gossip of the country-side, and resented the idea of anybody else being first in the field.

"You may not have heard the news," said the stranger, "but he's come for all that."

Just then the men emerged out of the dense shadows into the twilight, and immediately Roger Meyrick recognised his companion.

"Well indeed!" exclaimed Roger. "Sure enough 'tis Morgan Button himself! But what do you come this way for? Why don't you go to Sheepcote?"

"To tell the truth," said Morgan, lowering his voice, "I want to keep out of the way for a bit. My father is home, and I've been a bad boy—spent too much money, and he's angered about it. My mother asked me to keep away from the house for a few weeks."

"And where may you be staying?" asked Roger.

"With the people of Tinkin's Wood," was the reply.

"Oh! with the Powells?"

"The same."

The men walked slowly on in the growing darkness, until they reached the little bridge spanning the brook, and leading to the farmhouse known as Tinkin's Wood, close beside Castell Carreg.

Morgan talked much of his escape after the battle of St. Fagan's, and of his doings whilst abroad, and time seemed to fly, so pleasant was the conversation. The men lingered on the bridge until nightfall, and then Roger was loth to leave the wanderer.

"Come up with me to the house a bit," said Morgan. "'Tis early yet."

"Well, to be sure," said Roger, "I think I will. It can't be long after six, by the light."

At Tinkin's Wood, Roger was warmly welcomed. The inmates were hospitable people, and soon Powell the elder, Morgan Button, and Roger Meyrick were regaling themselves with cakes and *cwrw da* (beer).

In the midst of their rejoicing, loud knocking was heard at the front door.

A stranger begged permission to rest awhile, for the night was dark, and he had come a long distance.

"Come in, come in," said John Powell, throwing the front door widely open.

In strode a tall young man dressed in the fashion of the period.

"I have tethered my horse to a tree in yonder yard," said the strange visitor.

John Powell directed his men to see to the animal, and led the way to the kitchen.

Roger Meyrick could scarcely believe his own eyes, for there, erect as ever, stood his youngest son, Cyril!

"My son! my son!" exclaimed Roger. "My son returned from exile!"

Cyril warmly returned his father's embraces, and his friends' hearty greetings. Then they all sat down and talked, and quaffed large tankards filled with foaming nut-brown ale. Story after story was told, and the night was growing. Morgan Button quaffed the foaming ale and related his experiences abroad. Cyril Meyrick also heartily quaffed the ale, and talked much about his adventures, while John Powell and Roger Meyrick listened long and earnestly.

The hours flew like fleet-winged birds before a hurricane. It was eleven o'clock, and Roger said he must go, but Morgan Button and Cyril Meyrick urged him to remain.

"If you'll stay another hour," said Cyril, "you shall have my horse. I'll stay here, and you can go home and prepare mother for my coming."

What a kind and thoughtful son! Roger, mounted on a swift horse, would be home in "no time." It mattered little if he remained another hour. Again and again were the tankards replenished with the foaming nut-brown ale of Wales.

It was midnight! Still one more story, then Roger must go.

It was an hour later when he mounted Cyril's horse, and had the reins put in his hands by his long-exiled son. The knowledge was too good to be true.

How the kind wife at home would rejoice, "for this my son that was lost is found again."

"Cyril, my boy, what is the horse's name?" asked Roger Meyrick.

"Firefly," replied Cyril. "He's fleet-footed but quite safe."

Then Cyril lighted the small saddle lantern which he always used when riding in the dark.

"Good-night," said Roger.

"Good-night," responded the other men.

Down through the darkness and the narrow lane leading to the road went Roger. He was careful just there, for the lane was rough, and the horse was strange to those parts.

Presently he reached the road leading from St. Nicholas towards Duffryn. At first the horse went almost too slowly, but once on the good road, it went at a better speed. By-and-by it quickened its pace, and when Roger turned into the road leading from St. Lythan's, Firefly was going positively fast.

"It's a good horse," remarked Roger, stroking its head.

Soon afterwards he thought the horse went a little—just a little too fast. Firefly struck its hoof sharply upon the rocky road.

That was enough !

Firefly started at a race-horse speed, and the hands of the rider could not check him.

On, on went the horse and the rider, as though to win a wager.

Roger Meyrick used every effort to restrain Cyril's horse, but failed.

Although the night was dark, and the roads strange to the horse, the animal raced until Roger Meyrick felt as though he were being carried off in a whirlwind.

Northcliffe was passed, Sutton was reached, still on, on, through the darkness and the night went Firefly.

Up hill, down dale, clattering through villages silent as the grave; bounding over brooks; dashing past lonely churchyards where the dead slept oblivious of everything; and surmounting every obstacle, Firefly raced as if lives were at stake. Roger's brain whirled. He was almost too giddy to wonder how and where the race would end. What a terrible ride! He could never forget it—never! He longed for the first light of dawn to reveal where they were.

At last it came. A rift appeared in the grey November clouds, and Roger had sufficient light to see that they were on the Golden Mile, near Bridgend, and many miles away from home.

Firefly slackened its pace for a moment, during which time Roger Meyrick was able to turn the horse's head. But the next minute the animal was careering as madly as ever.

"The animal is surely bewitched," muttered Roger, as he heard the people in the village shouting, "A runaway! a runaway!"

The race was fearful, the noise of the people

along the thoroughfare became deafening. Clatter, clatter, went the horse's hoofs upon the road. Rattle and whiz went the whirlwind around Roger's ears, as the "bewitched horse" raced along. Suddenly the cock crew, and the horse stopped.

Roger Meyrick rubbed his eyes. He found himself in Castell Carreg!

The "bewitched horse" was the fallen cromlech on which he was seated. The ride was merely a dream engendered by copious draughts of the Welshman's beloved *cwrw da*.

Roger Meyrick went home a sorrowful but wiser man, and when he told his wife the story of the Firefly race, she said, "That will teach thee a lesson to come home straight instead of going to sleep in Castell Carreg!"

A year later the exiled son returned home, but Morgan Button's fate remained a mystery.

Early in the last century it was a folk-remark in that neighbourhood, when a man went to market, to warn him to "Take care thee dost not go for a ride round Castell Carreg on thy way home."

"Till the Day of Judgment"

A NIGHT IN THE CHAIR OF IDRIS

ELYN AP MADOC, a prince of Merioneth, had been reading the Triads, and afterwards pondered deeply upon the one in which it is recorded :—

" The three Blessed Astronomers of the Island of Britain—Idris, the Great ; Gwydion, son of Don ; and Gwyn, son of Nudd—so great was their knowledge of the stars, and of their natures and influences, that they could foretell whatever any one might wish to know till the day of judgment."

What attracted his attention most, was that " they could foretell whatever any one might wish to know *till the day of judgment.*"

At the same time, Belyn by no means wished to know future events so far as the day of judgment. In truth that was, he thought, going a little too far ; but his ambition was to know if ever he would become a great man, a "leader of men," like the renowned Glendower. Then he suddenly remembered the old story, wherein it was stated that whoever slept for one night in the Chair of Idris would, as people said, "go mad," or awaken gifted with inspiration—some said poetical, others said astrological, while some declared it was a little of each, seeing that poets, seers, and madmen are closely allied.

Whatever the inspiration was, Belyn coveted it, and set about the right way of obtaining, as he thought, a "peep into the future."

Belyn, taking sufficient provisions to sustain himself during his pilgrimage, started in ample time to reach the summit of Cader-Idris early in the afternoon. Very beautiful, though toilsome, was the route upward from Dolgelly; but, though the scenery was grand and impressive, few people in those troublous times heeded the beauties of nature. Grim chasms, beetling crags, and towering rocks overhanging solitary ravines, or looking downward over long stretches of rich pastures and thymy uplands where the heather was not yet in blossom, and the slopes were strewn with fading petals of the golden gorse—had little charm for the rough and uncultured mountaineers of that period, or for the men who were ready to take up arms with or against Owen Glendower.

D

Belyn, after many pauses to rest on the upward way, gained the summit, and for a short interval stood to look down upon the vast panorama below.

It was a grand and impressive scene. Amid warm mists and heated vapours the July sun crept stealthily, and almost thief-like, behind the western mountains, as though his golden orb was being watched and his precious darts had a price set upon them.

Belyn was dazzled by the sight, as he gazed and gazed, until the great sun sank below the peaks of the west. For him the western distance held no charms beyond the freedom of the sea, so like his own restless heart, and the grandeur of the wild coast, so like his own wild and uncurbed nature. The north was his home, and his soul clung to that with all the ardour of a Welshman. But the south, down there about and beyond the Berwyn mountains, held a wonderful charm for him, for there at present the great and renowned Owen Glendower congregated his followers.

As the last rays of the setting sun blazed above the purple mountains, and the last shafts of golden light glanced like lances between the sharp peaks and splinty spires of the west, Belyn moved towards the Chair, at the foot of which he took a seat.

Not far above him eagles poised on their wings, ready to descend in a "fell swoop" into the valleys below, and on the crags around him vultures congregated as if in solemn conclave, while, lower down, kestrel and kite wheeled wildly in the evening air.

Far, far below, lake and river and stream looked like orbs and ribbons of silver in emerald settings, while over all the tardy twilight threw a veil of pale and delicate opal and purple tints. Soon the light, circling clouds, like masters of magic, wove spells around the great mountains, and then Belyn felt himself altogether cut out from the lower world.

Soon afterwards, nerving himself for the occasion, Belyn took his seat in what is called the "Chair."

Night approached, and while dark clouds circled below the peak, above, in the clear purple sky, the stars came out and sparkled like jewels. And then Belyn thought within himself, No wonder that Idris Gawr (Great) had come there in dateless days far above the world to watch the stars. Then there came to his mind once more the enthralling words of the ancient Triads—"Idris the Great; Gwydion, son of Don; and Gwyn, son of Nudd. So great was their knowledge of the stars, and of their natures and influences, that they could foretell whatever any one might wish to know till the day of judgment."

" So far," he whispered under his breath, for the very thought overpowered him with awe. " So far," he repeated, as a shudder passed through his frame and the night wind played around his fevered brow, and cooled his heated brain that throbbed with a wild unrest.

At last, when the first sense and symptoms of drowsiness began to oppress him, he tried to ward them off. For, in truth, although he came up there to get the magic sleep,—ah! now it had come to the rub, he feared the nameless horror of—madness!

What if he should go mad—yes, mad, and die out there on the heights alone, and far from kith and kin; or worse still, become a wild and sense-reft wanderer among the mountains, or a time-driven and brain-consumed skeleton, to descend like an evil spirit among his people, and prove himself to be a living example of one who had dared more than a mortal should?

No; he would not sleep in the Chair of Idris. He would remain awake, and descend from the great and gloomy peak as soon as the day-dawn appeared.

Suddenly, and without warning, he found himself in utter darkness. Oh, the horror of it! He stretched forth his hands as if to grasp some friendly rock or ledge, but in vain. What was worse, it was a thick darkness, in which he gasped for breath. He thought he must soon be suffocated.

One moment he shivered with the cold until his teeth chattered ; the next he was burning with fever heat, until his pulse throbbed as though ready to burst with liquid fire.

Alas ! that he ever was so foolish as to venture to the Chair of Idris, and, after all, be unable to sleep in it.

Surely they were mad who had said, that " he who slept for one night in the Chair of Idris would awaken gifted with poetical or astrological inspiration," when there was no sleep to be had in the hated spot.

Presently to his great relief the darkness seemed to decrease, and he hailed a faint grey glimmering light, as one who, clinging to a shattered spar on mid-ocean, greets a distant sail.

Belyn was almost frantic with delight.

The grey light developing revealed gigantic forms, and Belyn began to think of Idris the Great, of Gwydion the son of Don, of Gwyn the son of Nudd, and last, but not least, of the Brenin Llwyd the Grey King, who, they said, seated himself among the mountain peaks and discovered the secrets of the stars.

Belyn then heard the sound as of uncurbed

floods let loose, and the rushing of waters, and the noise of many conflicting winds. He remembered he truly was near the " fountain of the waters, and the cradle of the winds."

Out of what he thought to be the dim morning twilight, a voice came, and this is what it said : " When thou hast secrets to keep, dost thou know where to keep them ?"

Another voice answered in hollow tones, " No."

" Trust them to the depths of the ocean ; trust them to the rocky fastnesses of the mountains ; trust them to the lone star distance, but not to fellow-mortal ! "

Belyn sighed. It was a relief, and yet not quite a pleasure, to hear these strange and unearthly voices.

" Hast thou ambition ?" again questioned the greater voice.

" Ay ! ay ! " responded the lesser voice.

" Place it on the flower of the field, and it will wither ; plant it in the furrows with the grain, and it will be blighted ; set it in the sweet affections of thy heart, and it will turn to wormwood and gall ; let it follow the warrior, and it will end in conflict, in death, in dust ! "

Then another voice chaunted :

> " Few win renown !
> The monarch's crown
> Is worn in pain !

> The warrior's strength
> Is spent at length,
>   In vain, in vain!"

Belyn almost groaned. His ambition was to follow Glendower, and, like him, to become a leader of men—a mighty warrior—an everlasting world-name.

One of the mysterious people appeared to divine his thoughts, for, after a pause, the greater voice cried : "Beware, rash youth, beware of warfare, of battle, of woe, while yet no thread of silver is seen in thy dark curling hair. We know thy wishes. They are to go forth to battle—to earn a mighty name, and to come home victorious and triumphant. Be not rash. Many will go forth and few will return. Go home, and try not to learn the secrets of the stars. The greatest inspiration is to do good to thy neighbours as to thyself, to be true to thyself and thus be true to all men—to help the helpless, to comfort the sorrowful, to give food to the hungry, and to do well in the sphere of life in which thou wast born."

Then the voice ceased, the gigantic figures slowly vanished with the morning mists, and the sun was shining when Belyn aroused himself. He was stiff and sore after the night spent in the Chair of Idris, and he began to wonder that during the unearthly watch, or sleep, or dream, or whatever it was, he had not truly " gone mad." As for inspiration, he was quite sure he had received sufficient never again to venture upon such a foolish and daring expedition.

Slowly, but in a thankful spirit, he descended homeward.

"Where hast thou been?" asked the few wayfarers who met him on the downward path.

"Up the mountain-side," said Belyn.

"He's been sayin' his prayers," said some jeering fellows lower down.

Yet Belyn left them alone.

"Hast been among the eagles?" asked a neighbour nearer home.

Belyn remained silent. At length he approached home, and by this time the twilight began to descend slowly upon the earth. He paused to look back, and upwards towards Cader-Idris, and it seemed to him as though the grey and gigantic figures once more stood there and gazed kindly downward. Distance softened their outlines, and, instead of being objects of terror, they appeared to be stretching forth their arms as if breathing a benediction upon all below.

When he reached his father's partially ruined stronghold beyond Dolgelly, sad thoughts once

more oppressed him, for the home, which had
been a noble fortress in the days of Edward
the First, bore many traces of stern resistance
and pitiful defeat; and Belyn wondered after all,
if it were not better to live in peace, and let the
chances of war to the brave, but wild warriors of
Wales.

Musing in this manner, he paused where the
dark portcullis threw its sheltering shadows
around him, and night wandered soberly into
the deserted courtyard.

Suddenly he heard sounds of revelry in the
banqueting-hall, and the words of Owain Cy-
veiliog, the poet-prince of Powys, rang in his
ears:—

"Fill thou the horn, for it is my delight in
the place where the defenders of our country
drink mead, and give it to Selyt the Fearless,
the defence of Gwygyr. Woe to the wretch
who offends him, eagle-hearted hero, and to the
son of Madoc, the famous and generous Tudwr,
like a wolf when he seizes his prey, is his assault
on the onset. Two heroes, who were sage in
their councils but active in the field, the two
sons of Ynyr, who on the day of battle were
ready for the attack, heedless of danger, famous
for their exploits. Their assault was like that
of strong lions, and they pierced their enemies
like brave warriors; they were lords of the

battle, and rushed foremost with their crimson
lances; the weight of their attack was not to be
withstood. Their shields were broken asunder
with much force, as the high-sounding wind on
the beach of the green sea, and the encroaching
of the furious waves on the coast of Talgarth.
Fill, cupbearer, as thou regardest thy life . . .
the Hirlais drinking horn, . . . and bring it to
Tudwr, the Eagle of Battles ; . . . give it in the
hand of Moreiddig, encourager of songs. . . ."

Belyn marvelled as to the meaning of all this
noise and revelry, the sound of the harp, the
voice of Gruffydd, the family harpist, and the
wild and frequent bursts of applause. In a
pause of the song he went onward, and, wishful
to remain unseen, sought the shadows where,
like an eavesdropper, he lingered beside the
least-used and garden entrance of the great
hall.

Once more Gruffydd swept his fingers along
the harp-chords, and resumed his song :—" Pour,
cupbearer, from a silver vessel, an honourable
badge of distinction. On the great plains of
Gwestine I have seen a miracle, to stop the
impetuosity of Gronwy was more than a task
for a hundred men. . . . They met their enemies
in the conflict, and their chieftain was consumed
by fire near the surges of the sea. . . . Pour the
horn to the warriors, Owain's noble heroes, who

were equally active and brave. They assembled in that renowned place where the shining steel glittered ; . . . hear ye, by drinking mead, how the lord of Cattraeth went with his warriors in defence of his just cause, the guards of Mynyddawc, about their distinguished chief. . . . Pour out, cupbearer, sweet and well-drained mead . . . from the horns of wild oxen covered with gold, for the honour and the reward of the souls of those departed heroes. . . ."

Then there was another pause, more like a sacred and solemn hush than anything else, in which only the sounds of the swords as they were being sheathed could be heard, after which the tune was changed. Instead of wild martial music, Gruffydd played a soft and subdued interlude in a minor key, which seemed to soothe the warlike spirits of all present. A moment later, the aged and snowy-haired harpist recommenced singing :—" Of the numerous cares that surround princes no one is conscious here but God and myself. The man who neither gives nor takes quarter, and cannot be forced by his enemies to abide to his word, Daniel the valiant and beautiful. Oh, cupbearer, great is the task to entreat him; his men will not cease dealing death around him until he is mollified. Cupbearer, our shares of mead are to be given us equally before the bright shining tapers . . .

Cupbearer, slight not my commands. May we all be admitted into Paradise by the King of Kings!"

Song ceased, and, looking through the doorway, Belyn saw that the warriors' lances had been laid aside, swords were in their scabbards, and gold- and silver-bordered shields were heaped together in a corner of the hall. He heard his father Madoc calling, " My son—where is Belyn, my son—why tarries he so long—we wait his coming, as the thirsty flowers wait the approach of the life-giving dews, or the refreshing rain ! "

It was enough for the wanderer, who rushed forward, and immediately found himself locked closely in his father's arms.

When the mutual greetings were over, Madoc, whispering a word to the stern warrior sitting beside him, placed his son's hand in his.

" For the sword and the honour of Wales !" shouted Madoc, and all the warriors united in one wild outburst of applause.

Belyn looked bewildered.

" My son—my only son," exclaimed Madoc. " I proudly give thy hand, and, if need be, thy life, into the keeping of our noble leader—Owen Glendower ! "

Belyn dared scarcely glance upward.

So much for his dreams of peace !

Unasked, he was placed—and by his own father—in the hands of Owen Glendower, whose deeds he so recently wished to emulate.

After some formalities, he found himself pledged to accompany wherever he went, and to defend the leader of the great rebellion against the English king, Henry the Fourth.

When Belyn took his seat beside his father, the words of the mysterious speaker rang in his ears : " Many will go forth, and few will return."

He was not a coward, but his new dreams of peace were dispelled, not by his own wish, but by his father's all-powerful will. Then he thought of the grim monitor who said, "Do well in the sphere of life in which thou wast born," and, taking up the broken threads of his hopes, he made a resolution to try and do his best, even in taking up arms under the direction of Owen Glendower.

.   .   .   .   .

Fiercely the conflict raged. Wild yells and frenzied shouts of the living, and the sighs and groans of the wounded and dying, mingled with the ringing clash of arms, made day discordant, and, as evening approached, they increased rather than diminished.

Only the sea was at peace.

Scarcely a ripple marred the serene surface of Cardigan Bay, and the wavelets seemed almost too lazy to roll along the sands, or to glide in and out among the rocks under Harlech.

On sea and land, the red sun shed a lurid glow that deepened towards the setting, and illuminated the distant peaks with its beacon fires.

Darkly in the crimson sunset, the serried hosts fought and wavered, each pause being only the signal for still more desperate attacks.

Here and there, on the fringes of the field, cowled monks and solemn friars waited the result of the warfare—waited ready to administer reviving cordials and soothing remedies to the wounded and the dying.

Here and there, hovering around the mountains, fierce eagles and hungry vultures waited, ready to descend for prey, while hoarse-voiced ravens croaked in response to hooded crows that stalked the lonely shore while waiting for carnage.

In the front of the fray, Owen Glendower urged his men to unceasing action, while the opposing hosts fought and faltered, then rallied and wavered weakly before the overwhelming force of the enemy.

On, on pressed Glendower and his men, as they scaled the heights and looked down on their comrades.

Suddenly the red sun seemed with renewed

strength to glare upon the terrible scene, and, as
a vivid flash of sunset light shot across the field,
a fierce, ringing cry rent the air, and the warriors on the heights signalled victoriously to
their comrades, who rushed forward and upward
in ecstasy.

The vanquished forces wavered for a moment,
then rallied, and made one supreme effort onward, but it was too late. They were crushed
back by superior and overwhelming numbers,
and fell lifeless on the field.

Harlech was taken, and Owen Glendower held
the castle.

That night, when the slender crescent of the
new moon pierced the dark blue sky, and the
star of strength shone steadily above Harlech
Castle, and the star of love gleamed peacefully
over the calm waters of Cardigan Bay, Belyn
the son of Madoc lay wounded among his comrades. Two years had passed since his father
gave him to Glendower and warfare, and there
was not a braver soldier in the service of rebellion. He had fought in several great battles,
yet, in this—which they only regarded as a
skirmish—he was wounded, and as he thought—
"unto death."

He found himself, with others, among some
mounds close under the castle, just where the
grass was thickest, and the shadows were darkest

Belyn felt as though he had been in that position for nights instead of about two hours, when a voice aroused him with—" If thou wouldst have comfort and shelter, follow me."

" I cannot," he murmured wearily. " My wounds are great and will not permit me to move."

Whereupon the stranger said, " I will lift thee ;" and forthwith Belyn found himself raised in the great arms of one who appeared to have Herculean strength.

It was but a short way across the fields to carry the living burden, and the stranger soon deposited him in the comfortable and spacious kitchen of an ancient farmhouse.

Belyn was surprised at his good fortune, but his wounds were so great, and his strength so little, that he could not question nor make comment of any kind.

In a few days those that remained of the vanquished left the neighbourhood, and Glendower's men held the castle while their leader pressed onward.

When all was quiet again, and the wounded had either recovered or died on the field, and Belyn was able to sit up, he found that he was in the house of an old friend whom he had not seen since his childhood.

Gwilym ap Howel had been his father's firmest

friend in days gone by, and had left Dolgelly for Anglesea to inherit estates.

"Thy father would little look for me here," said Gwilym sorrowfully. "Fallen fortunes and loss have brought me to this place, where I would fain live during the remainder of my days in peace, surrounded by my good wife and children. Mine has been a life of trouble and foolish expenditure of time in fighting, and all to no purpose, save that of diminishing my means."

At that moment a merry-eyed maiden entered the room, and, tripping gaily up to her father, asked when the stranger would be able to join them "at meals."

Without answering her, Gwilym said, "This is my little daughter Elined. As soon as thou art able to quit thy couch, I will give thee into her care. She is as good a nurse of those that are on a fair way to recovery, as her mother is to those who are wounded or in dangerous illness."

Thus it proved.

When Belyn was able to walk a little, who should lead him but Elined, and by and by it came to pass that the two became inseparable companions.

Hours ran into days, and days merged into weeks, still Belyn remained there. Love and

E

peace went hand in hand, while rebellion, and the sound thereof, vanished from the shores of Cardigan Bay.

But the longest day has its end, and the time came when Belyn, the son of Madoc, must go from under Gwilym ap Howel's kindly roof.

When the morning for the young man's departure came, shadows lurked around Elined's dark eyes, her red lips drooped unusually downward, and instead of her sprightly manner, her movements flagged.

Noticing this, Gwilym tenderly said, " We are all sorry to see thee going. But come again. Thou wilt always be well received."

Belyn saluted his host and hostess and their family in the fashion of those days, and with a suitable escort went homeward.

For many days afterwards, Elined drooped like a flower bereft of sunshine, and then her parents knew that her heart had gone with Belyn the son of Madoc.

In the stronghold of Madoc there was great rejoicing at the only son's return, and when the feasts were over the father said, " Thou shalt go no more in the train of the great Glendower, but take to thyself a wife, and remain here in peace."

Then the truth came out that the world held but one woman for him, and when the son of

Madoc named her, his kinsman said, "It is but right that Belyn—from Beli, the sun—should wed Elined, Luned, or Lunet—the moon."

Belyn, accompanied by a brilliant retinue, soon returned to Harlech, and asked Gwilym ap Howel for his daughter's hand, at the same time adding mirthfully, he knew he had "already obtained her heart."

When Belyn returned home with Elined his bride, few wondered she had charmed him, for she was "passing fair."

In the future Belyn had every reason to be thankful that his father "gave him to Glendower," for thereby he obtained a good and beautiful wife.

Belyn never again troubled himself about the Triad that says—"So great was their knowledge of the stars, and of their natures and influences, that they could foretell whatever any one might wish to know *till the day of judgment.*" But ever to his dying hour he remembered that night in the Chair of Idris.

The Ransom of Sir Harry Stradling

DOWN to the wave-worn stretches of rocks under the cliffs and crags of Tresilian and St. Donats, the laver-gatherers go when the tide is high, and, as the waters recede from the long ledges, the women begin working.

Brown, and glossy, and beautiful are the long leaves of the sea-liverwort, called by the Welsh country-folk laver, which, when cooked, is known as laver-bread.

In the glorious hours of April, May, and June the laver-gatherers are always very busy, lingering among the rocks and smooth ledges where the liverwort spreads its leaves, and stretches them out and down into the clear sea-pools.

It is the custom of the women to fill large baskets with liverwort, and then bring their burdens shoreward, where, in deep pools, they wash and free the laver from all traces of sand.

After that, the toilers rest awhile on the shore and in the caves before proceeding homeward.

Close beside Tresilian is a lofty, long, and spacious cavern, which can only be entered when the tide is out. The inhabitants of the neighbourhood call it Reynold's Cave, which is supposed to be a corruption of Reynard's or Fox's Cave. It faces the sea, and its most remarkable feature is a natural arch which spans the cave a little below the general roof. Even in the present day, it is the custom for visitors to try their luck in throwing pebbles over the arch, so as to fall on the opposite side, but many people fail to do so owing to the great height of the cavern. The number of unavailing efforts —after preliminary practice—made before the arch is surmounted denotes the period of years that must intervene before the person throwing the pebbles will be married, or, if married, be released by death to make another choice.

This cavern was known to the ancient Britons as Dynwen's Cave. Dynwen was the daughter of Brychan Brycheiniog, who flourished about A.D. 45. The British votaries of Love were supposed to supplicate Dynwen, who discountenanced celibacy, and presided in the cave near Tresilian. The arch was formerly called Dynwen's Bow of Destiny, and through hoary centuries, many men and maidens have consulted the wave-resisting oracle. Although the arch appears to be very close to the roof, a boat could be rowed over it easily, and about half a century ago a man swam above it at springtide.

Old and young, rich and poor alike, still try their luck in Dynwen's Cave.

In this beautiful cave, when the June sun was shining with almost tropical fierceness, and the younger laver-gatherers washed the contents of their baskets in the fresh sea-pools, the older women rested awhile.

Cool and pleasant were the shadows in Dynwen's Cave. Sea-swallows, sand-martins, and wagtails darted and flitted over the Bow of Destiny, or dipped down to drink of the rockbound streamlets that slowly trickled from ledge to ledge, and fell with musical cadences to the pools below.

Among the rocks, just where small pebbles and sand mingled on the floor of the cavern, sat the old women, surrounded by a group of merry girls, who, treating laver-gathering as holiday work, toiled a little and rested long.

While the laver-gatherers either worked in the burning sunshine, where the yellow sands fringed the rocky ledges, or rested where shadows were cool and refreshing, my thoughts went back to

the days of old, when other generations wandered
along the shores. Like drifts of brown sea-
laver thrown up on the sands of Time, the old
traditions and stories of this part of Glamorgan
came to my mind, and deftly as the laver-
gatherers worked among the shelving rocks, I
penetrated the nooks and crannies of the past,
and with the following results.

In the memorials of the ancient Stradling
family, who, in an unbroken line, from the time
of the Norman Conquest until the year 1738,
were owners of St. Donats Castle, Glamorganshire, it is thus recorded—" Sir Harry Stradling,
in the sixteenth year of the reign of King
Edward the Fourth, journeyed like others of his
ancestors to Jerusalem, where he was honoured
with the order of the Knight of the Holy
Sepulchre like his father, grandfather, and others.
This Sir Harry died in the island of Cyprus on
his return homewards, in the city of Famagusta,
and was buried there."

The family had an estate at Coombe Hawey
in Somersetshire, where they occasionally lived,
but their favourite residence was at St. Donats.

St. Donats Castle is one of the most ancient
in Wales. It is beautifully situated on the side
of a lovely but narrow glen sloping to the Severn
Sea. Cradled, as it were, among luxuriant trees,
its mossy lawns descend in terrace after terrace

down to the old sea-wall, where in former times the barracks stood.

Before the ancient castle the calm sea glitters in the golden glow of summer, and the foam of the cold grey waves looks like driven snow when winter winds swell the waters, and lash them against the rocky barriers of the dangerous coast.

On the west of the glen stand the remains of an ancient watch-tower, which was built by Sir Peter Stradling, " to give light to his galley at nights when the family returned from Coombe Hawey to St. Donats."

Other authorities said that Sir Peter—from whom Sir Harry was sixth in descent—erected the tower and placed a light therein, " to decoy vessels to the dangerous rocks that extend along the coast for some miles east and west of St. Donats."   " But," says an old writer, " this kind-hearted and charitable family were far indeed from entertaining any such intention. It is, however, said, that the light in the tower led some vessels astray, that were ultimately lost on the bordering rocks; but so far were the Stradlings from plundering the cargoes of such wrecks that, instead, they preserved and protected them to the utmost, for the rightful owners—affording, also, every succour to the crews."

In the days of Sir Harry Stradling, a notorious

pirate, known as Colyn Dolphyn, a native of Brittany, scoured the coast, now making raids on the English side of the Bristol Channel, then crossing over to Wales and plundering the country there.

According to the old chroniclers, Colyn Dolphyn was a tall, athletic, and mighty man, "like Saul in Israel." He " towered head and shoulders" over the Welsh and English alike.

Colyn Dolphyn's name was a terror in South Wales. At the sound of it children crouched around their mothers, and stalwart men trembled, and even in the present century the name of the great pirate is a power in the home, for the Welsh mothers and nurses still say, " Hush ! Be good children, or Colyn Dolphyn will come again !"

In the reign of King Henry the Sixth, a strange beldame appeared in the neighbourhood of St. Donats. During the day she groped away to the shadows of gloomy glens, dark caverns, or deep dingles, but at night she came forth and wandered about. Her real name, the race from which she was descended, and the manner of her life or source of sustenance, were unknown to any mortal. Because of her nocturnal habits, the peasants called her Mallt-y-Nōs (Night Matilda, or Matilda of the Night). She worked magic and witchcraft, and it was said—though in fear and trembling—that she was Colyn Dolphyn's spy, and a minion of the arch-fiend himself.

One evening, as Sir Harry Stradling, accompanied by his man Dewryn, went from the castle to the watch-tower, old Mallt-y-Nōs crossed their path.

"How now, beldame!" exclaimed Sir Harry, throwing her some money.

Leaning on her staff, the old woman paused, looked down at the money, and muttered under her breath, "Thee'lt want a fortune of that kind soon." Then, picking up the coins, she hurried quickly under the trees towards the church and village.

"Mallt-y-Nōs muttered some words, but I did not hear them," remarked Sir Harry to Dewryn.

The man repeated the words.

"What can the hag mean?" said Sir Harry.

"That I know not; but she means no good, we may be sure," said Dewryn.

Sir Harry and his man strode on, and soon reached the watch-tower.

Meanwhile, Mallt-y-Nōs made her way to the castle.

Although shunned by all, turned away from the doors of rich and poor alike, the witch was received kindly by Lady Stradling, who bestowed food, clothing, and sometimes money upon the wanderer.

It was whispered abroad, that the stately sister of William Herbert, Earl of Pembroke, and wife of Sir Harry Stradling, was superstitious, and fond of consulting the witch, for sometimes Mallt-y-Nōs was closeted alone with her ladyship when Sir Harry was away.

" My respects to your ladyship," said Mallt-y-Nōs, dropping a curtsey to Lady Stradling at the door of the great hall.

" Bid her come in," said Lady Stradling to one of the maids.

The witch entered. As she did so, Elizabeth, Lady Stradling, devoutly crossing herself, said, " Put food before her, and then send her in to my presence. I wish to consult her as to the properties of ground ivy."

After having partaken of the very welcome refreshment, the witch was conducted to Lady Stradling's room, the door of which was immediately closed.

" Your ladyship looks troubled," said the witch, dropping a very low curtsey.

" That I am," was the reply.

" It behoves me not to ask questions of my lady, but I should like to know what ails you, madam ? "

" Much," was the reply. " Sir Harry is going to Somersetshire, and it is my desire to prevent him."

" Why so, my lady ? "

"Because I like not the omen he had last night."

" What was that, my lady ? "

" He had a bad dream. In it he was on a solitary island, where an angry sea rolled and a tempest raged. He said I was crying and wringing my hands, and, standing in a ship beyond the surf, I begged the seamen to succour him, but they would not. I fear some harm will befall him."

Mallt-y-Nōs pondered awhile, then said, " That dream bodes no good."

" I fear me not," said her ladyship, " and yet I know not what to do."

" If Sir Harry will go, he will," said Mallt-y-Nōs ; " for he's a man of great determination."

" I know—I know," said Lady Stradling, impatiently, as though she wished the witch could do something, or work magic to prevent Sir Harry's departure.

Guessing this, Mallt-y-Nōs said, " I can warn Dewryn this very night, and that I promise you, my lady."

Then dropping a low curtsey, the witch went her way.

That night when Dewryn crossed the park, Mallt-y-Nōs accosted him.

" Beware ! " she said, raising her thin and boney finger ; " beware ! "

"What danger now, hag?" asked Dewryn, pausing to listen.

"Beware of dangers and troubles on sea and land, and soon—soon!" said Mallt-y-Nōs.

"Dangers, troubles, woe, and mischief, are always the burden of thy croak!" exclaimed Dewryn, striding away.

"Beware!" shouted the hag after him.

"Beware!" cried the mocking echo.

The next day Sir Harry Stradling and his men set sail for Somersetshire, where the party intended remaining for some time.

It was July when they went, and they purposed returning early in August.

Tidings were received of their safe arrival in Somersetshire, and Lady Stradling's mind was at rest.

Through July the clustering grapes ripened in the celebrated vineyards, and the deer browsed in the parks of St. Donats, where the monks and friars of neighbouring monasteries and abbeys were at liberty to wander at will.

Leland in his Itinerary writes: "In the which space bytwixt the Castelle and the *Severn* is a Parke of Falow Dere. There is a nother Park of Redde Deere more by Northe West from the Castelle. The Parkes booth and the Castelle long to Stradeling, a Gentilman of very fair Landes in that Countery."

August came, and with it the ripened fruits, and corn, and barley, and truly the *Gwlad ar Háv*—Land of Summer, as Glamorgan was called, looked radiant and beautiful.

August waned, and the September moon arose like an orb of beaten gold in the sapphire sky.

Day after day Lady Stradling took her three children, Thomas the heir, Blanche, and the baby, to the terrace to watch and wait for the return of Sir Harry, but still he came not.

In the evening of a glorious autumn day, a small sailed skiff was seen approaching, and in a few minutes two of the crew landed. They hastened to the Castle, and asked for Lady Stradling.

The first question they put was, " Is Sir Harry Stradling come home? " and were answered in the negative.

" Then," said the elder man of the two, " some ill must have befallen him."

" I fear me it must be so," said Lady Stradling, " though we have not had a storm."

" See," said the other man, " these things were found by the captain of a schooner off Nash, and brought therefrom to Minehead."

The articles were a light leathern package containing a valuable document belonging to Sir Harry, and the figurehead of *St. Barbe*, the Stradling vessel.

Lady Stradling was stricken with grief as to the fate of her husband.

The weather had been so calm and fair that the ship could not be wrecked, but its fate was a mystery.

" P'rhaps it has foundered on the Nash," said the people, and forthwith a search party went to the dangerous sands, which can only be approached in calm weather, and when the tide is out.

There they found many tokens of the *St. Barbe.*

It was evident that Sir Harry and his crew had been wrecked on the Nash Sands.

.   .   .   .

Meanwhile many weary months passed away. during which Sir Harry Stradling, his faithful man Dewryn, and the crew of the *St. Barbe,* were kept close prisoners by Colyn Dolphyn, on board his barque the *Sea Swallow.*

The *St. Barbe,* on the homeward voyage, had been seized by the notorious pirate, and scuttled near the Nash Sands.

In pain and sorrow, Sir Harry and his men were kept manacled in the *Sea Swallow,* wherever it sailed. Now the pirate barque, followed by other vessels belonging to Colyn Dolphyn, fleeted before the wind up-channel, past the Steep and Flat Holms, and on, higher up the Severn, then down again on the wind's wing, only pausing to seize some unfortunate ship, or running into lonely parts of England and Wales, and re-embarking with spoils from numberless castles and abbeys, monasteries and farms. The captain and crew of the *St. Barbe* were dispersed among the notorious pirate's various vessels, so that there could be no chance of mutiny or the escape of Sir Harry.

By-and-by, after one whole year of torture and privation for Sir Harry, it occurred to Colyn Dolphyn that more money might be made by releasing the owner of St. Donats than by keeping him. Thereupon he proposed that Sir Harry should find a ransom, but the sum named was so high that the prisoner knew his family would be reduced to want and beggary in order to pay it.

For several months, even though suffering the pangs of hunger, the pains of torture, and the taunts of the coarse and rough sea-thieves surrounding him, Sir Harry refused to pay the ransom. Later on he begged Colyn Dolphyn to reduce the sum. This happened at a time when "trade was dull" with the great pirate, who then offered to take 2200 marks—just half the sum he at first demanded. A messenger was despatched to Lady Stradling and other members of the family, who, in order to raise the sum wanted, were compelled to sell part of the Stradling property.

According to Sir Harry's directions two ancient manors in Oxfordshire, the manor of Tre-Gwilym, in the parish of Bassaleg, in Monmouthshire, together with the manor of Sutton, in Glamorganshire, were sold, and the money was sent from St. Donats to Colyn Dolphyn.

Sir Harry, his man Dewryn, together with the captain and crew of the *St. Barbe*, were landed, ragged, penniless, and without food or raiment, on a lonely part of the coast about ninety miles from St. Donats. Footsore and weary, the victims of the pirate's cruelty reached St. Donats Castle, where they were received with great rejoicing.

Soon after his return home, Sir Harry Stradling placed arms in the ancient watch-tower, and men who, according to an old writer, had " to watch at night for the sea thief, Colyn Dolphyn, who too frequently cruised along the Severn Sea on ship-robbing intent."

Many a weary watchman had waited in vain on both sides of the Severn Sea, for the English and Welsh alike longed to catch Colyn Dolphyn. But the old sea-rover was wary. He knew where schemes and traps were laid, and carefully avoided them.

In the course of time Sir Harry thought of the old report concerning the building and purpose of the ancient watch-tower. Pacing up

F

and down the terraces of St. Donats Castle, Sir Harry one day—when the white-capped waves hurried landward, and the storm-wind howled through the grim caves on the rock-bound coast —looked across at the watch-tower.

"Old Sir Peter kept a light in the tower," said Sir Harry to his faithful Dewryn, "and I think I will follow his example. If light fails to lure our old enemy, nothing will take him. See that a light is put there to-morrow night."

A strong lantern was accordingly placed in the tower, and Dewryn took charge of it. Every morning he trimmed the lantern. Every night he lighted it. The beacon light could be seen far out at sea.

Colyn Dolphyn saw it and swore.

"Ha, ha!" he cried. "Sir Peter's lamp re-lighted! Well, in times gone by it was a welcome beacon to warn mariners off the wild Welsh coast. A beacon it shall be to me henceforth. Good Sir Harry! He thinks of his days with us, and the perils of the sea!"

November fogs glided ghostlike up the Severn Sea, enveloping the coasts of England and Wales. November's drizzling rain fell on land and sea alike. Through fog and rain the old sea-rover fearlessly sailed, for too well he knew the coast to venture into danger.

December dawned, and with it at first came

sleet and beating hail, followed at the end of the
month by wild winds and blinding snow. The
storm raged furiously. Snow fell thick and
fast, filling the frozen sails of the *Sea Swallow*.
Icicles clung to the mast. Icicles fell in long
fringes from the figurehead of the pirate's barque.
Colyn Dolphyn's sailors dashed the icicles from
their long hair as it froze.

The old sea-robber paced the deck, now
shouting a command, then pausing to shake the
snow from his shaggy beard and matted eye-
brows.

"We must put in to land!" he yelled.

"But where are we?" shouted the man at the
helm.

"Off the Tuscar," responded the pirate, in
hoarse tones, as he peered through the increasing
gloom.

"A light! A beacon light!" cried one of the
crew.

Colyn Dolphyn gazed through the snow.

"Good Sir Harry's beacon!" he shouted.
"That will do. Now, make for Dunraven."

On, on, the plaything of the tempest, the frolic
of the waves, went the *Sea Swallow*. It was a
terrific storm! Now, creaking and groaning in
the snow and surf; now thrust back by the
force of the waves, then hurled forward by the
relentless winds, the pirate's barque was wrested

from the captain's power. On, like a sheeted ghost, the *Sea Swallow*, with sail and cordage riven, with frosted yard and spar, and with a half-frozen crew, was driven by the wind.

One more leap across the dark and yawning wave chasm—one more dip down into the depths of whirling surf and hissing spray—one more struggle, then, groaning, creaking like a human creature, the *Sea Swallow* struck on the Nash Sands.

It was a widely scattered wreck.

In the gloom of the wintry daybreak, through hissing spray and wind-blown surf, Colyn Dolphyn and his crew clung for dear life to drifting yard and spar, hoping thereby to reach the shore. Some of the crew were engulphed in the yawning waves, and some, by dint of clinging to the frozen wreckage, were saved, and that on the third day before Christmas.

Sir Peter's beacon light had done its work! Sir Harry Stradling was revenged! Dewryn, pacing the shore, looked keenly on. Malt-y-Nōs, groping among the snow-covered crags and rocks, that on this coast have been hurled in wild confusion, alternately groaned and sighed.

Sir Harry hurried to the shore. He had tidings of the wreck, and, ready to lend a helping hand to all "in peril on the sea," he was prepared for generous action.

Yet even he hoped the wrecked ship was the *Sea Swallow*, and the lost included the old pirate and his crew.

Foremost among those swimming from the wrecked ship to the shore, was one whose brawny arms and breast battled bravely with the angry waves, and at last succeeded in gaining a rock of safety. There, tall and erect, in the cold of winter and the snow, stood Colyn Dolphyn, with six of his crew. The old sea-robber gazed around and then shouted, " Where —where am I ? "

For answer, in the growing daylight, he was surrounded by Sir Harry's men, and, together with the crew of the *Sea Swallow*, Colyn Dolphyn was made prisoner.

The notorious pirate and his men were manacled and marched from the scene of the wreck to St. Donats.

Nothing daunted by the disaster, Colyn Dolphyn, on the upward way, playfully promised to call his confederates from the sea to join him in Sir Harry's Christmas sports. He fully expected that if he offered a good ransom, or the return of the sum paid for the release of Sir Harry, the owner of St. Donats would set him free.

All the captives were taken to the Castle keep, and there secured to wait until the morrow, when, according to the old chronicles, Colyn Dolphyn, without the aid of judge or jury, was sentenced to death.

In solemn tones Dewryn said, " Colyn Dolphyn ! we doom thee, by means of wind and twist, to writhe until thy soul and body part !"

It was Christmas Eve. Early in the afternoon the javelin men, aroused by a sudden trumpet blast, assembled in the court-yard of the Castle, and were then joined by a band of well-armed soldiers. Soon, as a search-party, they marched down through the glen to the shore, where, perhaps, some lurking ship waited to land others who would be ready to rescue Colyn Dolphyn. The men, however, returned with the tidings that all was clear.

At ten o'clock that night, from each battlement, court, and mound, hundreds of flambeaux blazed.

The guard turned out; the javelin men grimly surrounded Sir Harry, who, accompanied by friends, priests, monks, and friars, went in procession to the Castle keep.

Colyn Dolphyn and his crew were brought forth and led to the place of execution. On the right side of the notorious pirate, one of the Friars Minor urged him to repentance ; on the other side, a " White Monk " tried to soothe him by word and sign, and promise of pardon hereafter.

Presently the dark and gloomy procession halted before the fatal oak where the pirate was to meet his doom. Then, according to the ancient chronicles, a strange scene was witnessed.

The wretched man, with a terrific glare, appeared to gaze upon some fearful supernatural form seen only by him. They said he "held converse with the Fiend," and that he "invoked the 'Sire of Sin.'"

While crowds transfixed with horror listened, he delivered his invocation, which has thus been rendered in verse by Taliesin, the son of Iolo Morganwg :—

> "Oh thou ! full well whom I have serv'd,
> From whose commands I never swerved ;
> To help thy faithful follower speed !
> Nor stand aloof in hour of need !
> By years that bade remorse adieu !
> By deeds that ne'er repentance knew !
> By murder'd infants' parting breath !
> By pleading mothers dash'd to death !
> By hands, through life in blood imbrued !
> And by my soul ! with thee imbued !
> Come to my aid ! avert this fate !
> Our compact told a longer date.
> Thine am I ! pledg'd by deed and vow !
> Supreme of Darkness ! nerve me now !"

Silence deep and profound followed the invocation. Dewryn's band of armed men pinioned Colyn Dolphyn, and soon the crowd around saw the old sea-pirate suspended by his neck from the ancient oak.

Before he breathed his last a terrible tempest arose. In the words of Taliesin, the son of Iolo Morganwg :—

> ". . . Fierce the wild tornado grew ;
> Their maniac forks the light'nings fling,
> And demon hosts are on the wing ;
> The warring winds assail the deep ;
> The waves infuriate upwards leap ;
> The beetling cliffs, in frequent crash,
> Hurl downwards with impetuous dash ;
> Fierce thunderbolts the forests rend,
> And all the elements contend ! "

While the thunder pealed and the lightning flashed across the midnight sky, and the crowd stood in terror before the awful gallows-tree wherefrom Colyn Dolphyn's body was suspended, a solitary figure quickly threaded its way to the scene of execution.

It was Mallt-y-Nōs.

Under the heavy snow-encumbered branches of the ancient oaks, she waited until the curious crowd gladly and yet fearfully went homeward.

Some marvelled that such a storm of thunder and lightning should occur in the winter ; some said it was because Colyn Dolphyn invoked the Fiend, who was not satisfied with the pirate's latest adventures ; some said it was because the

holy Eve of Christmas was desecrated by the
execution of the sea-robber and his crew; while
others declared in sinister tones that it was the
vengeance of Heaven expressed against Sir
Harry Stradling for having despatched the pirate
without the privilege of trial by judge and jury.

When all was quiet—when the crowd had
dispersed, and the dead bodies drooped listlessly
in the frosty air, Mallt-y-Nōs crept towards the
oak where Colyn Dolphyn hung.

In the distance, the prowling fox yelped, the
hounds howled dismally in their kennels, and
down in the glen melancholy owls hooted to
each other.

Dewryn alone, unseen among the surrounding
oaks, watched the witch in her progress.

Afterwards he said she invoked the "Fiend,"
and that there, in the loneliness, darkness, and
snow, she collected the materials necessary for
preparing the gruesome "Dead Man's Candle."

"Then," said Dewryn, relating the story to
his fellows in the Castle, "she muttered strange
words, made strange signs, and uttered unearthly
sounds. And I saw that she was joined by three
witches of terrible aspect. They bound her hand
and foot, and, amid the smell of sulphur and
flames of fire, she was wafted out of sight."

From that night Mallt-y-Nōs was never seen
again. In the "Memoirs of the Stradlings" it

is recorded that for having executed Colyn Dolphyn without trial by jury, "Sir Harry Stradling, it cannot well be devised why, was bitterly pursued at law by Henry the Sixth."

Yet another story about this romantic and picturesque neighbourhood.

The last of the Stradlings to live in St. Donats was Sir Thomas Stradling, who was killed " in a duel" at Montpelier, in France, on September 27, 1738, and was buried at St. Donats on March 19, 1739.

Much mystery and suspicions of foul play surrounded his death. Young Stradling went abroad with his friend Tyrwhit, and they agreed in writing that, if any ill befell one of them, the survivor was to inherit the other's estates.

Some said that the body conveyed from Montpelier to St. Donats, and there buried, was not the mortal frame of Thomas Stradling. Litigation for more than fifty years followed the death of the last of the Stradlings. By that time Tyrwhit, the claimant, was dead, and the Castle was rented to a family named Thomas.

In the early part of the present century, when May blossoms filled the land with beauty, and nature looked like a fair young bride going forth radiant and gladly to meet her groom, a strange thing happened.

Lewis Thomas left St. Donats Castle in the

afternoon for Tresilian. After spending some time there, he decided to walk homeward along the shore instead of following the cliff line.

The tide was far out, and there was no danger of being wave-locked. During that delightful walk Lewis Thomas thought much and pleasantly of his son, who was "far out at sea." In this state of mind he wandered slowly along the lofty and inaccessible cliffs that towered above him.

Far over the sea a soft golden glory lingered, and slowly merged into the purple haze of twilight that deepened almost imperceptibly. When Lewis Thomas was within twenty minutes' walk of the Castle, he thought he felt somebody tapping his shoulder.

"It was only a fancy," he murmured, for on the solitary coast not a person could be seen. Only the sea-swallows darting to the cliff cavities, and the sea-gulls flying in their wake, were visible.

Again he felt a tap upon his shoulder, and this time, turning round, he saw beside him a tall bearded man, dressed as a sailor.

"What may you want?" asked Lewis Thomas accosting the stranger.

"This, only just this," said the man breathlessly. "I hurried after you as fast as I could to draw your attention to yonder cliff"

"And what of that?" asked Lewis Thomas.

"Before three days have passed there will be a slight, a very slight landslip there. Now, I want you to promise me something."

"And what may that be? I do not like making rash promises."

"You shall see; the land will slip and thereby lower the cliff."

"Indeed!" exclaimed Lewis Thomas doubtfully.

"When the land has slipped," said the stranger, "lose no time in making a stairway that shall lead upward from the shore to the fields beyond."

"And why?"

"Ask not," said the stranger, "but solemnly promise you will do as I bid."

"I solemnly promise," said Lewis Thomas.

"Then farewell. There's no time to spare—proceed with the work at once."

Before Lewis Thomas could respond, the stranger vanished.

Three days later the Castle servants reported a landslip on the very spot indicated by the stranger. Lewis Thomas went to see it. Yes; there was the slip which considerably lowered the cliffs in that part.

"This would be a good place for a way up from the sea, in case of shipwreck or being locked in," said Lewis Thomas, who forthwith directed his men to make the necessary preparations for a rough stairway there.

The work was completed, and the whole countryside sang the praises of Lewis Thomas and his work.

Months passed. September gales raged—the Severn Sea waves rolled majestically, and their thunders could be heard far inland. Breaksea Point roared in response to Sker, and the breakers around the Tuscar Rock sent their sad wave-messages to the eddies that whirled around the treacherous sands of Nash.

In the night of a rainy day, when the wind went down, and a dangerous white fog enveloped land and sea, a fog-horn was heard.

"A ship in distress," said the Castle folk, some of whom went down to the shore as quickly as possible. But by that time the horn ceased, and the fog, increasing in density, prevented the people from seeing the position of the ship.

"It has passed on safely," said one.

"Or struck somewhere," said another.

Then the party returned to the Castle. Two hours passed. The Castle clock struck ten. Half an hour later the fog had lifted, and the stars were glittering in the September sky.

About midnight loud knocking aroused the Castle people from their beds.

"Who is it? What is the matter?" asked Lewis Thomas, opening the door.

"We're shipwrecked mariners," was the reply. "Pray let us in."

"To be sure, to be sure," said kindly Lewis Thomas, throwing the door widely open, and thinking of his dear son "far out at sea."

He lighted the candles, roused the servants, and ordered fire, clothing, and food for the dripping sailors.

"Don't you know me?" said a bearded man, coming eagerly forward.

"No," said Lewis Thomas.

"Not know me!" exclaimed the man.

Lewis Thomas looked closely at him again. "My son! my son!" he cried; "my only son, whom I thought was far out at sea."

After the first joy of welcome had passed, Lewis Thomas asked where they were wrecked.

"We would have been overwhelmed by the tide," said the sailor son, "but I noticed in the half light a land-slip. We made for that, and there found a stair leading to the fields. The ship was wrecked, but by swimming after me towards the ship, the captain and crew were all saved."

Lewis Thomas then told the story of the mysterious stranger and his command. "And the stranger was no other than thou, my boy, for now I see thou hast grown a beard," said Lewis Thomas, who rejoiced in having performed the promise, and so saved the life of his son, then "far out at sea."

From that day to this, a steep and rugged pathway, now worn with age and partially obliterated, remains.

Leading upward from the shelving cliffs to and through a tangle where white violets, primroses, and blue bells grow in profusion, the pathway is lost among the elderberry bushes fringing the field beside St. Donats Castle. It is known as " Lewis Thomas's Stairs."

The Sweet Singer of Valle Crucis Abbey.

EXPERIENCES OF THE SUPERNATURAL.

OFT and filmy mists, through which the moonbeams occasionally strayed like arrows of silver, filled the beautiful Valley of the Cross, and lightly shrouded the ruins of the celebrated Valle Crucis Abbey, which was founded by Owen Gwynedd, Prince of Wales, in 1200.

Through the light veil of the mist the hoary ruins loomed like a grim warden, surrounded by a staff of sentinels guarding the resting-place of the illustrious dead and the sacred secrets of the past.

There, in solemn loneliness and grandeur, kings and princes have been laid to rest; and beside them mitred abbots, cowled monks, and humble friars are sleeping their long last sleep. There, too, where the shadows fall kindly, and the moonbeams quiver gently, Iolo Goch, the illustrious poet of Wales, has rested through the long centuries that have gone by since Owen Glendower lived at Sycarth, and the comet which appeared, auguring good fortune and success for the intrepid leader of Welsh insurrection.

Slowly through the mist and the early morning moonlight, two pedestrians wended their way through the silent valley, and paused occasionally to rest awhile, now on one of the stone stiles still so numerous in Wales, and again leaning against a gate to look back as far as they could see. They were tired already, having come a long distance, but consoled themselves by saying, "Two miles more and we shall be in Llangollen." There they were to join a friend who had offered them seats in his dog-cart, bound for a distant town.

These solitary travellers were itinerant preachers, and like many of their brethren in the present day, they often had to walk far and sometimes fare badly.

The name of the one was Robert Owen, and the other was Richard Rhys, both ministers of that large community known in Wales as Calvinistic Methodists.

In their days men were obliged to be good walkers, for the century was young and coaches

G

were unknown in the remote parts of Wales.
Sometimes the itinerant brotherhood had the
loan of a mountain pony, but more frequently
they had to walk.

Robert Owen and Richard Rhys had already
walked twenty miles when they reached the
sacred Valley of the Cross. During their journey
they had whiled away the time by discussing the
views of the day, the state of religion, the spread
of infidelity, and lastly, they related anecdotes
and stories of fellow-ministers.

A great number of the itinerant preachers of
Wales are born story-mongers. All the good
and bad stories of the Principality are included
in their repertoire, and if any Englishman wishes
to increase his knowledge of "gallant little
Wales," let him spend a holiday among the
people there in the wild highlands or the lonely
lowlands of Wales, where the itinerant preachers
are still to be found as "thick as leaves in Val-
lambrosa."

In the ancient farmhouses of Wales, where
once devout men of another creed—men whose
carved crucifixes, quaintly bound missals, and
curious rosaries, proved like a talisman everywhere—the itinerant preachers of Wales are to
be seen. Cowled monk, mendicant friar, and
wandering priest, who wended their way through
the gloomy glens, shadowed ravines, or mountain

passes, have been succeeded by the great dissenting brotherhood for which Wales is celebrated.

In the days of Robert Owen and Richard Rhys, people believed in ghosts, though the old faith in fairy folk was gradually but steadily waning. Long before the travellers had reached the abbey, conversation turned to these subjects.

" Do you believe that there ever were such beings as fairies ? " asked Robert Owen.

" You ask me a question difficult to answer," said Richard Rhys in his quaint and slow fashion. " There were such beings—as giants—in times gone by ; that we know—for a certainty. And —if there were—giants—why—should not there have been—dwarfs ? "

" But surely it would be impossible for such tiny little creatures as fairy-folk to exist. I have heard my mother talking about the Tylwyth Têg and Bendith-i-Mamau as if she knew them well."

" Perhaps she did," said Richard Rhys, the elder man of the two.

" I couldn't believe it," said Robert Owen.

" Not believe your own mother ! Oh !" said Rhys.

" Very likely it was only a fancy of hers," continued Robert Owen. " Her great-grandmother, her grandmother, and her mother believed in fairies, and it was only natural that my mother should inherit the belief. Did your mother believe in fairies?"

"She did, and my grandmother too. I will tell you a story about my grandmother," said Richard Rhys. "I've heard her tell it many a time. In the early days of her married life my father, a small farmer, had a hard struggle to get along. Times were bad, the family was increasing, and the harvests were small. One day my grandmother lamented to herself about the near approach of rent-day, and no money to meet it. My grandfather was out working on the farm, and the children were playing in the yard. Just as my grandmother was thinking like this, she heard a knock at the door. 'Come in,' said my grandmother, and in walked a little old woman dressed in a green gown, with a red cloak and hood, and a tall extinguisher hat. She was one of the 'little people,' she said, and had come to help my grandmother. The fairy told grandmother to go in the dusk of the evening to the cross roads, and turn to the one leading to Ruabon. Grandmother went, and was met by a fairy man, who gave her sufficient money to pay the rent, and afterwards, whenever she wanted money, she went there, and the fairies supplied her."

Robert Owen discredited the story, but did not make any comment on it.

After a brief silence Robert Owen said, "Well, come now. Turning from fairies, do you believe that disembodied spirits return to earth—that ghosts haunt any particular spot or person ? "

" I do," said Richard Rhys firmly.

" And I do not," said Robert Owen decidedly. " But I would like to have the proofs of your belief."

"That you shall," said Richard Rhys. "Twenty-five years ago I had to fill another preacher's place in the Association held at Machynlleth. When I got there I found nearly every house filled with strangers from all parts, and the deacon had so many visitors himself that several of us had to sleep out. I was one of them. But first let me tell you that I had never been in the town before, and I knew nothing about it at all. The house I had to put up in was very ancient, and I could see it would soon tumble down. Soon after supper the first night I went to bed early. My room I found to be very large—too big for a bedroom. In it was a great four-posted bed, a good-sized round table of solid oak, and other furniture besides. Tired after the long journey I soon fell asleep, and suppose I must have slept for several hours, when a noise in the house disturbed me. At first I thought something had fallen to the floor in the next room, but by-and-by, when more sounds came, I could hear the tramp of many feet on the stairs. Suddenly the door of my room flew open, and in walked a troop of men. I could see them as plain as possible, because the moonlight was as bright as day. And what I thought most odd was that all the men were dressed as armed men of hundreds of years ago. One of the men planted himself by the chimney-piece, and the others stood before him. Although I was very fearful, I sat bolt upright in bed to look at them. Some were fierce-looking, others were milder, but all were armed, and all wore swords. The men seemed to be debating, and the leader was apparently giving directions, when one of the number rushed forward, and lifting his sword attempted to kill the leader. In the twinkling of an eye the head man sprang aside, and the assassin was foiled. Terrible noise followed, and I could hear the clatter of arms, and the clash of swords as the men crowded around the fellow, who had tried to slay their leader. Then, as strangely as they came in, they tramped out of the room, and I heard the sound of their feet going downstairs and out to the road."

"And what followed?" asked Robert Owen.

"I got up at once," continued Richard Rhys, "and I looked out, but all was as quiet as the grave. Before I left the town I told the deacon what had happened, and he had heard the house was haunted."

" Did you ever find out anything more about the place ? " asked Robert Owen.

" Not then," replied Richard Rhys, " but a year later I met a preacher who saw exactly what I had seen. It appears he found out that the old dwelling was called the ' Parliament House,' and there in 1402 Owen Glendower narrowly escaped being assassinated by Sir David Gam, the Fluellin of Shakespeare."

" Have you another proof of your belief in ghosts ? " asked Robert Owen.

" Yes ; one of my own and one of my fathers," said Richard Rhys. " Seven years ago I was down in Aberedwy, dear Builth, Breconshire. I had to preach twice on the Sunday and one week night in Builth. The deacon was a blacksmith, and lived next door to the smithy. The weather was very cold, and everybody believed snow would soon fall. It was late when I got to Aberedwy on the Saturday night, and late when we went to bed. In the dead of the night I felt cold, and got up to put some more blankets that the deacon's wife had placed on a chair by the bed. Just then I heard a voice by the blacksmith's shop, and it sounded to me as though the smith was shoeing a horse, but it could not be that at two o'clock on a Sunday morning. I got up and looked out.

Snow was covering the road, and the moon was
shining.   Down by the forge a man was standing while the blacksmith shod the horse.   I
thought it something important, or a man would
never come to shoe his horse at such an untimely
hour.   Well, I saw the stranger remount his
horse, and ride off, and when he was gone I
saw a curious sight.   In the snow, the mark of
the horse's hoofs were the wrong way around.
The smith had shod the horse backward.   I
didn't then tell the deacon a word about what
I saw, but next time I went to Builth, I heard
that another preacher had seen the same sight:
I was told it was the ghost of Prince Llewelyn,
who rode to the smithy at Aberedwy to have his
horse shod backward in order to defeat the
enemy.   Now, the other ghost story was told
by my father.   In his age, he was then over
seventy, he preached one Sunday night at
Meifod in Montgomery, and after service he
had to go to Llanfyllin on the Vyrnwy, six
miles away.   It was a dark, wet, and windy
night in December.   My father, mounted on a
merlyn, rode on very comfortably for two miles
or more.   Then the horse stood quite still.   He
tried to make it go on, but it would not.   Then
he heard a rustling noise in the hedge on the
roadside.   A minute later, a very tall gigantic
figure appeared on the road.   It stretched out

its arms as wide as ever it could, and made a
kind of barrier across the way. My father rode
nearer to it, and implored it in the name of the
Lord to speak. He heard a sound like the
rushing of a flood, and then the phantom, without moving, said, "For your life go back." My
father was so much astonished that he turned
the horse's head, and rode back to Meifod. It
was lucky he did, for next morning the news
came to Meifod that about the time my father
was stopped on the road, a man was attacked
and murdered by a gang of highwaymen. If
my father had ridden on, he would have shared
the same fate. The spectre on the road was a
warning from the Lord. Now, what have you
to say about ghosts?"

Robert Owen did not reply.

"Do you believe in special interposition of
Providence?" asked Richard Rhys.

"I have no reason to disbelieve, seeing I
never had any experience in that way," said
Robert Owen.

By this time the preachers approached the
ruined Abbey of Valle Crucis.

"It is many years since I last saw the old
place," remarked Richard Rhys.

"And I have never been here before," said
Robert Owen. "There is time to take a look
around, I suppose?"

"Plenty, plenty," said the older man.

By this time the mists began to melt away, the morning moonlight faded, and the shadows grew longer and deeper among the ruins as day-dawn approached.

"It's a grand old place," remarked Robert Owen.

"Very," said Richard Rhys, who began moral-ising on the vanity of human desires and the scattered vestiges of what he called "ecclesiastical extravagance."

Just as he came to a peroration on the subject a sound was heard coming from the distance.

It was the voice of a singer, singing in the ruined choir.

The preachers listened for a few minutes, and then Robert Owen said, "Let us go and see who it is."

"No, no," replied Richard Rhys, "if we do that we shall stop the singer."

Robert Owen obeyed his friend; at the same time he ventured, as the children say, "to have a peep."

He just caught a glimpse, no more, of the long and somewhat broad shadow, apparently of a man, across the spot where once costly marble chancel pavement was to be seen.

Then, fearing to disturb the singer, he drew back.

The preachers withdrew to a secluded corner of the ruins, and there listened as if spellbound.

To the humble and simple preachers the singing was mysterious, and in a language unknown to them.

At first the singer appeared to be practising a few bars, then he went on, and by-and-by began singing the grand old *" Dies Irae"* in Latin.

Although the preachers did not understand a word of the hymn, the melody and the manner of singing enthralled them, especially when the singer sang the more pathetic parts. Both Richard Rhys and Robert Owen would have felt greater sympathy had they known the meaning of the words—

> " Recordare, Jesu pie
> Quod sum causa tuæ viæ,
> Ne me perdas illa die,
> Quærens me sedisti lassus,
> Redemisti crucem passus,
> Tantus labor non sit cassus."

The singer threw wonderfully deep and pathetic expression into the hymn, and when the sweetly sad but powerful voice ceased, Richard Rhys grasped Robert Owen's hand, as though he felt shaken to the soul by the grandeur of the singing. There was a pause for a moment only, and it seemed to the listeners that the heavens had

opened, and a voice from on high began singing
another hymn, but still in the same unknown
tongue. It was the sixth "Penitential Psalm,"
the grand "*De Profundis,*" truly the cry of a
contrite heart imploring the Divine mercy. Then
as if to fully practise the beautiful Psalm, the
singer commenced singing in English—

> " Out of the depths have I cried unto Thee, O Lord.
> Lord, hear my voice. . . .
> . . . With Him is plentiful redemption . . .
> . . . Let perpetual light shine upon them . . .
> May they rest in peace ! "

Then the singer ceased. Tears fill the eyes
of the preachers, who, although they understood
very little English, knew enough to recognise
some of the leading passages.

How long they had stood listening to that
wonderful and melodious voice, neither Richard
Rhys nor Robert Owen could tell.

This they knew, and this alone. Morning
moonlight filled the land with chastened splendour
when they entered the ruins of Valle Crucis
Abbey, and when they turned to proceed to
Llangollen the sun was fairly high in the heavens.
And they knew at last, such had been the power
of the singer of those holy and mystic melodies,
that hours had passed by like a dream of delight.

" Did you ever hear anything like it ? " asked Robert Owen in enraptured ecstasy.

" Never," exclaimed Robert Rhys. " It was truly wonderful, wonderful."

" Whoever the singer was he had a grand voice," said Robert Owen.

" Yes," said Richard Rhys, " but I fear me we have tarried too long, We shall not get to Llangollen in time to go off with Morgan Wynne. That is a pity."

" Well," said Robert Owen, " a voice like that is only heard once in a lifetime, and I'd rather miss the dog-cart than lose hearing those divine strains divinely rendered."

The preachers left the ruins and passed by the ancient fish-pond, where once the friars fished and abbots partook of the contents of the anglers' baskets; then they walked from the lovely Valley of the Cross, and reached the road leading to Llangollen.

They arrived at Morgan Wynne's house, on the outskirts of the town of Llangollen, to find their friend had taken his departure without them.

" How long is he gone ? " asked Robert Owen.

" About three hours ago," replied Mrs. Wynne.

" That is all because we listened so long on the way," said Richard Rhys. " It was foolish to do so."

"I don't know so much about that," said Robert Owen.

After refreshment and rest, the preachers were obliged to resume their journey. It was somewhat annoying to have to walk when they had an opportunity of being driven.

How foolish they were to loiter on their way! How foolish it was to listen to the sweet and mysterious singer!

But were they foolish?

For answer they met a horseman half way between Llangollen and their destination. He was riding post haste.

"Bad news," he breathlessly shouted, and halted a moment: "Morgan Wynne and his brother have met with an awful accident. The horse took fright and ran away. John was thrown out and killed on the spot; Morgan has been badly injured, and is only barely sensible."

Then the horseman rode on with the news to Llangollen.

Robert Owen and Richard Rhys proceeded to the place where the accident occurred. In a cottage close by, they found Morgan Wynne just able to recognise them, and poor John's dead body laid on a bed in the next room.

The preachers in one voice offered up their prayerful thanks to God for their safe deliverance from peril, and perhaps death.

Richard Rhys declared his belief that the voice in the ruined abbey was the special and merciful interposition of Providence to retard their progress and shield them from danger.

Robert Owen attained a good old age, and to the end of his life he attributed his safety on that perilous occasion to the wonderful, mysterious, and sweet spirit-singer of Valle Crucis Abbey.

The Ghost of the Gate=House.

JACK, the stable-boy at the Old Farm, had been asked to do something very strange, and he puzzled his head as to "what the world was coming to," but having promised to remain silent, he kept his word.

His young master, Meredith Gwyn, told him to saddle the roan mare Ruby as soon as the old master was safely in bed, and to say "nothing to nobody." The old gentleman farmer, who was also a J.P., seldom retired much before midnight, and it was about a quarter after twelve when the young master appeared, booted and spurred, with hunting-crop in hand, and fully dressed for riding.

Jack thought it "uncommon odd," for the young farmer to be "goin' off like that between twelve an' one o' the mornin'."

"The mare's in splendid trim for a long ride," ventured Jack, as his master mounted.

"Hold you're tongue, will you?" said Meredith

Gwyn, in a rough whisper, as he gave a piece of silver to the boy. "Don't say a word to anybody."

"Right, sir," said Jack, touching his cap.

"Now, lead the mare quietly out," said Meredith, "and when I'm gone, see that the gate is shut. Be here again at four to the minute."

"Right, sir," said Jack, who, after his young master had gone, turned into the stable-room, and began to muse.

"P'rhaps he's in love," he murmured to himself, "but 'tis an odd time to go a courtin'."

After speculating for more than half-an-hour, Jack fell asleep, but was awakened by the thought that his master must be admitted as quietly as he made his exit. So he rubbed his eyes, and began to think of his sweetheart, who was the prettiest girl in the village, or for the matter of that, in the whole Vale of Glamorgan.

It was four o'clock in the starlit morning when Meredith Gwyn returned home, and gave his horse into Jack's charge.

"Not a word," said the young master.

"Right, sir," repeated Jack.

At the same time he had his "thoughts," when he observed that Ruby was covered with mud, and bespattered even to her ears. He then remembered that Master Meredith looked

H

as though he had been out hunting in the worst of weathers.

"It's a rum go," muttered Jack in his own rugged way.

The morning passed, and breakfast-time came.

"Thee'rt half asleep," said Will Morris, the general man, to Jack.

"I kept awake half the night," was the reply. "I had the rheums that bad——"

"Who left the hay-loft door open last night, I should like to know?" continued the old man.

"I didn't," said Jack.

"Nor did I," remarked Will Morris, with something like a nasty jeer.

After breakfast the old man went to the stables, and, when there, called Jack to him.

"Take thee care," said Will Morris, "that thee'st got nothin' to do with Rebecca and her daughters, or, as sure as I be alive, I'll be the death of thee."

Will Morris, the general man at the Old Farm, was Jack's uncle, and therefore felt he had a right to do as he liked with the lad.

"I've never had any dealin's with Rebecca and her gang," said Jack sulkily.

All he knew about Rebecca was what he heard first hand in the Old Farm from his uncle, or second hand in the village from the idlers.

While the master of the Old Farm and his family were seated at dinner, the news came that one of the turnpike gates, near Peterstone, had been destroyed, and the gate-house was burnt to the ground.

A few minutes later the gate-keeper himself came, and asked to see the farmer and magistrate.

"Bring him in here," said Mr. Meredith, who was too eager for news to wait until after dinner.

"Well, what about it, Daniel?" asked Mr. Meredith.

"It did happen like lightning," said Daniel. "They did ride up thirty or forty of 'em, all in women's dresses, an' their faces was as black as the chimney backs, an' they did lay hold on me, an' carry me off to the blacksmith's shop, an' there they did keep me, while they did break down the gate, an' did burn the house to the ground."

Daniel, having delivered his message, went his way.

"It's bad business," remarked the master after the old man had taken his departure. "Something must be done to put a stop to it. But what can be done, bothers my head."

Day by day the demolition of the toll-gates increased; brutality was frequent, and occasionally murder was committed.

One morning in December news reached
Peterstone, that all along the main coach road,
from Carmarthen upward, the gates were being
destroyed, and sad havoc was wrought. People
in terror bolted and barred their doors, barri-
caded their windows, and prepared for the
coming of Rebecca and her daughters. Children,
almost frightened to death, cowered in safe
corners, and women whimpered and turned pale
with fright.

"It's cruel times," said those quiet men, who
felt it their duty to leave work and stay at home
to protect the women, the children, and the
helpless ones.

All along the main road, from Cowbridge to
Cardiff, people were ready to receive Rebecca
and her daughters. The gate-houses were forti-
fied as best they could be, and the keepers
thereof, while still remaining true as possible
under the circumstances to their posts, acted as
a rule upon the principle of the man who
sang—

> " He who fights, and runs away,
>   Will be able to fight another day."

In the "dead of the night," Cowbridge toll-
gate was destroyed, and, tired after arduous
work, Rebecca and her minions disbanded for
what they called "a few days' rest." Where

they went, nobody knew; but even these riotous ladies needed a little respite, and naturally nobody begrudged it them. People only wished they would always rest, and never resume their nefarious occupation. Those who waited in the neighbourhood of the next toll-gate—that of Bonvilstone—shivered in their shoes, for they knew well that Rebecca would soon be with them.

The day after the demolition of the Cowbridge toll-gate was bitterly cold. It had been freezing for days, and the leaden sky promised snow. Pedestrians were glad to turn in to the " Old Post," a well-known and ancient hostelry near Bonvilstone, on the main road between Cardiff and Cowbridge. Travellers driving gave their horses a feed, and meanwhile went in and warmed themselves awhile before continuing the journey westward to Cowbridge, or eastward to Cardiff.

Conversation naturally turned on the tyranny of turnpikes, though people felt that Rebecca went "too far" in injuring harmless gate-keepers, and frightening innocent women and children.

" I got to pay six turnpikes 'fore I can get a penn'orth of coal," grumbled a coal vendor present. " An' what's more, I do pay eight turnpikes 'fore I can sell a bit anywhere."

The man lustily cudgelled the table with his whip.

"Well, then, why d'ye grumble about Rebecca?" asked a hoarse-voiced cattle-drover, bringing his blackthorn down with a thud upon the arm of the settle.

"'Cause he do want the turnpikes to come down, only for him not to be in the pickle," said a farmer, poking the landlord's dog with his ash-staff.

Party feelings ran high, and when the commotion was on the verge of a brawl, the thin, weazened little tailor of the village entered, and in a squeaking voice said, "I'll venture my life, Rebecca 'll be 'fraid of our turnpike."

This remark immediately diverted the attention of the brawlers.

"Why should she be 'feard o' your turnpik' more'n any other?" asked the coal vendor.

"Is it fire-proof?" croaked the cattle-dealer, who suffered from chronic hoarseness.

"P'rhaps 'tis going to surrender without a word," sneered the farmer.

"Neither," replied the tailor. "It's jest this. There's a mystery 'bout *our* gate-house, that's all."

The men were angry, and clamoured to know what the mystery was.

"Think I'm goin' to tell?" asked the tailor

provokingly. "No, not I. P'rhaps you be daughters of Rebecca, for all I can say."

The noise was greater now, and the men were for "screwing the tailor's neck off," as they said, but the landlord interfered, and matters were amicably settled by the explanation that the gate-house was haunted.

"At least, so they do say," said the landlord of the "Old Post," and his word was a bond that the county would accept.

"Well, all I can say is that Rebecca will lay the ghost," said the drover.

"Ghosts," corrected the tailor.

"Ghostesses, if you do like," said the coal vendor. "But I've come this way all hours o' day an' night, an' I never see'd a ghost there yet, though "—and he lowered his voice—" I've seen one on the road by Llantrythid church. They *do* say 'tis the ghost of one of the Aubreys who comed to his end 'bout there."

So the conversation ran on, from Rebecca to ghosts, and from them to all sorts of nonsense, until the afternoon waned, and people resumed their various routes.

White, and staring, and bald, the turnpike gate of Bonvilstone looked in the haggard twilight, when the dark grey snow-clouds gathered, and from the north-east a withering wind came searchingly along the highway.

As night approached the cold increased, and before nine o'clock the wind, rising higher, prevented the expected snowfall.

Just before midnight, when darkness was greatest and the roadway was almost deserted, two men passed the "Old Post," and walked towards Bonvilstone. As they approached the gate-house, and were within about a hundred yards from the cottages near it, one of the men said to the other, "Ben, did you hear that noise?"

"What noise, Tom?" asked Ben.

"Like a groan."

"Go along with you—I didn't hear any noise."

"Well, I did."

The men stood still.

"There; I heard it again," said Tom. "Keep quiet, Ben, and you'll hear it."

Tom and Ben paused to listen.

It was a groan—a deep, wretched groan, that made the men shiver, and imagine all sorts of dreadful things. The sound appeared to come from a distance, and to proceed from the east rather than the west.

Then there was a pause, during which the wind whistled in the trees, and sobbed around the scattered cottages near the gate-house.

"I can never go by," said Tom.

"Bless me, you ninny," said Ben. "Come on.

'Tis only the wind ;" and making a brave effort, they strode on.

Presently they came again to a " standstill."

" There 'tis again," said Tom.

It was the groan as of one in mortal pain or soul agony, and as it fell off into a kind of wail, the men clutched each other's arms in terror.

Strange sounds had been recently heard in that neighbourhood, and report gave them the credit, or otherwise, of being supernatural.

As the men approached the gate-house, they found something worse in store. In the dense darkness of the night, they both, and at the same moment, saw what was locally known as " the ghost of the gate-house."

There it stood, as though undaunted by mortal gaze, and waved its arms to and fro in the night, while its deep and heavy groans made the strong men tremble.

Tom and Ben turned back as quickly as they could, and when within a fair distance they paused.

" I'd rather walk every step of the way home again than pass there to night," said Tom, and Ben agreed with him.

Yet they were ashamed of their cowardice.

While the men pondered as to what was best to be done, they heard the sound of horses, and turned aside just in time to escape three of

Rebecca's scouts, who rode up within a hundred yards of the gate-house, remained there a few seconds, and returned as quickly as possible.

" 'Twas some of Rebecca's men," muttered Tom.

" Are you sure of it ? " asked Ben.

" I'm too used to the sound of them," said Tom.

The men then retraced their steps, and sought shelter for the night in the " Old Post."

In the morning they related their experiences to the landlord, and much amusement was created when the men stated their belief that Rebecca's scouts had been frightened by the ghost.

Soon after twelve o'clock the next night Meredith Gwyn mounted Ruby, and this time Jack thought he would be equal with his master. In the evening of the previous day, he laid a plan with a friend to have a horse ready near the foot of the hill leading to the main road, and there he intended mounting and following the young master, who of late went either to Bonvilstone or St. Nicholas.

It was a daring resolution, but Jack had sufficient pluck for anything excepting to face his uncle's anger, and this time he risked even that.

Jack ran as quickly as he could after his

young master, and mounted the horse that waited for him. The night was dark, and all Jack could do was to follow—cautiously, and at a safe distance—the sound of Ruby's hoofs.

Meredith Gwyn ascended the hill, and then rode hard and fast along the highway, until he reached the eastern side of the toll-gate at Bonvilstone. There he was joined by several other horsemen, who, congregated together, appeared to have been waiting his coming. Two of these men rode westward to the gate-house, and quickly returned. A conversation was held, and a few minutes later the whole company rode onward a few paces to the toll-gate. There they quietly, and without noise, removed the gate from its hinges, threw it over into a field, and rode on towards Cardiff.

Jack at a discreet distance followed until the party reached Cotterell, and then he returned to Peterstone, gave the horse to his friend, and then went home to wait for his young master.

In great sorrow of heart, he had discovered that Meredith Gwyn was a friend of Rebecca, if not actually one of "her daughters," and the knowledge was almost more than he could endure.

At four o'clock Meredith Gwyn returned, not in the least the wiser as to the part of spy that had been played by his servant.

Three days later all the toll-gates from Cowbridge to Cardiff were totally destroyed and burnt with their respective gate-houses. Only the gate-house at Bonvilstone escaped. That was left intact and untouched, and the barred gate was found in a field close by.

Then the question arose, why had that obstacle been left unmolested, and the tailor said it was because of the ghost. A few years afterwards it was reported that the ghost and the tailor were one and the same person.

Meredith Gwyn was " suspected " immediately after his latest midnight ride, but money saved him, and he quitted Wales for America, never to return.

Rebecca subsequently returning, totally demolished the Bonvilstone toll-gate, and thus laid the " ghost of the gate-house."

The Flight of the Merlyn.

IN the year 1789 there was no prettier village in North Wales than Llanwddyn, which formerly stood between Llanfyllyn and Bala. It was a secluded and solitary spot, surrounded by bleak moors and grand but gloomy mountains that cast their shadows across the country, and looked like sentinels of grim secrets locked in the plains below. The old Llanwddyn is no longer in existence.

In former days it was like a fairy oasis in a region that at first sight appeared dull and dreary, but afterwards revealed scenes of varied beauty and unsurpassed grandeur.

Round about Llanwddyn the farms and houses were badly built and untidily kept, but the village itself was compact and orderly, each cottage having its flower-garden and orchard, which in the season of blossoms caused the little spot to look like a glimpse of Eden among the dark and dreary barriers of the world.

All the farms in the neighbourhood were— as they still are in that district—chiefly famed for their pasture lands, upon which were reared hundreds of black cattle of a small kind, and a peculiar sort of ponies called merlyns. Great trade in cattle, sheep, and ponies was carried on between the farmers and the cattle-dealers, who visited the district periodically for the purpose.

Cattle-dealers from the South, pausing on their way to Bala, always praised the housewives of Llanwddyn for their clean and orderly houses, which, though antique in design, and for the most part bearing evidences of the ravages of time, were at least domestic strongholds with walls, in most instances from three to five feet thick. Some of those houses dated back beyond the days when Owen Glendower rebelled against Henry IV., and, with a strong body of sturdy and desperate men, scoured the country, and attacked castle and cottage alike.

Llanwddyn, in the year 1789, bore a few traces of Glendower's rebellion and Cromwell's scouts, but the village escaped grave mutilation because the wandering rebels were bound for Bala or Dolgelly.

Not far from Llanwddyn, and just where the bleak and heather-crowned moorlands met the base of one of the grim mountain ranges, there was a narrow ravine. In the topography of Merionethshire the name of this ravine was not recorded, but from time immemorial it had been called the Nant-y-Garth, which means the ravine or dingle leading to a ridge, a hill, or a mountain. Nant-y-Garth was a steep ravine, winding upwards from the moorlands to the mountains. Its grey cliffs were covered with richly-tinted mosses, and in every nook and cranny all kinds of ferns grew in profusion. Gnarled and ancient oaks stretched forth their arms, as if yearning to reach the light that fell brokenly through the trees on the tops of the high cliffs. It was a very lonely spot. The morning sunlight penetrated half-way through the ravine, and then passed away, leaving the shadows to grow darker and the grey cliffs to look more foreboding than ever. In the winter, the mountain streamlets made a broad pathway in the rocky road, and kept the place clean and free from earth, and in the summer, pedestrians, wishing to ascend to the heights, could do so with comparative ease and comfort. Down through Nant-y-Garth the shepherds brought their sheep from the sheep-walks among the mountains, and the cow-boys, driving their herds of small black cattle from the higher table-lands, selected this ravine as the nearest way home.

Nant-y-Garth was about half-a-mile long, and terminated near the first ridge of the mountain range. At the summit of the ravine, sheltered by a grove of stunted and weather-beaten oaks, was a little half tumbled-down cottage, which had once been a small and poor farmstead. The mountain streamlets passed it by, but the rains and the action of the weather had battered the outhouses, and only the house itself remained. It was the dwelling-place of a farmer's herdsman, whose father and grandfather had occupied the habitation.

Twm O'Garth, as he was called, was a bachelor of sixty, living with his mother, who was known in Llanwddyn as Betty Barebones, a beldame of eighty. People were afraid of Betty, because she was supposed to have supernatural power, and to be able to dispense good or bad luck to willing or unwilling recipients. The gossips said where she willed it, she could do great good or do evil with equal power.

Between the months of March and September, Betty, even at the age of eighty, would descend to the valley villages. After that she was seen no more until the month of wild winds brought the crocuses and catkins.

In the winter Twm O'Garth looked after the merlyns, or mountain ponies, and worked in the woods for his master, a gentleman farmer in

Llanwddyn, but in the summer he attended to the vast herds of small black cattle that browsed upon the mountain sides.

Very few people ever visited Twm at home. Betty Barebones was the obstacle in the way. But Twm regularly descended through Nant-y-Garth to the "King's Head" in Llanwddyn, there to smoke his pipe, drink his *cwrw*, and hear the latest news from the cattle-dealers and drovers that frequented the old Tudor tavern.

In the earlier days of her son's life, Betty remonstrated with Twm upon the frequency of his visits to the "King's Head," but the habit inherited from three generations of ancestors remained unbroken, and the herdsman at last went his way unreproved.

Betty spent the greater part of her time in collecting herbs, and making infusions thereof, which she sold for a good price in the surrounding villages, and once a week from "spring-time to fall," she went with the carrier to Bala—a distance of about eight miles—and there disposed of her herb teas and herb beers. Rue tea for epileptic patients, dandelion tea for affections of the liver, tonics for the weak, and cooling concoctions for the robust, with other infusions, were prepared and sold by her. She made all sorts of healing and soothing ointments, plaisters,

I

embrocations for the "rheumatics," drops for the "rheums," and liniments for sprains, strains, broken bones, and bruises.

The old woman obtained her sobriquet of Betty Barebones because she was tall and thin, and, as the villagers said, "more like a skileton" (skeleton) than a living woman. There was "a bit of the witch about her," the people said, and everybody believed her to be gifted with second sight, and the power of foretelling future events. She made a rhyme, which ran thus—

"Llanwddyn's tower shall tumble down;
    A llyn (lake) shall fill the moorlands brown;
    A llyn shall flood the pasture lands,
    And waters shall be where earth now stands.

"House and home, and orchard wall,
    By the hand of man shall fall;
    Llanwddyn shall become a llyn,
    Then may Bala shake within."

The cattle-drovers in the "King's Head" kitchen ridiculed Betty Barebones' rhyme, and the horse-dealers and others in the tavern parlour declared the old woman was witless.

"Twm O'Garth, dost thee believe thy mother did mean what she did put in the verses?" asked a cattle-drover.

"Iss inteed to goodness, I do believe it as sure as I be a livin' man," replied Twm. "She's uncommon odd, an' wuss as she do get older. Mind you now, 'tis no great shakes livin' with her."

" Why ? " asked the drover.

" She do talk most parts of the nights, an' lately she's bin sayin' such odd things," continued Twm.

" What's she bin sayin' ? " urged the drover.

" I never can tell," replied Twm.

" Have another drink," said the drover.

" Man alive, I've had two," said Twm.

" Three won't hurt thee," continued the drover.

By and by Twm was willing to double the three quantities of beer, and then the drover's object was attained. Other drovers came and crowded the old oaken settles in the kitchen, and all present wished to hear what Betty Barebones had been saying.

" Come now, Twm ; tell us all about it," clamoured the men.

" Well," said Twm, " one night a bit ago I did go home, an' I s'pose I was purty dirty lookin', an' up an' says the old woman, 'Thee'st bin at the " King's Head " again.' An' if I was never to move again, the inside of the 'King's Head' hadn't seed me that night. So says I, I did slip just in front of Nant-y-Garth, an' that was cause of a rollin' stone. 'Well,' says I, 'you be the oddest woman for a mother as ever was. When a man do come home full of bruises, an' bruises is worse than broken bones—you——'

"'Hold thee tongue the old c-nock,' says my mother, 'best thing for bruises is snail's-foot oil. Thee look for some of that t'morrow an' thee 'll soon mend.' An' with that she did go to bed. An' I did sit up a spell. An' if I was never to move again, I didn't have one spot of liquor in me. Well, that night 'bout two in the mornin' I did hear the old ooman talkin' to herself. An' I did listen. An' this is what she was sayin', 'There's nothin' like snail's-foot oil for bruises. An' by an' by there'll come a bruise, that Twm O'Garth 'on't get over, n-ither. An' when he's dead, dead as a nit, his body 'll be tied to a pony's back, and the merlyn 'll fly away with his corpse. An' there'll be a rumpus!' Then the old ooman did begin a-singin' to herself the same piece you did hear me repeat just now."

The drovers laughed heartily, and persisted in calling Betty Barebones moonstruck.

Although Twm often acknowledged to himself that his mother was, as he called it, "hipped," he did not like anybody else to revile her. So he keenly resented the drovers' insolence, and a noisy brawl ensued.

It was late, or rather early in the morning,

when Twm reached home. During his progress through Nant-y-Garth, he had fallen several times, and presented a woe-begone appearance as he sat down in the arm-chair beside the hearth, where a smouldering fire still remained. He slept heavily for several hours, and when he awoke, the sunlight was streaming in through the little windows of the cottage.

"Thee'lt save a sight o' money, only give thee time, Twm," said Betty, as she prepared the breakfast.

Twm remained silent.

"Art hard o' hearin'?" asked Betty.

No answer.

"'Tis well when a man o' sixty do begin to think 'bout savin'," persisted Betty, adding, "Thee'rt lookin' copper this mornin'."

Twm, who had indulged too freely the previous night, was by no means in a good humour, and at length he said, "Thee'rt anuff to make a man mad! How ken I save when thee dost take every penny of my wages. Last night I did go down without a penny in my pocket, an' the others did say, 'Thee'rt tied to the mammy's apron strings,' an' that's how I've bin all my life, an' I s'pose that's how I shall be to the end of my days!"

"The end's nearer than thee dost think. Thee'lt go to the 'King's Head' once too often," said

Betty Barebones. "Take thee warnin' in time. Next bout will be the last for thee."

Betty Barebones clenched her fist in her son's face, and almost hissed at him.

After breakfast Twm went to his work, but all through that day, and far into the next night, his mother's words kept ringing in his ears. "Next bout with them drovers will be the last for thee!"

The words rang in his brain like a funeral knell, and for days Twm moved about like one in a dream.

For many months after that, Twm avoided the "King's Head" whenever the cattle dealers and drovers came to Llanwddyn. As chief herdsman of the farm he was obliged to meet these men, but he was careful not to go to the "King's Head" with them.

Summer with its brilliant sunshine, its birds and flowers, passed away, and a rainy autumn flooded the lowlands, and filled the woodland hollows with water.

Autumn was succeeded by a wet winter, and the Welsh villagers said, "A green winter makes a full churchyard."

Just before Christmas a hard frost set in. It lasted four days, and then rain came again. The rain falling upon the frozen earth made the roads and pathways very slippery, and locomotion became both difficult and dangerous. For a week or more men were continually falling, sometimes with bad results and broken bones.

It was Christmas Eve.

The clouds hovered heavily over Llanwddyn.

Towards night a wild wind arose, howling drearily among the mountains, and wailing around the bleak moorlands.

It whistled among the bare branches of the gnarled oaks in Nant-y-Garth, and it sighed wearily around the herdsman's lonely cottage.

Betty Barebones replenished the fire on the hearth, and then busied herself in making ointments, always much in demand during the winter.

Now and again she paused to look out into the storm, which was rising to almost a hurricane.

Not a star was to be seen, and before seven o'clock rain began to fall.

About an hour later Betty was startled by a loud knock at the door.

It was most unusual for anybody to come to that lonely spot at night, especially in the winter.

"Come in," shouted Betty.

In response, a big, rough-looking youth of about seventeen entered, accompanied by his dog.

It was Ivor the cowboy.

"I wouldn't 'a' come up heer if it hadn't 'a' been for the missis, an' if I did think it would rain I wouldn't 'a' come up 't all."

Ivor the cowboy was strong, stalwart, and tall. Hereditary tendencies, life spent in the open air, and continual active exercise, made Ivor more sprightly than the majority of youths of his class. He was famed in the neighbourhood for his fearlessness, both as a rider and walker.

"What's up now?" asked Betty.

"The missis has got the rheumatics dus'prate bad, an' she do want some o' your stuff for it. She's been bad for more'n a week now," said Ivor.

Betty had often treated the farmer's wife for rheumatism, and she quickly prepared the lotion.

"Here's the stuff," said Betty. "She must rub it where she do feel the most pain. An' she must keep on with it constant all through the winter. 'Tis no good to rub a drop in to-day, an' then leave it off for a week or so. She must rub, rub, rub every day, whether she's got the pain or not. There's nothin' wuss than the rheumatics."

"Thank goodness, I don't know what they be," said Ivor.

"Thee'lt never know much 'bout 'em," said Betty. "There's nine lives in thee, like in me."

"Ay, ay," said Ivor, "they do say there's nine lives in every cat."

Betty, shaking her fist at Ivor, said, "Never mind. Thee'lt do me two good turns yet 'fore I do die."

"Don't know so much 'bout that," said Ivor. "Thee don't give anybody the chance to do good for thee or thine."

"Thee'lt have two chances for all that," said Betty, indulging in a wild, unearthly scream, startling Ivor, who mentally remarked how dreadful it must be to live with such a hag. "'Tis a dark night anuff," said Betty, opening the door and peering out into the little garden. "Hast got a lantern?"

"Iss," said Ivor; "who'd come up Nant-y-Garth of a night like this without one? I put it by the gate."

"Then 'tis blown out," said Betty, "for I don't see no sign of a light anywhere."

And so it proved.

When the lantern was re-lighted, Ivor, accompanied by his dog, set forth on his return through Nant-y-Garth. The wind was not quite so high, and the rain by this time had ceased.

Ivor strode on as quickly as it was possible,

because everybody was afraid to venture that way after dark.

Some said Nant-y-Garth was haunted, others declared that unknown witches came there to meet Betty Barebones at midnight, and it was whispered that the witches' Sabbath was kept inside and outside the herdsman's cottage.

With a shiver Ivor remembered all these sayings, and his flesh began to creep with unnatural coldness as he more firmly clutched his ox-goad and whistled to his dog.

When about half-way down the ravine he heard the owls hooting and the wind wailing among the trees on the top of the cliffs.

Still another sound, and one that made Ivor's heart to beat wildly.

It was a blood-curdling sound. It now resembled the deep baying of distant hounds; then it sounded like a mighty groan.

Ivor hurried on. He began to think of the Crwn Annwn, or spirit-hounds, and the groaning of the Gwrach-y-rhybin—the hag of the midnight mist.

Stricken with terror, Ivor thought he could see goblins and hobgoblins grinning wherever his lantern light flashed.

Again he heard the strange sounds. As he strode quickly forward he imagined he heard footsteps following him; but he had not the courage to turn round and look back.

Perhaps it was some of the witches who visited Betty; perhaps it was Betty Barebones herself, following him with some additional recipes for his mistress. If so, she must come to him, for he could not turn round to her.

Ivor quickened his pace, and, as the strange sounds still continued, the cowboy began to run. As he ran, it seemed to him that the sounds grew louder, and the footsteps following him became swifter too. Ivor ran without ceasing until he reached the entrance to Nant-y-Garth, where the sounds and footsteps suddenly ceased. Then, utterly exhausted, he paused to rest on the way-side.

From dark cloud-rifts the moon looked down upon Llanwddyn, and Ivor was glad to see in the distance the welcome lights of the village, and soon he reached home, vowing that never again would he go through Nant-y-Garth at night.

When he related his experiences to his fellow-servants, one of the elder men said, " 'Tis Christmas Eve, an' I've heerd say that all sorts of noises ken be heerd in Nant-y-Garth 'bout this time, and again on the 'tier nos ysprydion' (the three spirit nights)."

" If I was never to move again, I do b'lieve

Betty Barebones is a witch," said another servant.

" An' ought to be burnt for a witch," chimed in one of the farm boys.

The next morning Twm O'Garth did not appear to fulfil his duties, though the master had said he need not on Christmas Day come so early as on ordinary days. But when ten o'clock came, and the chief herdsman did not appear, the farmer ordered Ivor to go to Twm's cottage.

The cowboy said he was afraid to go alone.

" Afraid, and by daylight ? " exclaimed the farmer.

" You'd be 'fraid too," said Ivor, " if you'd bin through Nant-y-Garth last night."

Ivor asked Wat the ploughboy to go with him, and they set out at once.

When half-way through Nant-y-Garth, Ivor told his companion where he first heard the strange sounds.

" 'Twas uncommon odd," said Wat.

" You'd have said so if you'd been there," said Ivor.

They walked silently on for some time, and then Wat exclaimed, " Look there—d'ye see that ? "

" What ? " asked Ivor, looking in the direction indicated by Wat.

" Can't you see, boy," replied Wat, peering at the stones on the pathway.

" One might think you'd caught sight of a snake," said Ivor, stepping forward. " But what is it ? "

" Why, 'tis nothin' more nor less than blood ! " said Wat.

The boys went on. The blood-marks increased in number and size, and when the boys were three parts through Nant-y-Garth, they saw a good-sized pool of blood.

" Murder ! " exclaimed Wat.

" It looks like it," said Ivor.

About a hundred yards from the herdsman's cottage, the boys saw Betty, who appeared to be dragging a burden towards the house.

Seeing the boys, she cried out, " Come, come ; be quick, he be just dead."

The boys soon reached her, and immediately drew back in horror, for the burden that Betty Barebones dragged homewards was the lifeless body of Twm O'Garth.

Twm's blood-bespattered face was pallid with death, and from a fearful gash in the back of his head a gory stream issued.

Betty Barebones gave a strange unearthly shriek, then said, " Twm didn't come home last night, an' I did look an' listen an' wait, but no sign of him did I see. Surely, says I, he's

stayed down in the master's, 'cause 'tis Christmas
Eve, an' he'll be up by breakfast.   But when
the clock did strike nine, an' I did see no sign
of him, I did start to come down to the village.
An' when I did get half-way down Nant-y-Garth,
who should I see but Twm lyin' in a heap by
the elder bushes.   'Twm,' says I, all in a fright,
'how did'st thee come heer?'   But he did give
no answer.   So I did look, and then I did see his
head was bleedin'.   By an' by he did open his
eyes, and then he did groan.   An' all he did say,
'home—— to die.'   But he did die there and
then, an' I did try to lift his body, but couldn't.
'Twas too heavy.   Then I did try to drag it up,
an' did faint twice on the road.   I did thank my
stars when I did see you comin'."

The boys then bore the body onward.   Betty
following, kept muttering to herself all the
time, "I did warn him of it.   I did say the
next bout will be the last for thee, but he did
take no heed."

Having laid the body on a bed, Ivor and Wat
prepared to return home.

"Thee'st done one good turn for me—didn't
I say thee would'st?" said Betty to Ivor.
"Thee'lt do another in a bit.   Thee didst help
to carry poor Twm home to his mother, sure
anuff."

Then Betty began to cry, but her tears soon

vanished, and leaping about a foot from the ground, she shrieked so suddenly and sharply that the boys were startled.

Ivor and Wat returned home, and Betty Barebones was left alone with the dead.

As soon as the news spread through the village, nearly everybody accused Betty of having murdered her son.

But even Betty Barebones found friends in need, in the persons of her son's master, and, strangely enough, the landlord of the "King's Head," who declared that, although Twm was very drunk, he persisted in going home. A neighbour led him so far as Nant-y-Garth, but feared to go beyond, and the neighbour said Twm was sufficiently sobered by that time to go home alone. The doctor said Twm had stumbled, and, very likely falling on the back of his head, received his mortal wound.

He must have been soon insensible, and the groans that Ivor heard were evidently the dying agonies of Twm O'Garth. Three days after Christmas the funeral was to take place.

Many people wended their way up through Nant-y-Garth who had never been there before, and all agreed it was a lonesome place to live in.

The herdsman's cottage was in a very awkward situation. Vehicles could never approach it, and the only means of access to it from the village, was by a narrow, steep, and very rough road leading to the labyrinth of sheep-walks, or *via* Nant-y-Garth.

When Twm's father died there, the bearers failed to traverse the sheep-walks, and they knew it would be impossible to descend through Nant-y-Garth. So they had recourse to a custom prevalent in some parts of Wales to this day. The coffin was securely strapped upon the back of a merlyn or mountain pony, and the animal was led slowly from the heights to the village of Llanwddyn.

Betty decided that Twm's body was to be borne in the same way.

Twm was much respected in the neighbourhood, and the number of people attending the funeral was unexpectedly large. The herdsman's cousins and friends, who, under ordinary circumstances, would have been bearers, strapped the coffin to the merlyn's back, and then the animal was cautiously led along the sinuous sheep-walks.

The long procession had moved onward about half a mile, when a sudden and sharp turn in the sheep-walks caused the people to halt. The first half of the cortège was lost to sight by huge crags and boulders on the mountain side, when those behind heard a shout or cry of alarm from those in advance.

"What is it?" whispered everybody as the procession was obliged—owing to the narrowness of the way—to go in Indian rank and file.

The turn in the path revealed all.

Fleeting down the mountain side went the merlyn with the coffin on its back. The animal, stumbling beside the boulders, became frightened and escaped its leader.

It was a strange and gruesome scene.

The mourners crowded together speechlessly, and looked over the mountain - side to the lower sheep-walks whither the fleet-footed and frightened merlyn speeded.

On, on, with the rapidity of lightning the animal went, until it was lost in the dense windings of the woods at the base of the mountains.

The mourners could not give chase, because the descent was dangerous. They walked quickly on, and only hoped that the pony would be caught in the village.

Still, onward speeded the merlyn. Now it galloped, then it stood still, only to start away more wildly than before!

On it went, its burden still securely strapped to its back. It fled so madly through Llanwddyn that it could not be caught, and then it sped along the road leading to Bala.

Pedestrians paused and gazed in wonderment

K

to see a merlyn with a coffin strapped on its back, running as if for a wager or a race.

The day passed, but no news came of the merlyn. It was a terrible and gruesome flight.

Through daylight and into the darkness the pony speeded onward, up hill and down dale, while some people regarded it as a weird and dreadfully uncanny spectacle, and others looked upon it as an apparition, rather than a living object bearing the burden of death.

All agreed that Betty Barebones had "bewitched" the merlyn.

Two days later, news about that awful flight were brought by a minister from below Bala. He said that a merlyn answering to the description given of the Llanwddyn pony, with loosened straps, was found dead just where the Treweryn joins the Dee, and still lower down a coffin was seen floating on the waters, and people in one of the villages in pity buried the body.

And that was the last heard of Twm O'Garth.

Betty Barebones never recovered from the shock of her ill-fated son's funeral.

The people in Llanwddyn tried to persuade her to go and live in the village, but she would not, and afterwards, twice a week, the farmer and his wife sent provisions up to their faithful herdsman's mother. Sometimes Wat went up, and sometimes Ivor would go, but never again in the night.

In the February after Twm's death the weather became severely cold. The wind groaned and howled among the mountains, and every day the frost became more intense. Rivers were ice-bound. Llyn Tegid, as Bala lake is called, was completely frozen over; streamlets were petrified, and from the summit to the base in Nant-y-Garth silver-green icicles were suspended, and fantastic icework transformed the gnarled oaks into traceries and designs of Gothic grandeur.

It was bitterly, bitingly cold. Even the howling wind seemed to be frozen.

After a dark and windy week, with a leaden sky, snow began to fall, and continued to do so without intermission for four days and nights.

The snow assumed every shape of white magnificence.

The Welsh mountains everywhere appeared like grand monarchs rising one above the other, surrounded by pale warriors and lordly citadels. The sternness of the storm-beaten cliffs and crags was beautifully softened, and each towering mountain peak was clothed with graceful draperies of white.

Humble alder and black-thorn, stately oak and elm, graceful chestnut and lordly fir were veiled with fairy-like woof and warp of snow, and with fringes of flashing icicles.

Almost all work and traffic were totally suspended.   Mankind congregated around the blazing hearths ; womankind longed for the frost to break up, and take the men out of their way.

On the fifth day, when the blinding snow ceased falling, the thoughts of the people reverted to Betty Barebones.

"What about Betty ?" asked Ivor's master.

"We did take her a basketful of things up on Monday," said Ivor.

"And 'tis Friday to-day," said the farmer.

"I sent enough food to last about a week," said his wife.

"She must have a fresh supply to-morrow," said the farmer.   "But who can get at her in this weather?   Much better if the wilful old woman had come down long ago as we wanted her to.   I don't know what is to be done."

"I'll go up," said Ivor.

"I don't see how it can be done," said his master.   "Nant-y-Garth is choked with snow, and it would be sheer madness to try the mountain paths."

Few men who hold human life as their dearest possession would have attempted to effect an entrance to Nant-y-Garth, much less to scale the mountain sides, in such weather.

Yet, knowing the dangers well, Ivor, on the morrow, started patiently to make his way through the desolate ravine, and that too at a time when perhaps the storm would recommence with renewed severity.

Before proceeding, the courageous cowboy took a hearty meal—eating it as a soldier arming himself for warfare. As the last crumb disappeared he said, "Now, lads, the next meal will be with Betty Barebones if I shall ever reach her cot."

Was her old life worth the risk of a young life? asked the farm-folk.

Ivor knew it was a perilous errand, but he started with a light and brave heart, though the chances of wind and weather were against him.

Seizing a long pole, he called out gaily to his fellow-servants—

"Joy go with me, and a pottle of moss,
 If I never come back 'twill be no loss!"

He knew that one of the worst parts of his journey would be to reach the entrance of Nant-y-Garth from the main road. The route lay along very rugged uplands filled with deep hollows, around which he was obliged to feel his way, now using the long pole, and then creeping on his hands and knees in the most slippery places.

Before reaching Nant-y-Garth, the snow began to beat pitilessly in his face, and strong gusts of wind frequently forced his steps backward.

Ivor consoled himself by remarking that once in Nant-y-Garth, he would at least be sheltered from the relentless wind and the blinding snow.

Half a mile from the ravine he found himself up to the shoulders in snow. By means of his long pole he extricated himself, and with considerable difficulty reached the entrance of the ravine, there to be obstructed by a huge sloping barrier of snow. The surface was frozen as hard as it could be, but the cowboy feared to trust the treacherous crust, which might at any moment give way and prove to be a snowy grave.

For a moment Ivor stood in a sheltered corner, and closed his aching, snow-blinded eyes.

How to get over that snowy barrier, was a problem difficult to solve.

Suddenly he remembered that the ancient oaks at the entrance of the ravine were as strong as iron. If only he could get hold of the branches he would be able to ascend.

By means of his long pole he took a long leap forward, and was able to clutch one of the snow-encumbered branches.

Now courage and confidence were returning. He was not cold any longer.

Swinging himself from one frozen branch to another, he soon reached a ledge in the rocks overhanging the snow barrier. Once there, he planted his pole in the top of the ridge, when suddenly, and with great noise, an avalanche descended from the upper rocks, and went thundering down into the mouth of the ravine.

Ivor was then able to descend from the cliff side into the ravine.

There, in some places the snow was deeply drifted, while in other parts the rocks appeared as slippery as glass.

Now Ivor was climbing around huge boulders —now he strode along spaces blown bare of snow —and now he sank into drifts that every moment threatened to bury him. Now he would pause to rest and look back down through the ravine.

What a grand sight!

With that solemn and almost melancholy religious feeling which Welshmen possess in common with the Hebrews, Ivor thought of the judgment, the great white throne, the archangels and angels clad in snow-white raiment. And, as he passed onward, the snow-enshrouded oaks reminded him of hoary Druids clothed in the spotless raiment that distinguished them on the borders of the battlefield from the ancient British warriors.

A fearful feeling of desolation came over him.

In temporary despair he sank down suddenly on the slippery rocks, as if he would gladly embrace death to escape the loneliness and hunger and thirst for life.

Then, again, he seemed to hear voices calling him higher up the ravine—kindly voices of angels and Druids, mingled with the urging tones of ancient warriors.

It was then—his own strength flagging—that Ivor looked higher for the first time, calling on his Master for help.

He staggered on his journey, and soon approached the top of the ravine. Only another turn of the grim cliffs and crags, and the herdsman's cottage would be in sight. Onward he went, clasping a slippery boulder to avoid falling into a miniature avalanche.

But what was this in the snow? His pole struck something hard, and stooping down he found it to be an old crook, and beside it a three-legged stool. He wondered vaguely what they meant. Then he found a saw, a shovel, a pan, and a large old-fashioned flannel apron blown across the frozen branches of low-growing hazels.

Breathing in heavy gasps, not daring to guess what was before him, Ivor pressed on towards the cottage. But, alas! it was not there!

An avalanche descending from the upper ranges of the mountains had swept over the cottage, and left it a ruin. Only one wall of the house built against the cliffs alone remained, and part of the broken roof lay before it.

Ivor called out loudly, but was only answered by echoes. He made his way to the site of the cottage, calling and shouting at every step. Straining his ears to catch some answer to his cries, he heard a faint sound coming from the snow-buried garden. He listened.

"Here," a feeble voice said.

He called again, "Betty! Betty!"

"I be here," answered the voice, as that of some one expecting help.

Ivor hurried on in the direction of the sound. In a moment he was on the spot, digging the snow away with his hands.

"Who was it?" came the cry.

"Ivor—the cowboy," was the answer.

"Oh, Ivor, boy! I did feel sure God wouldn't leave me to die here all alone. I've been prayin' all along to Him," and poor old Betty Barebones' pinched face had a smile for the cowboy. "How good God is!"

Tears rolled down from the cowboy's semi-blinded eyes to his frost-blistered cheeks. He could not speak. Loosening the old woman from the snow and wreck of the cottage, he clasped her in his arms. The movement gave her acute pain. One of her arms was broken, and her body was crushed and lacerated. He hastened with his burden to the wall that still stood against the cliffs, and laid Betty under its shelter. Then he took off his greatcoat and covered her with it. As he did so, her eyelids slowly lifted.

"I did tell you you'd do me another good turn," said Betty, while the tears rolled down her wan and wasted face. "Ivor, I did think 'twas the Judgment-day, an' that the world was come to an end, an' I was up here—left alone to face my Maker."

"Can you tell me all 'bout it?" asked Ivor, kneeling beside Betty.

A long pause followed, her eyes closed, and occasionally she compressed her lips, as if to overcome pain.

By and by she said, "It did come when I was makin' a bit o' breakfast this mornin'. Just as I was turnin' from the fire to the table I did hear a dreadful noise like thunder. Everythin' seemed to be breakin', as if the mountains was comin' on top o' me, an' then, in the twinklin' of an eye, the roof did fall, an' I was stunned. I did know no more till I did find myself in the snow jest as thee did'st find me. God did send thee here, Ivor!"

She lifted her withered hand and passed it over the lad's brown and blistered face.

"Listen, Ivor," the old woman whispered. "When the snow is gone, thee can'st look for the old chest what used to be by the chimney, thee'lt find there 'bout three hundard pounds. That'll pay thee for thy trouble. 'Twas very well to look on it once—'tis no good to me now !"

Ivor buried his face in his hands, and his whole frame shook with sobs. Never before had Ivor seemed so helpless.

Suddenly he remembered that in the wallet he carried on his shoulder his mistress had put a phial containing a comforting cordial, which she told him to use "to keep out the cold." He gave some of it to Betty, and took a little himself.

The cordial appeared to revive the old woman, who firmly held one of his hands, while Ivor for the first time realised the situation.

To move Betty was a sheer impossibility, and to go for help was to leave her to meet certain death alone.

Betty looked up. She seemed to guess what was passing through his mind.

"Ivor, boy," said she. "Don't thee mind. I did heer the call—I got nothin' to fear now—it won't be long—the end is a-comin'."

Her eyes closed again, and tears slowly found their way down the deeply furrowed

checks—not tears of rebellion, but bitter drops
of sorrow for a life wasted in miserable and
unnecessary loneliness.   Had she mingled with
her fellow-mortals, and come down to the world,
she would have died in her bed.   She now felt
that her life had been as far removed from
human kind as if she had lived in a tropical
desert, or among the ice fields of the polar
regions.

"Ivor," said Betty slowly, "if thee can'st
lift me a bit, I do think the pain would come
better."

The cowboy lifted her, and rested her poor old
head on his shoulder.

"Ivor, my boy—tell 'em all down there I did
mean well to 'em.   Only I was always odd like,
and did keep from 'em.   But—" she faltered, " I
was never a witch, nor hadn't no dealin's, as they
did say, with the old Satan.   No, no! An' when
the snow do go—you come an' take the old chest,
an' the money's yours."

Ivor remained silent.   He did not want, did
not hope for reward.

"Promise me, Ivor," added Betty.   "'Tis a
dyin' wish, an' we in the old country do always
respect the dead.   Promise me."

"I promise," said Ivor solemnly.

Betty's eyes looked radiantly up at him.

"They're a-comin'," she said, "they're a-comin'

—the angels an' the holy ones, an'—peace—everlastin'—peace!"

And with a sigh, and a tear of joy, Betty passed away.

Ivor laid her body to rest where her poor wasted frame would be protected until it could have decent funeral.

Never was mortal placed in a fairer grave than that which Ivor made among the desolate mountains of Wales for Betty Barebones.

It was down near the cottage wall in the shelter of projecting cliffs, and crags, and, as he laid the poor old body to rest in its snowy grave, for shroud he placed her Welsh flannel apron upon her breast, there to remain until the mountain fastnesses and sheep-walks were released from winter's thraldom.

Looking down for the last time upon the wan and upturned features, the desolation of the place, its solemn grandeur, and the painful loneliness of the death scene seemed suddenly to pass away, and the words from the Revelation came back to Ivor's memory: "*God shall wipe away all tears from their eyes: and there shall be no more death, neither sorrow, nor crying, neither shall there be any more pain!*"

.   .   .   .   .   .

When Ivor returned to Llanwddyn, the

shadows of the early twilight were falling across the frozen snow, and the welcome lights of the farm were as friendly beacons to the shipwrecked mariner. The cowboy told his story in solemn silence, while tears rained in showers from the eyes of all who listened.

Snow fell almost continually for fourteen days after Betty's death, and it was April before any attempt could be made to reach the ruined cottage among the mountains. Even then, the snow remained in many places, and still covered Betty Barebones' remains.

May, with its sunshine and songs of birds, came, and then the men ascended the mountains, at the foot of which a large funeral procession waited for the coming of the body of Betty Barebones, who was buried with her husband in the little village churchyard.

Five hundred pounds were found where Betty said three hundred were stored, and Ivor, who was advised by his master, kept the sum he promised to take, and gave the remainder to the old woman's next of kin. Ivor the cowboy set himself up in a small farm near Llanwddyn, and years afterwards his eldest son became an earnest and hard-working minister of the "Corph," as the Calvinistic Methodists are called in Wales.

According to poor old Betty Barebones' prophecy, the ancient Llanwddyn was demolished, and the place where it once stood is submerged beneath the Vyrnwy Waterworks—that huge artificial lake from which Liverpool receives its daily supply.

The Man of the Moat House.

HE lived alone, and gloried in it. His home was called the "Moat House," and that name it bears to this day, though nobody knows why, because there does not appear to be a vestige of a moat near the place.

In his Moat House he reigned supreme as an absolute monarch, and when they told him that Oliver Cromwell, having already made turmoil in England, was about to proceed to Wales, Michael Giles exclaimed, "More's the shame for him—a Welshman—to try and beat Welshmen! But never fear. The Royalists and the Roundheads will pass by little Lisworney."

So he leaned back in his chair, and enjoyed himself like a king. He ate and drank alone, worked and rested alone, and declared that he never suffered from bodily ache or mental pain, simply because his life was unruffled by a companion.

When the old women came around offering their herb infusions, he would laugh heartily at them, and say, " If you want to live well and long—live alone. 'Tis livin' with other people an' bein' bothered with 'em that brings on the indigestion an' the black bile an' the rheums. Here am I, as happy as the lark, and as rich as I wish to be, an' all because—I live alone ! "

People who were allowed to go so far as the threshold of the Moat House said it was spotlessly clean, just as if " a woman kept it."

When this remark reached the ears of Michael Giles, he said, " Some men be tidier than women. As a rule, women is much like peas in a pod : there's no tellin' which is the best till you come to shell 'em, and then like enough you'll find the bigger the pod the fewer the peas. So you mustn't judge a woman by the outside nor the threshold of her house. Sometimes the finer the windows the bigger the cobwebs."

Michael farmed for himself. He had never been known to have hired help in his lifetime. His dairy-work, house-work, and farm-work were performed single-handed. He drove his own flocks to market, and there sold them, and as a purchaser he had the reputation of being a hard-bargain driver. He had been known to take his cattle thrice to Cardiff market, and bring them back again, because of the difference

L

of sixpence ; for which the country people would call after him, " Thee'lt need to shoe thy cattle, to go long distances for the splitting of a hair."

Michael Giles only laughed, and would answer, " Perhaps in the long run it would pay to have them shod. Worse things than that have been done."

His house, or as much of it as should be seen, was clean ; his garden was well kept, and his farm was always in an orderly condition ; but he had many peculiarities, as might be expected.

One of his whims was to strew the floors with leaves, whereat the good people of Lisworney laughed.

Michael, seeing no laughing matter in that, said, " What could be more beautiful than fresh leaves and woodland flowers in spring-time and summer : brown bramble leaves and ferns in autumn, and fragrant pine spikes in winter? Are they not nature's carpets, and better than those supplied by the hand of man ? "

" Now, Michael," said the lord of the manor, " what would you tell King Charles if he came here ? "

The lord of the manor was a staunch Royalist.

" Tell the king ? " said Michael. " I'd tell him that if he'd learnt the way to reign alone, he'd have had no trouble. 'Tis company that brings trouble. An' if the king was to come here, I'd not let him put foot over my threshold unless he begged permission."

"What would you tell Cromwell?" asked the lord.

"The very same thing. Only I would add to Cromwell, that more's the shame for him, a Welshman, to try an' beat an buffet his countrymen."

The lord of the manor rode away.

"Men that live alone are generally morose, but——" remarked the parson of Lisworney.

"Do I look morose?" interrupted the man of the Moat House.

"Nay, nay, as I was going to remark, I——" said the parson.

"Do I talk like a morose man?" asked Michael.

"Nay, nay, friend," replied the parson.

"I'm no friend of thine," said Michael, "for thou'rt both morose in looks an' in talk."

The parson smiled and walked on.

"There's nothin' like livin' alone," said Michael to a neighbour. "If one has a quarrel with oneself, it can't become the talk of the village. When I count up my money, there's nobody to look on through keyholes and cracks, an' when I sit down to have my food, there's nobody to say it isn't done to satisfaction. When I laugh, I enjoy it alone. When I sing, I'm all alone, an' there's nobody to say I am out of tune. An' when I do—which is seldom—run down anybody, I do it alone, an' there's nobody to hear."

His panacea for all the ills of life was to—live alone.

As time passed political matters were getting more complicated, and it was necessary for the Royalists to form an organisation in order to support the king and resist the enemy.

The lord of the manor called upon Michael Giles to ask his assistance.

"I'll give thee no aid," said Michael. "But come in and sit down, an' we'll talk the matter over."

The lord of the manor entered.

"I've never asked thy aid, or the king's yet," said Michael, "an' what's more, I never intend to while I've breath in my body. I've lived alone all my lifetime, an' mean to as long as I live."

Then he laughed heartily.

"I don't understand how you can be so happy," said the lord of the manor.

"Why, sir, that's easily understood," said Michael. "I've nobody to ruffle my temper, nobody to oppose my wishes, nobody to frustrate my designs, nobody to thwart my intentions, an' nobody to say 'No' to me!"

The lord of the manor went away, wishing he too lived alone!

"I fear me there are dangers ahead," said a neighbour, a little later on, when news came that Cromwell was in Cardiff.

"P'rhaps so, but they'll never come to little Lisworney," said Michael.

"But s'pose the troops *did* come here," said the neighbour. "They'd ransack the place an' p'rhaps turn us out of house an' home."

"Wait till they do come," was Michael's reply. "Living alone hath made me hopeful. I've nothing to fear, nobody to trouble me, an' little to lose."

But the day came, when the lord of the manor and other gentlemen had to seek the aid of every man in the neighbourhood, and they claimed, almost pressed, Michael's assistance.

The man of the Moat House flatly refused, and the others had to go without him.

During the absence of all the men in the neighbourhood but the parson and himself, Michael became the protector of Lisworney. In that capacity he acted like a veteran Field Marshal, and, with keen eye, closely watched all who came in or passed through the village.

One day a small party of Royalist soldiers trooped in, and during Michael's temporary absence in the fields, entered the Moat House.

Seeing from a distance their movements, Michael promptly returned, and ordered them out of his house. This they refused to do, and declared their intention of remaining there as long as they thought fit.

"I'll make ye clear out," said Michael.

The men laughed, and, leaning back in their chairs, ate and drank the best of everything in the house.

"How wilt thee do it?" asked one.

"Thee'lt see how, time enough," answered Michael.

"By means of a watch-dog?"

"Nay," answered the man of the Moat House.

"By means of firearms?" queried another.

"Nay," said Michael. "What good would one firearm be against six?"

"By burning down the house?" asked another.

"Nay; I would not ruin my property for such little sakes as thine," said Michael, with a touch of scorn. "And would ye all willingly sit down to be burnt alive! No, no. I'll use more effectual means to clear ye out of my house, an' save your skins too."

The men laughed at his threat, and in fun waited to see what means he had at hand for ejecting them.

In the room in which the soldiers regaled themselves there were three doors, one of which

led upstairs, and the other opened into the dairy.
The third was the parlour door. Without attract-
ing attention, Michael Giles went out through
one door, and made a slight noise upstairs, then
descending as quietly as possible he went into
the back yard, took a hive of bees, and crept
behind the settle. Then quickly turning the
hive over, he gave the bees their freedom. Like
a dense cloud they swarmed the room, and be-
sieged the intruders. With great difficulty, and
not without severe stings either, the soldiers
rushed out of the kitchen into the open air, only
to be followed by the persistent bees. In pain
and misery, with swollen faces, eyes, and hands,
the men mounted their horses and hastened
away anywhere from Lisworney.

Not without a parting shot from Michael Giles,
who at the top of his voice shouted, "I found
effectual means of getting rid of ye all. There's
nothing better than a siege of bees!"

The event became the talk of the country-
side, and the people declared in jokeful fashion,
"There's nothing like bees for driving enemies
away."

A few weeks before the great battle of St.
Fagan's, the lord of the manor came begging
Michael Giles to accompany them to Cowbridge,
where all the Royalists were to assemble, in
order to proceed to the scene of conflict.

"It's your duty to come," said the lord of the manor.

"I call it my duty to remain at home," said Michael determinedly. " I've always lived alone, never had a companion, and why should I go out amongst others? No, I'll stay at home, and mind the Moat House and Lisworney."

He remained true to his post, and waited anxiously for news of the great and terrible battle fought at St. Fagan's, after which the Parliamentary forces did much damage in and around the neighbourhood of Cowbridge.

One evening in May, soon after the Battle of St. Fagan's, a party of Parliamentary soldiers rode into Lisworney.

Michael Giles, like a Field Marshal, immediately spied them.

Seeing the stalwart Welshman, the leader of the party rode up to him.

" We would fain rest awhile," said Captain Garland, "and have what private provision we can. Will you direct us?"

This was spoken in a tone of such refined courtesy, that Michael Giles, even though a Royalist himself, was much touched. Honour be to the magnanimity of the Welsh Royalist, he immediately conducted them to his own Moat House, and regaled the captain and his men with the best provisions he had in his possession.

Then Michael Giles discovered that the leader of the band was no other than the well-known Captain Garland, who was mentioned in Colonel Horton's despatches to the War Department.

Captain Garland and his men halted at Lisworney for the night, and early the next morning took their departure for Bridgend. Before going, the captain ordered his men to give three ringing cheers for "Master Michael Giles, of the Moat House, Lisworney, and may he live long and prosper!" And the men cheered to an echo.

"He'll prosper as long as he lives alone!" shouted Michael, whereupon all the soldiers laughed heartily.

"I crave a boon before you go," said Michael, resting his hand on Captain Garland's horse.

"Anything you may wish to name," said the captain, "and it is in my power to give."

"I crave thy gauntlets," said Michael.

"And you shall have them," replied the captain, forthwith handing them to Michael, who promptly returned thanks for the boon.

The Royalists then rode away, and long after the civil war was over, Michael Giles would tease and taunt his own party, by saying, "The Roundheads paid for their place with a pair of gauntlets; but, for their insolence, I paid the Royalists with bees!"

In the course of time Michael Giles was gathered to his fathers, but, about forty years ago a gauntlet, containing coin of various reigns, was found in the thatched roof of the Moat House.

The Lady of the Lake

BRYNACH AP HOWEL, a prince of Montgomery, was in a gloomy mood. His lands were fair, his flocks were large, his herds were vast, and his palace near Welshpool was very beautiful.

Yet, he was a man with a grievance. His fair domain must fall into the hands of an enemy, unless Owain, his son, married a rich woman.

Unfortunately all the pretty princesses of Montgomery were very poor, while the only rich women were Gwenllian of Craig-y-Mwyn, who was already promised in marriage, and Olwen of Carno.

Owain ap Brynach was one of the most handsome men in Montgomery — a kind-hearted neighbour, and one of the best huntsmen in Wales. He knew his father's grievance, and put off the evil day as long as he possibly could.

But there was no help for him. The beautiful

maidens of Montgomery were poor, and Olwen of Carno possessed untold wealth. At last they were married, and the estates were saved.

Olwen was old enough to be Owain's grand-mother, and her figure was bent and bowed with extreme age. Her parchment-coloured skin was wrinkled, crows' feet surrounded her eyes, and her lips were thin and compressed.

Day after day Owain, as he sat down to the banquet, grieved bitterly over his condition. What was the good of all the wealth in the world and no happiness? Like a skeleton in a cupboard was Olwen to him, and as time passed, the worse matters grew. He disliked her at first, he hated her in the end.

When in a maddened mood Owain, without a word to Olwen, would angrily stride out of the banqueting-hall, and go away hunting. It was only in the chase he found any pleasure now.

Sometimes he wandered listlessly through the pleasant woodlands, where he sought, but always failed, to find solace for his heart-ache.

One day, when he was more than usually gloomy in mind, he threw himself upon a mossy bank in the woodlands, and there, half asleep and half awake, he mused over his condition. Overhead, the interlaced branches of the trees waved gently but solemnly to and fro. Around him, the white anemones quivered in soft summer air, and away in the distance the blue-bells looked like a sea of azure. Slowly through the long and natural woodland avenue a lovely maiden came. As she drew near, Owain observed that her face was fair and extremely beautiful. Long golden hair fell in profusion far below her waist. Her hands were like the white anemones, and her lips were red as the summer rose. She came quite close to him, so that he could almost touch her robes. Her eyes were like violets gleaming darkly under the long-fringed lids.

At last she spoke.

" You are sad," she said, in bewitching accents.

" I am," he replied.

" And why ? "

" Because I am tied for life to an ugly partner," said Owain, as the maiden sat beside him.

" Why don't you get rid of her ? " asked the beauty wickedly.

" Because it is written, ' Thou shalt do no murder,' " replied Owain, who thereupon poured forth a torrent of laments to the lady who so enthralled him.

" I must go," said the maiden.

Owain besought her to stay, but she would not

" I'll come again to-morrow ! " she cried gaily and then vanished.

Day after day Owain and the beautiful maiden met, until at length the prince determined to marry her.

But how was he to get rid of his ugly wife?

Even the beautiful maiden could not suggest any better or more effectual method than— murder!

One day Owain strode angrily homeward, and was in a sufficiently mad state of mind to thrust his sword there and then through his ugly wife's heart. Accordingly he went to her room, but she was not there. He searched the palace from battlement to basement, but she could not be found.

Where the ugly Olwen was gone nobody knew, and nobody cared.

Forthwith Owain went for his new and beautiful bride, whom he brought to the palace amid much rejoicing.

Henceforth life was like a summer of delight.

There was only one mystery about the fair lady. She agreed to become Owain's wife only on one condition. On the eve of every seventh day from the date of marriage she was to go away, and not be asked whither she went or what she did. The lovely lady then added— " If you agree to this your riches shall increase, your wine shall never fail, and my beauty will

never wane. But, if you once begin to doubt
me or oppose my wishes—

" Rushes and reeds, both rank and tall,
    Shall flourish in Owain's stately hall,
    And all that now may be therein
    Shall sink in the waters of a llyn !" (lake).

Owain agreed, and the long years passed joy-
ously. His bride still retained her wonderful
beauty. Her violet eyes were as. bright and
clear as ever ; her complexion was as fair as when
Owain first saw her, and in her long golden tresses,
not a single thread of silver could be found.

With the flight of time Owain, growing old
and careworn and wrinkled, noticed with a touch
of jealousy, how marvellously his wife retained
her wonderful youth and beauty. He grew
querulous and fretful, and was troubled with
visions. His mind reverted to Olwen's mysterious disappearances, and he pondered deeply
about his beautiful bride's strange absences.

It was a dull and gloomy day in December.
Not a gleam of sunshine could be seen, and the
leaden sky promised snow. A bitter biting
wind whistled through the bare branches of the
stately trees in the park, and with every gust,
the last remaining dead leaves whirled around
the palace porch.

In the early twilight, when the logs were

glowing brightly on the hearth, and the hounds, resting at their master's feet, started in their dreams, Owain's wife entered the great hall. She was richly robed, and jewels sparkled on her fingers, around her neck, and in her golden hair. She looked more beautiful and youthful than ever. On her arm she carried an outer and hooded garment of silk lined with costly furs, and Owain knew what it meant to see her attired thus. It was the eve of the mysterious seventh day.

"It is very cold," remarked Owain.

"Yes," replied his wife with a slight shiver.

"I fear we shall have snow," said Owain. "The sky is dark, and the wind is bitingly cold."

"It is," meekly murmured the fair lady.

"It is not fit for man or beast out this eve, much less for a fair lady," continued Owain, impatiently kicking one of the burning embers on the hearth.

The violet eyes glowed with a strange unearthly light as the lady answered—

"You remember the promise! Don't ask me to break it unless you wish

> "Rushes and reeds, both rank and tall,
> To flourish in Owain's lordly hall,
> And all that now may be therein
> To sink in the waters of a llyn!"

Owain frowned, and looked gloomily into the fire.

"It is getting late," said his wife. "I must go."

She had not long been gone, when snow began to fall, and in an hour's time the park and the fair lands around the palace were white and gleaming.

Owain impatiently strode up and down the hall. He was in an unusually gloomy mood, and could hardly restrain himself from putting a watch upon his wife. But he feared the consequences, although he fretted sorely about his wife's absences, and her perpetual beauty.

Absorbed in these thoughts, Owain did not observe the presence of his dearest friend.

Into the lordly hall, Wylan the monk had come silently, and with almost stealthy tread.

"Thou art sad, my son," remarked Wylan.

"That I am," replied Owain.

"And almost too pre-occupied to receive thy friend with kindly greeting," remarked the monk.

"Wylan!" exclaimed Owain harshly and impatiently, "I am tired of all this."

"All what, my son?" queried the monk.

"All these goings on," was the reply.

"Of whom?" asked Wylan.

"Of my wife, of course," said Owain.

"It can't be helped; and, moreover, she tells

M

you what the consequences would be if she failed to keep her tryst," said Wylan.

"I verily believe I am united to an evil spirit," said Owain angrily.

"Perhaps so," calmly remarked the monk.

"She will never grow old, and that's mysterious," continued Owain.

"It is," responded Wylan.

"She has not lost a tooth, or obtained a single grey hair, and she's sixty, if she's a-day by now," said Owain.

"Quite so," provokingly said Wylan.

"I am tired of her beauty," continued Owain. "One wouldn't like the moon to be always shining."

"Certainly not," said Wylan.

"What can I do?" asked Owain.

The monk paused for answer.

Meantime it must be said that Wylan, the monk and religious man, coveted his neighbour's wife.

"I have an answer for thee," said Wylan, as the two friends seated themselves besides the fire on the hearth.

"And what is the answer?" asked Owain harshly.

"Resign thy fair wife to me, with as much wine, and sufficient of thy flocks and herds, as may be needed by the monks of yon monastery.

Without the flocks and herds, without the wine,
I will not take thy lady."

"Agreed," exclaimed Owain.

Then the friends parted company.

That night Wylan the monk crossed the park,
but not towards the monastery. His pathway
was in another direction. He sought the Llany-
mynach Rocks, and the far-famed Cave of Ogof,
where the devil was supposed to hold terrible
orgies. The monk invoked the fiend, and promised to give him his own soul, if only Owain's
wife should become his. To this, the legend says,
the devil was quite agreeable.

At some distance from the Cave of Ogof there
stood a cross, which is known in the present day
as "Croeswylan," or the Cross of Wylan.

The devil promised the monk that, if he went
to the cross on the eve of the next day, Owain's
wife should be his. But there was a condition.
Wylan must legally, and in proper order, marry
the lady.

The eve of the seventh day came, and, as usual,
Owain's wife went to keep her tryst.

Wylan the monk went to keep his tryst at the
cross. According to the devil's promise, the
beautiful lady appeared. Jewels sparkled on her
white fingers, around her neck, and in her golden
hair, and she was enveloped in her flame-coloured
silken outer garment, lined with costly furs.

In order to make the marriage proper and legal to the satisfaction of the devil, Wylan had invited a neighbouring priest to perform the ceremony.

At the conclusion of the marriage service, a loud rumbling noise was heard in the Cave of Ogof; thunder pealed in the wintry heavens, and forked lightnings darted from the gloomy sky.

Wylan shuddered, and hurried his bride homeward. The lady gathered her hooded robe closely around her, for the night was bitterly cold, and they had to walk to the monastery.

Wylan, accompanied by his wife, entered the great hall, where, when the lady threw off her cloak, a mystery was revealed.

There, before all the brotherhood, stood Wylan's bride, Owain's lost wife Olwen.

Horror of horrors! Instead of the beautiful woman who had graced Owain's lordly banqueting-hall, there stood the toothless and crooked-back hag who had mysteriously disappeared from the palace.

Wylan was outwitted.

He had Owain's aged wife, the flocks and herds, the wine also, and, to make matters worse, he had parted with his soul for—the hag Olwen.

In the thunderstorm the foundations of the palace of Brynach ap Howel fell to the earth, and Owain, with all his household, perished, and soon afterwards—

> "Rushes and reeds, both rank and tall,
> Flourished in Owain's lordly hall,
> And everybody that was therein
> Sank deep in the waters of a llyn!"

Where the palace stood a small pool or lake may now be seen. It is called the Pool or Lake of Llynclys.

At one time the people of the neighbourhood firmly believed, that when the waters were *clear enough* the towers of the buried palace could be seen.

Unfortunately the day has yet to come when the darksome waters of Lake Llynclys shall be clear!

Sweet Lydia Fell

A STORY OF THE WELSH QUAKERS

WHEN it was announced by the deacon that Joshua Morgan, "a man from Abergele in the North," was to preach in Bethel in the South, there was quite a stir in the chapel.

"Who is he?" whispered one man to another.

"Don't know," was the reply.

"Have you ever heard him?" asked one aged woman of her neighbour.

"No, not I," was the answer.

"Is he young?" asked the girls, almost in a breath, as they fluttered up to Rhys Robert, the "leader of the singing."

"Well," said Rhys, slowly and deliberately, in his usual provoking way, "Well—I did hear —him—singing—when he was—let me see— 'bout eighteen—I should think—and——"

"He's 'bout sixty-six now, I s'pose," interrupted one of the girls.

" Wait—till I do—tell you," continued Rhys, slower if possible than before. " You gells do—want to—jump—down a man's—throat. Joshua—Morgan—did sing—well, there then—like a——"

" Angel," put in another girl.

" No," said Rhys; " no such—thing. He did sing——"

"Hoof to the man," exclaimed an impatient girl. " Out with it. You do drive us mad, waitin' so long. If you don't tell soon, I'm off."

" Well," continued Rhys, " the long—and short—of it—he did sing—like a L-A-R-K," said Rhys, spelling the word.

" If he did sing like a lark at eighteen, how do he sing now ? " asked one of the elderly women.

" Like a crow, now, I s'pose," said one of the girls, saucily tossing her head.

" I'll find out all 'bout him 'fore this time to-morrow," said Gwladys, Rhys Robert's daughter.

" Not you," said Mary Jenkin of the Shop, as the girls separated, some going homeward and others going to join their sweethearts.

All the unmarried women of Quakers' Yard were quite excited about the " man from the North."

Lydia Fell heard about the preacher, though she did not attend Bethel, for Rachel David, cousin to the pretty Quakeress, brought the news.

"Joshua Morgan of Abergele," remarked Lydia Fell, musing awhile. "Thy mother, Dinah Fell formerly, Dinah David now, and my father, Zebedee Fell, were first cousins to Abigail Fell, who married John Morgan of Abergele."

"Have you ever seen Joshua Morgan?" asked Rachel.

"Not since I was quite a child," said Lydia.

"What was he like then?"

"A very fine and beautiful boy of about fourteen, and I was nine."

"Oh!" said Rachel absently, while mentally calculating the minister's age. "Then he is only about thirty-six now?"

"Yes," said Lydia. "That is all."

"Is he dark or fair?"

"Dark, with very black curly hair, and dark glowing eyes. If Joshua Morgan has grown up, as he promised, he must now be handsome—very," said the Quakeress.

Lydia Fell was the only daughter of Zebedee Fell, a member of the Society of Friends. Zebedee's grandmother, Lydia Fell, was the owner of the northern portion of the Llanfabon estate. When a burial-place for the Friends was necessary in the neighbourhood, Lydia Fell gave a piece of land for the purpose in the year 1670, or

1680. The village now known as Quakers' Yard takes its name from the ancient resting-place of long departed Friends.

Zebedee Fell lived upon a small independency inherited from his grandmother, but the former wealth of the family dwindled to a mere nothing with the flight of time. Zebedee and Lydia were the last surviving of a long race bearing the name of Fell. All the others were married out of the fraternity, and their names were lost among Welsh families.

When Zebedee heard that Joshua Morgan was coming to Quakers' Yard, he said, "Thou must see the young man, and if he will not sojourn with us, maybe he will break bread here. Dost thou hear what I say, Lydia?"

"Yes, father," replied Lydia.

The aged man, dressed in the sad-coloured clothes common to the fraternity, rested on his staff, which, from father to son, had descended through long generations. For a time he mused in silence, and sighed deeply.

Then he asked, "When is the young man expected?"

"On the sixth day."

"Go and see thy Aunt Dinah about it, and tell her what I say."

Lydia's Aunt Dinah was the wife of Deacon David of Bethel.

It was arranged between Dinah and her niece Lydia that Joshua Morgan was to be the Deacon's guest, but the bread-breaking was to be left to the young minister's inclination.

In a few hours the girls in Quakers' Yard had heard all about "the man from the North," and eagerly looked forward to his coming.

At length the sixth day came, and the minister arrived.

He came in the April twilight, when the land was dim and shadowy. Through the soft and balmy evening air the young man saw the cherry blossoms glimmering like stars, those of the pear falling like snow-flakes in the orchards, and the pink and white petals clustered upon the branches of the apple trees that drooped down almost to the verge of the silvery Taff.

Although here and there, a girl modestly concealed herself behind the purple lilacs or under the orchard trees, not one could boast of having seen more than the shadowy outline of the minister's figure sitting beside Deacon David in the gig.

Dinah David came to the door to welcome her nephew, and Rachel peeping shyly on from the end of the passage. Instead of the short and thick-set man she expected to see, there appeared a tall and stately minister.

Joshua Morgan of Abergele was a stalwart

and handsome man, standing six feet in his stockings—and in those days much attention was attracted by masculine legs and feminine feet and ankles. Fine legs with ample calves, gave a man a better footing in society, than his neighbour who possessed thin and lean limbs. For that reason men with poor legs frequently adopted false calves. This practice caused some people's legs to be regarded as impostors when they were really *bôna fide*. Feminine feet and ankles fared better. There was no disguise for them. Big feet may be crushed into shoes a size too small, but then the ankles would bulge out and reveal the cramping. In those days women wore clogs and pattens, and the pretty foot looked prettier still in low shoes, to which dainty pattens were strapped. And women then were very proud of their highly-polished pattens, which kept the feet so nicely out of the mire and clay.

To return to Joshua Morgan. His fine legs were encased in drab gaiters when he arrived and was conducted by Aunt Dinah to his room. When he reappeared, the gaiters had been removed, and as he entered the parlour Dinah David mentally remarked, "What a handsome man—what splendid feet and legs!"

Joshua Morgan wore knee-breeches, fine white stockings—such as gentlemen only wore in those

days—low shoes with plain silver buckles, and a
cutaway coat. His linen was frilled, and his
dark, thick, and naturally curly hair was tied at
the back with black ribbon.

"He's quite the gentleman," thought Deacon
David, as he greeted his nephew-in-law.

Joshua made himself thoroughly at home, and
when Dinah, introducing her daughter, said,
"This is thy cousin," the minister, taking the
outstretched hand, said tenderly and slowly,
"Rachel, Rachel, for whom one waited through
weary years!"

A thrill of pleasure speeded through Rachel's
heart.

Joshua's voice was so tenderly sweet, so
musically clear, and yet by no means effemi-
nate. It was strong and powerful, but governed
according to the necessities of time and circum-
stance.

After a substantial supper Deacon David
settled down in his old arm-chair, and, taking
out two pipes, offered the minister one.

"Thank you," said Joshua; "I never smoke."

"What a nice man," mused Rachel.

"Thy father smoked," said Aunt Dinah.

"He would smoke against my mother's wishes.
Ever since his death my mother will not allow
pipes or smoking in the house."

"Ah!" sighed Dinah, as one before whom the

long gone years passed in review. "Time hath not changed thy mother, my cousin Abigail."

"And never will," responded the minister.

"As thou dost not smoke," remarked the Deacon, "perhaps thou would'st like to go and see thy uncle Zebedee Fell. Dinah, wilt thou go with Joshua?"

Aunt Dinah assented.

"What about society affairs?" asked Joshua.

"They'll keep till thee dost come back," said the Deacon.

Rachel accompanied her mother's cousin to Zebedee Fell.

The candles had only just been lighted, when "the man from the North" entered and was warmly welcomed by the Fells.

Cheerful firelight flickered on the hearth, and in the ruddy glow sweet Lydia Fell looked very beautiful. Her neat gown of drab material and her snowy kerchief were highly becoming to her style of beauty. Soft little wisps of light golden brown hair persisted in straying from under the cap, and the deep violet eyes, with their long sweeping lashes, were now turned steadily and candidly towards Joshua, Aunt Dinah, and Rachel in turn.

More than once Rachel caught Joshua gazing intently at Lydia, behind whom the dark wainscotted wall, and the oaken side table with its blue china Dutch vases, looked like the background of a beautiful picture.

"He admires Lydia—everybody admires her," murmured Rachel within herself. "And yet, she's ten years older than me."

It was getting late, and the visitors did not remain long, but Zebedee and Lydia promised to spend a day at the Deacon's.

"Perhaps we shall have thy company on the first day of the week?" asked Zebedee.

Joshua looked at Aunt Dinah.

"Do as thee dost please," said the Deacon's wife.

"Then I will come," said Joshua.

"And Uncle and Aunt, and Rachel too," added Lydia.

To which proposition all agreed.

On the way home Aunt Dinah asked Joshua how long he could stay amongst them.

"I have fourteen days to spare now," said Joshua, "but you would be tired of having me all that time."

"Tired!" exclaimed Aunt Dinah warmly; "tired of dear Abigail's son? No; never!"

Joshua silently pressed his aunt's small white hand, in thankfulness for the warmth of her hospitality.

Deacon David was delighted to hear that Joshua could remain fourteen days, thus giving

the Bethelites the advantage of two sermon
Sundays instead of one.

On Sunday morning, as Joshua Morgan
ascended the high pulpit stairs, all the girls
present looked at him in amazement. First at
his handsome head and face, next at his fine
stature and "bettermost" style of dress, and
last, but not least, at his fine feet and shapely
legs.

But for some reason there were several unbelievers in those legs.

"He's got false calves," said Martha Jones of
Llanfabon when the meeting ended.

"No, no," said Mary Morris of Quakers' Yard;
"he's a shapely man from head to foot."

"The man from the North" pleased the con-
gregation beyond expression, and when Joshua
Morgan arrived for the evening service, Bethel
was crowded to overflowing, and people were
willing to accept standing room.

The sermon was grand, impressive, and the
young minister's oratory was of the old Welsh
order—impassioned, and glowing with flowers of
rhetoric.

At the end of the service the minister opened
the pulpit door and descended a step, but found
the stairway occupied by numbers of his fair
hearers.

They immediately moved back to allow him

just sufficient space to descend, and, as he moved downward, Martha Jones of Llanfabon quickly and slightly pricked in succession the minister's calves.

He never winced—never moved a muscle, but went down as though Martha Jones had not touched him.

That decided the question.

Martha Jones of Llanfabon had proved to the satisfaction of all the women in Quakers' Yard that Joshua Morgan of Abergele wore false calves.

"Never mind what he do wear," said one loyal woman, "he do preach beau-ti-ful!"

But next day Rachel David declared that her cousin said he felt the "mischievous pricks," though he was equal to any fun, and resolved "not to wince under them."

Joshua spent Monday with Zebedee and Lydia, and the beauty of the Quaker maiden impressed him more than when he first saw her.

Sweet Lydia Fell!

Her fair face pleasingly haunted the minister's dreams.

Her melodious voice charmed his waking hours.

In the afternoon of the third day of the week, Joshua Morgan spent several hours with Zebedee, but all the time wondered at Lydia's absence.

He waited patiently for her coming, but she did not appear.

At last, looking out through the parlour window, he saw Lydia returning from the fields and entering the orchard.

Joshua Morgan passed down the garden pathway leading to the blossoming orchard, and, for a moment, paused beside the lilacs to look at his cousin.

"Sweet Lydia Fell!" he sighed. "Thy presence makes this earth an Eden."

Slowly and thoughtfully, Lydia Fell wandered through the orchard.

April sunshine, woven with shadows of leaf and blossom, fell upon her snow-white cap, and intensified the glory of her golden brown hair.

Suddenly she turned back, and seeing the minister, came swiftly across to greet him.

"I did not know that thou wert here," she said.

"I know it," said Joshua. "My uncle said you had gone to the fields."

"Yes; but had I known that thou wert here, I would not have remained so long away," she said, in sweet and winsome tones.

"I am pleased to hear you say that," said Joshua; "yes, pleased more than I can tell."

"Art thou?" asked Lydia, looking up.

N

Her violet eyes met her cousin's admiring glances, and, in that moment, the beautiful Quakeress, and the "man from the North" became conscious of a mutual though unuttered love.

Silently Lydia and Joshua returned to the house, and presently the minister departed.

That evening, when the apple blossoms fluttered down upon Lydia Fell's clasped hands, only the birds singing in the laburnum branches, and the bees humming among the lilacs, heard the fair maiden saying, "The Lord knows what is best."

Sweet Lydia Fell !

The minister remained the fourteen days, and then returned to Abergele in the North.

But his love for Lydia Fell remained unuttered.

"He will come again in the summer," thought Lydia. "It is well he does not act hastily. Words once spoken cannot be recalled."

One day, when autumn leaves filled the deep valleys of North Wales, and September gales sent the mountainous waves rolling wildly landward across the sands of Abergele, Joshua Morgan quitted his study table, and went out for a stroll.

Sea-mists and salt spray driven by the wind, came across the solitary sands, where the minister chose to take his walk. His head throbbed and his heart beat with the spirit of unrest. The time had come when he could no longer conceal his love for Lydia Fell.

An invitation had been received from Quakers' Yard, and the surrounding district, imploring him to preach there at Christmas time.

Aunt Dinah pressed him to come. They had " such a blessed time in April," she said.

"And I had too !" he responded.

He would go—yes, he would once more go to Quakers' Yard, and see sweet Lydia Fell.

But the time had come when he must tell his mother of his intentions, and it was in preparation for this, that he paced the sands, and sought strength from the voices of the winds and the waves, who seemed like messengers of the Most High.

When he returned home he sat on one side of the hearth in the twilight and firelight. His mother was cosily seated in her easy-chair opposite him.

" Thee dost seem much pre-occupied," remarked Abigail Morgan.

"That I am," replied the minister.

" And wherefore ?" questioned his mother.

Joshua pondered for a moment. " You know what God hath said," remarked Joshua, pausing.

"It is not like my son to hesitate," said Abigail.

"It is not good that man should be alone," remarked Joshua.

"So—so," said Abigail somewhat testily; "the long and short of it is, I suppose thee dost contemplate marriage."

"I do," said Joshua candidly.

"And with whom?" asked his mother.

"Guess," said he.

As Joshua was called "a lady's man," she knew of several fair aspirants for his heart and hand.

"With Miss Lloyd? It would be a good thing for thee to marry her. She's worth her thousands," said Abigail.

"Not worth half as much as the woman I love."

"Is it Miss Robert of Rhyl?"

"No."

"Miss Price of Denbigh?"

"Wrong again."

"Well, it must be Miss Rees of Llanwrst."

Joshua shook his head.

"Miss Preece of Rhuddlan?"

"Somebody further south," said Joshua.

Abigail pondered.

"There was a Miss Llewelyn of Brecon thee wast attentive to once," said his mother. "Thee dost know thee'st spoken of them all to me. And I know for certain thee'st paid attentions to them all."

"Just because they liked it, and they were

very attentive to me," said Joshua.   " But things are altered now."

" Well, it seems to me," said Abigail, smiling, "it is reserved for the seventh woman to lay hold of thee, and conquer."

Joshua—remembering his six flirtations—for all the girls loved to flirt with the handsome minister, laughed and said, " It seems so."

" And the seventh—who may she be ?" asked Abigail.

" A kinswoman of mine," he said.

" Rachel David, daughter of my cousin Dinah?" guessed Abigail.   " She is too young for thee."

" No ; sweet Lydia Fell, daughter of Zebedee Fell," was the reply.

A dark cloud, an angry scowl, passed over Abigail's face, which turned pale and ghastly even there, where the firelight gained mastery over the deepening twilight.

" Mother !" exclaimed Joshua, starting back from his seat, and gazing at the angry and pallid face upturned to him.

" Mother !" he repeated.   " Speak, I beseech you !"

Slowly, very slowly, her lips opened, and bringing the clenched fist of her right hand down with force upon the arm of the chair, Abigail, in withering tones, exclaimed, " I would rather look on thy dead face—thy coffined body

—thy closed grave, than see thee the husband of Lydia Fell !"

Joshua Morgan felt stunned, and for a time was like one dumb. At length he remembered that on his return from Quakers' Yard she did not take any notice of his remarks about Zebedee Fell.

When he recovered his voice he mustered courage, and said, " Mother, let me know why this bitter antipathy to a woman you know little about ? "

" Listen," said Abigail harshly, though now more composed, but still pallid in the face, and severe in tone. " Listen : When I was seventeen the world held only one man for me, and I then believed I was the only girl on earth for him. He was twenty-three, and should have known his own mind. We loved each other devotedly for three years. When I was twenty, Dorothy Raymond, the Sassenach (Saxon) Quakeress, came to our home. She robbed me of the man I loved, and I never forgave her or him ! That man was my own first cousin —Zebedee Fell ! Three months later, I was married to thy father. Dorothy's eldest child was born the same year as thee, but it died soon. That was their first punishment. The second and third children were born, and died directly. They had three punishments. Thou wert six years old when Lydia was born, and six months later Dorothy Fell died. After this, wilt thou wish to marry Lydia Fell?"

"Sweet Lydia Fell!" murmured the minister. "It was not her fault. Surely, mother, in the years that are gone, you could have buried the bitter past."

"Joshua," exclaimed the relentless mother, "if thou dost wish to bring down my grey hairs with sorrow to the grave—if thou dost wish to bring bitterness into my dwindling life—to gall the end of my existence with a revival of the old sorrow, the old hatred—marry Lydia Fell! But one thing I ask thee. If thou dost marry her, bring her not to my sight. Once she is thy wife, my doors are closed against thee and her."

"Mother!" gasped Joshua.

Abigail once more grew white with passion, and going to the depth of bitterness, she continued—"If thee dost marry Lydia Fell, not one penny shalt thou have after me. My doors shall be shut against thee; then go—go, and live upon the miserable pittance thou has got as a preacher. Hear what I say, and take heed, for I mean it."

Joshua Morgan strode to his study and locked the door. At first he sat down by the table, leaned his head upon his arms, and wept as only a man can weep.

The struggle between duty and love was fierce and of long duration.

At length duty was triumphant. He rejoiced that he had not told Lydia of his love. Now, she should never know it.

He sought his mother, but she was nowhere to be found.

He asked the servant where she was gone.

"Mistress is gone to her room," said the maid.

Joshua ascended the stairs, and knocked at his mother's door, but he did not receive an answer. Turning the handle, he entered.

His mother was laid on the bed, and looking more like a dead than a living body.

"Mother," he cried, stroking her cold hands and kissing her pallid face and brow.

At first he thought she was dead, because the warmth of his hands failed to revive her. He called the maid, and asked her to bring him a cordial. As he wetted his mother's lips therewith, he told the maid to go for the doctor.

The minutes seemed as long as hours, and yet no symptom of life appeared. The doctor came, and presently declared that the minister's mother was suffering from a shock to the heart.

"She will recover," he said, "but must be kept very quiet, and not allowed to be excited in the least."

Through an illness extending over many weeks, Joshua Morgan nursed his mother as tenderly as if she were a babe. At times her mind slightly wandered, and then she said the hateful face of Dorothy Fell haunted her.

Abigail recovered and came downstairs again, but Joshua made a vow never to speak of marriage while his mother lived.

He wrote to his uncle, Deacon David, declining the kind invitation to visit Quakers' Yard at Christmas time. In a private note to his Aunt Dinah he told all—screening nothing. The most precious part to her was where he said, "I shall never marry. But there is only one woman in the world for me, and that is—sweet Lydia Fell."

Lydia looked eagerly forward to seeing Joshua at the Christmas time, and when she heard that he declined the invitation, she wondered why.

"He gives no reason," said Deacon David.

"But he supposes we take it for granted that he could not leave his mother after so serious an illness. And it is a tedious journey, from the North to the South," said Dinah.

"We were very thoughtless to forget Joshua's poor, suffering mother," said Lydia tenderly. "Duty should always come first."

And Lydia folded her hands, while she mentally said, "The Lord knows what is best."

"If she only knew the truth," said Aunt Dinah mentally. "But it is better she should not. Her thoughts about Joshua's mother are pure and good, and I am truly thankful that Lydia Fell is in no way like Abigail Morgan."

. . . . . .

Years passed.

Joshua never went to the South again.

Time and stern duty soothed, if they did not heal, his wounds of sorrow, and he went about preaching as of old.

He settled down into confirmed bachelorhood, and enjoyed the mild attentions of the six ladies who had "set their caps" at him, but, in turn, each got married, and it was left for them to amusingly remind him of his "willow cap."

Joshua Morgan had been keeping appointments in Montgomeryshire, and the last place against his name in "the publication" was hill-encircled Llanidloes, where, after the service, he found himself snow-bound. Locomotion over the hills was impossible, and foot-passengers were unable to reach even the nearest villages because of the deep and dangerous snow-drifts.

In the ruddy glow of the firelight, as the gloaming deepened into darkness, Joshua Morgan sat alone, moodily watching the fast falling snow.

He heard the sonorous ticking of the old clock in the hall, the purring of the cats on the hearth, and now and again, faintly from the distance, came sounds of active housewifery.

Outside, as the twilight merged into early night, all was snowy and frigid—inside all was warm, cosy, and glowing.

Joshua's reverie was disturbed by a rapping at the door, and his partly audible "Come in" had an immediate response.

He looked around.

There, standing beside him, was Miss Lloyd of Abergele.

"You here?" he asked in amazement.

"Didn't you know I came yesterday?" she said, sitting down in the arm-chair.

Another rap at the door, and Miss Roberts of Rhyl entered.

Joshua looked bewildered, as he greeted the new arrival, who, after shaking hands with him, took a seat beside him.

By-and-by Miss Price of Denbigh, Miss Llewelyn of Brecon, Miss Preece of Rhuddlan, and Miss Rees of Llanwrst, entered.

All these ladies at the same time in Llanidloes!

It puzzled the minister's brain.

Then Joshua thought to himself, " Perhaps they happen to be visiting the town just now, and, knowing I am snow-bound, have kindly come to look after me, for the sake of old times."

Aloud, he thanked them for their kindness in coming, especially " in such weather."

The ladies almost simultaneously smiled and bowed. There sat they who, in the years gone by, had been so " attentive to the minister," and with whom he had so willingly flirted.

Joshua Morgan was embarrassed.

He endeavoured to talk, but to no purpose, and seeing the ladies appeared to be preoccupied, Joshua relapsed into silence, hoping that soon his kindly hostess would come and explain matters.

Suddenly, a gust like a hurricane rattled the windows, and the door flew open.

Joshua shut it, and then went back to his deep and cosy arm-chair.

For a few moments he closed his eyes, and when he reopened them the ladies had vanished. and in their stead beside him stood Lydia Fell !

Yes ; there she was, smiling and as beautiful as ever.

In the ruddy fire glow her fair face looked radiant with joy. Her violet eyes, with their long sweeping lashes, were bright and undimmed, and her golden brown hair showed no traces of the touch of time.

How lovely she looked, with her pretty hair nestling around her forehead, and in some places escaping from under her cap. Her snowy-white kerchief was, as of old, folded over her bosom, and the folds of her neat drab dress fell softly around her figure.

Sweet Lydia Fell!

The past revived, the present faded wholly away, as Joshua, after long years of heart agony and sorrow, clasped his lost love in his arms, and kissed her.

"Come, come quickly," whispered Lydia. "There is no time to be lost. Oh, Joshua, Joshua, thy mother is dying!"

"My mother dying?" he said in broken accents.

"Yes, and she would see thee before she goes hence. Come, I beseech thee, come."

In the hour of sad tidings and sorrow the minister's heart went back to the past, and, as he once more clasped sweet Lydia in his arms, whether the message bore a larger portion of joy than woe, who shall tell?

The Quakeress moved to go, and Joshua followed his beautiful lost love, sweet Lydia Fell.

He went with her into the hall way, and just as he was taking his hat off the peg, his hostess called him, " Please come to tea."

"To tea ?" he asked in bewilderment.

" Yes, it is half-past six o'clock. But I didn't like to wake you before."

"Wake me ?" queried Joshua, amazed. "Have I been to sleep ?"

" Yes, ever since about four o'clock."

"Dear me, dear me," said Joshua aloud, but to himself he murmured, " It was only a dream, after all !"

The dream made the minister uneasy, and a day later he started on his perilous journey homeward, with the greatest possible difficulty reaching Abergele just one day before his aged mother died.

She had been seized with a serious illness about six o'clock, when, in a dream, Lydia Fell told him his mother was dying.

.   .   .   .   .   .

In April the "man from the North" went down to Quakers' Yard, where he arrived one evening quite unexpectedly.

He reached Aunt Dinah's in the dusk of the evening, and quite unrecognised by the few people who passed him.

"Joshua Morgan !" exclaimed Aunt Dinah,

tenderly greeting him. "So thou'lt come at last!"

When they reached the parlour Joshua said, "Time has dealt gently with you, dear Aunt Dinah."

"It hath indeed, and with my husband also."

"And Rachel?" asked Joshua.

"She is married, and has four children."

"Ah!" sighed Joshua. "These eight years have seemed like a century to me."

Joshua could not yet bring himself to utter the name nearest his heart.

"And how is Uncle Zebedee?" asked Joshua, drawing nearer the subject that was all in all to him.

"Uncle Zebedee! I thought thee didst know, but there, we have not written to thee since February. He died on the first of March."

"And Lydia?"

"She hath been low, and weak ever since. For two months she nursed her father day and night, and her strength gave way."

Not waiting to take refreshment with Aunt Dinah and Deacon David, Joshua went to see Lydia.

Finding the front-door wide open he strolled noiselessly in, and turned to the parlour.

A bright fire was burning on the hearth, and

beside it on a couch was the wasted form of Lydia, propped up with pillows.

The glance was too much for Joshua, so he stepped out into the hall to dash the tears from his eyes.

Lydia, hearing the retreating footsteps, feebly cried, "Aunt Dinah dear, is it thee?"

With that the minister entered, and gently said, "Lydia."

The Quakeress moved among her pillows.

"Who—who is it?" she asked.

Joshua stepped forward.

"It is Joshua, come at last!" exclaimed Lydia, extending her thin worn hand, which the minister took and held within his own.

Then he drew a chair beside the invalid.

At that moment he first observed the real alteration in his cousin.

She looked thin and worn. All the delicate colour had left her cheeks, and they were hollow and wasted as her poor little thin hands.

"I am sorry to find you thus," said Joshua, "but you will get better soon. Time is a great soother."

"Nay, Joshua, I shall never recover. For two years I have felt the end coming, but my poor father's death was the finishing stroke," said Lydia. "The Lord knoweth what is best. I am prepared to go whenever He calls me."

"You shall not go," said Joshua passionately. "You must live—live for me, Lydia."

Then, like a mountain torrent, he poured forth the story of his love, and the conquest of duty, screening not even his dead mother in the intensity of his passion.

"Thou hast suffered much," said Lydia tenderly, "and I would I could live, for thy dear sake."

There, in the fire glow, they plighted their troth, and Lydia felt conscious it was only the union of souls for a short time on earth but for ever in heaven.

When summer roses died in the old home garden, Lydia the beautiful passed away, and Joshua Morgan returned to Abergele, feeling like one from whom life's sunshine had been cruelly wrested by a fate relentless as the grave.

For years after that he annually visited Quakers' Yard, and the burying place of the Friends, where, so late as sixty years ago, a moss-grown stone still bore the partially obliterated name of Lydia Fell.

This story was taken from an aged minister's note-book. Therein it was stated that in his childhood he knew a sad-faced, but powerful

Q

preacher, named Joshua Morgan, who, even at the age of ninety, travelled from the North to the South, and ever spoke to his friends of the duty that vanquished love, and martyred sweet Lydia Fell!

The Welsh Merry-Man

IF the "Merry-Man" was not one of the best in his profession, ask the sailors who surrounded him in the inn at Port Dinorwic, known formerly as Felin Hen—ask the children from Mona to Montgomery—ask the girls from Snowdon, westward or southward to the sea—ask the mothers from St. Asaph to St. David's.

He was a veritable Welsh wag, or, as the country folk would say, a "Merry-Man." To call him a clown, or an acrobat, would be to libel him, even though he sometimes appeared among a troupe of strolling players, and went in for what the people called "a lot of antics and capers," but he more frequently went about only with a man and a dog. The man played the harp, and the dog danced to any gay or melancholy tune from "Hob-y-deri-Dando," to "Ar-hyd-y-nos."

Wherever the "Merry-Man" went he was welcome. Rough and ready sailors, in all the seaport towns of Wales, greeted him with friendly hand-grasp and a tankard of *cwrw-da*. The housewives on the dusty roadsides were ever ready to let him rest awhile from the heat of summer, or to shelter from the rains of early autumn.

Where he went in the winter was a secret known best to himself. In May he re-appeared and continued his peregrinations from north to south, until the fading and falling leaves proclaimed the approach of November.

Nobody knew his name, and when asked he would say—

> " Elecampane, Elecampane,
> 　If you ask me again,
> 　I will tell you the same ;"

or, laughing heartily, he would say, " Don't you know ?—why, the Sassenach do call me 'Our Taffy.'"

One wet afternoon in summer, when the inn at Port Dinorwic was crowded by noisy sailors, the Merry-Man appeared.

He was accompanied by his friend with the harp, and a dog.

" Where'st been this long time ? " said one and the other.

" Where I've been before," replied the Merry-Man.

" You do come in poor times for these parts," said the landlord.

" 'Tis always poor times in May," said the Merry-Man. " Spring cleaning is uncommon dirty work, and the women get that fractious over it—don't they, missis ? "

The landlady smiled.

" The worst week I did ever spend was with Morgan Lloyd in Dinas Mawddwy, when his wife was took with the spring cleanin'."

" Now for it ! " exclaimed the auditors, almost in one breath, as the sailors sat down before their tankards of beer.

The landlord took his seat in the arm-chair ; the landlady seated herself in the corner of the settle farthest from the fire.

" Well, I wass tell you," said the Merry-Man, using a common Welsh provincial expression, " how Mary Jones was took with the spring cleanin'. Soon after twelve of a Sunday night I did hear odd sounds ; crockery did rattle—glasses did jingle—an' by three in the mornin' Mary Jones was rampin'. Things was taken down from dirty shelves—clean crockery to be dusted was put on one side, and crockery to be washed was put on the other. Come Tuesday, nothin' was in its place. Well, the dirtiest thing I do know of

is spring cleanin'!   We was told that there was
to be no dinner 'cause the kitchen grate was to
be cleaned, an' the saucepans was to be scoured.
Wednesday there was no breakfast, 'cause the
kittles was to be cleaned inside and out.   The
beds was taken to pieces—ticks an' all—an' we
had to sleep on the floor.   Thursday we was
told to take off our boots and walk barefooted,
'fraid we'd dirty the floor, an' same day we'd to
eat the food in our hands to spare the plates.
'Twas cruel bad times.   She did blacklead the
outsides of the saucepans and kittles.   She did
clean the clock by taking out the works and
boilin' them.   She did rub beeswax on the
chairs, on the tables, on the posts of the bed-
sticks, on the floors, till they did come as slippery
as ice itself—and true as I be sittin' here, she
did beeswax the bellows!   I did ask if she'd like
to beeswax me!

"Well, well, the dirtiest work I do know of
is spring cleanin'.   But, to go on with my story.
Davy Jones did go out, an' worst of all, he did
go to the public-house, an' he did get drunk—
like all of us do get sometimes—and fust thing
on comin' home at night was to ask for his
fiddle.   'You kent have the fiddle,' says Mari,
'you bean't in a fit state to touch it.'   'I will
have my fiddle,' says he, and off straight he did
go to look for the instrument.   It did belong to

his greet-grandfather, an' he did set greet price
on it. In the twinklin' of an eye back he did
come. 'Mari,' he did bawl as loud as he could,
'Mari, what hast thee bin an' done with the
fiddle?' 'Bin an' done, to be sure,' says she,
flouncin'; 'I've bin an' cleaned it—that's all.
Time for it to be cleaned, I should think. 'Twas
thick with dirt, an' as black as the chimbley
back.' 'But, Mari,' says Davy, 'how did'st thee
clean it?' 'How, indeed! I'll tell you how in
a minute. I did put it in a tub of rain water,
an' I did scrub an' scrub it till I did jest get the
skin off my hands. 'Twas that dirty.' Davy
did jump with temper. 'The 'ooman's mad,'
says he; 'who did ever hear of any 'ooman in
her senses scrubbin' a fiddle! There—'tis ruined
for life!' 'No, 'tisn't,' says Mari, 'I did take it
out an' wipe it, an' then I did dry it before the
fire.' 'Before the fire!' says Davy. 'Iss, to be
sure,' says Mari, 'where would you have me dry
it—in the sun? Then I did beeswax it, an'
look at it now!' Mari did take the fiddle from
him, and did hold it over to me. Sure anuff,
there was the fiddle beeswaxed from stem to
stern, as you sailors do say. Davy Jones of
Dinas Mawddwy did hang his fiddle behind the
door, an' from that day to this he did never
touch it again. An' Mari was never took again
with such a bout of spring cleanin'."

Loud laughter and applause succeeded the Merry-Man's story, which, after all, was only a " good skit," as the Welsh sailors said, on the extremes of spring cleaning in some parts of Wales.

Soon the sailors clamoured for another story.

The Merry-Man readily granted the request, and he explained that he spoke in imperfect Anglo-Cymric dialect, so as to keep his stories to the letter and life as far as possible. Sometimes he would imitate the Anglo-French, sometimes he imitated the American dialect, but the people more thoroughly enjoyed his descriptive stories of their own land.

" Well," resumed the Merry-Man, " there was a greet big man from the North did go to Llundain (London). The man from the North did speak wonderful, all things considerin'. For he did know very little English, poor fellow, but he did do his best. Now he did learn his speech perfect before he did come, but he did want to say ' a few remarks' before he did begin his greet address. ' I did feel greet wish to see the greet City,' says he, ' an' I did say if mountain won't come to Ma'omet, Ma'omet will go to the mountain, an' here I did come. An' as I did come down for the first time in the train, I did say England got not half bad mountains, but they be little, an' poor anuff. And I did say to myself, If all the little mountains in

England was put together, that would be a big mountain, but not so big as one of the mountains with us, the mount called Y-Wyddfa (Snowdon), or Carnedd Llewellyn, or Carnedd Davyd. Well, after all, I do see you are so dull here. You don't know what 'talcen ty' is in English; 'tis the forehead of the house. You don't know what 'coes bren' is in English; 'tis timber leg! And then there's another bit I do see dull in you, for all you do live in the big City; an' I will tell you all 'bout it. When I was come to the deacon's, they did welcome me kind anuff at first, an' I did set down by the tea-table feelin' comfortable an' homely. An' after tea—I didn't like to mention it before— I did say as quiet as possible, 'If you will please to excuse me, Mr. Morgan, in takin' the liberty to say so, but I do want you to get the small-pox.' 'Get the smallpox?' asks he. 'I hope to goodness I shan't get it.' 'Now I do think that uncommon unchristian-like, for I do want you to get the smallpox,' says I, determined. 'An' I do think it unbecomin' of *you*, a minister of the gospel, to want me to get the smallpox.' We did get to high words—iss, indeed, look you; for all the time I did want him to get the smallpox. Well, I did go out, and I did go to the stasshoon, an' I did say to the—what do they call him, what runs 'bout up an' down

with a truck most of the time, an' calls out
somethin' I don't understand at all. There,
I do know now—'tis the Sassenach for Irish
stout. So says I to the man, 'Excuse me
speakin''—an' I did try to be as genteel as I
could—but I do want you to get the smallpox.'
There's a look he did turn on me! 'Twas anuff
to curdle vinegar. 'You can wish me to get
nothin' worse than the smallpox,' says the man;
'I hope I shall get nothing of the kind.' So I
did go off to the man that do go to shut the
doors of the trains when they do come in and
go out, an' I did begin as civil as possible, for I
was getting dusprad 'fraid of the people here in
the greet City. So I did try to speak mild to
the man what the English do call a watch-
chain—'I do want you to get the smallpox.'
'You'le a kind fellow,' says the man, 'to want
anybody to get the smallpox, I must say.' An'
he did turn on his heels. Well, I did never
think anybody would treat a stranger like that,
in a strange land, too. By-and-by I did go to
where there was a greet number of the men that
do go in the Sassenach by the name of Irish stout,
an' I did say, 'I do want you to get the smallpox.' You did never hear such a noise in your life!
One did tell me to go to Jericho, another did say
somethin' 'bout sending my granny to shoe ducks.
'Shoe ducks?' says I; 'do they do such a thing

in Llundain as shoe ducks.' Then they did laugh outright; but never fear, I didn't mind 'em a bit, so I did go on—'In Gwalia, where I did come from, they do shoe horses an' asses, but a Welsh donkey, leave alone a man, would laugh to see a duck in shoes!' I did think myself uncommon clever to turn the tables on them like that. But they—why they did laugh worse than ever. An' I did ask them what for? 'What for!' says one of the men, 'I'll give you what for soon if you don't clear off this platform.' Well, I did never feel more put on in my life. But the old Welsh blood was up in a minute, an' boilin' over too. I did only say I did want them to get the smallpox, an' with that the man did take me by the collar and go to put me out of the stasshoon. Well, I did turn on him, an' somehow or other we did come to blows, an' the end of it was, they did take me to the lock-up for insulting the man in the stasshoon. Next day I was took 'fore the magistrates, an' I did tell them plain anuff how it did all come about jest because I did say I did want them to got the smallpox. The magistrates did laugh outright. An' one of them did know the old language, an' he did say to me, 'They thought you meant the *frech wen.*' I did laugh fit to kill myself, an' there was no wonder they did think me mad to be wantin' the people to get the *frech wen* (smallpox), when all the time I did only want my little small—Box, they did spell it. 'Twill be the first an' last time for me to go to Llundain!"

Loudly laughed the company and eager were the demands for more stories, and, after the Merry-Man had rested awhile, he resumed his art, which, if not always so amusing as his antics, was, to some at least, entertaining.

He did not always talk in that quaint and queer *patois* of Wales, reserving that chiefly for stories illustrating the peculiar idiosyncrasies of the Principality. Sometimes he ran on in fluent English, which often pleased the people beyond measure, for the Welsh dearly delight in listening to a skilled conversationalist.

"You know but few of the old stories of Wales," said the Merry-Man. "If I could I'd make a book on them, like great writers do about England and Scotland and Ireland. I've got a story that will stand side by side with any of them, and I only wish I could write it. It is the story of the Robber's Leap. Rhys Coch, or Rhys the Red, was one of the celebrated 'Men of Mawddwy,' who were robbers in days gone by. A price was set on his head because he was the leader or chief of the robbers. The price was large and tempting, and it tempted one of his own band of robbers to try and capture the leader of the men of Mawddwy. But, by-and-bye, Rhys the Red began to have suspicions about his men, and one day he told Iolo, his chief man, what he thought.

" 'There is little faith in any one of them,' said Rhys the Red ; 'one can scarcely trust a man.'

" 'The times are bad,' said Iolo, who felt deeply the persecution of the law.

"Just before this time the King of England had passed laws for the destruction of the men of Mawddwy, and there was no peace for the robbers.

"Rhys began to fear his own men, and was continually changing his quarters. Sometimes he would suddenly go down to the lowlands, and sometimes he would keep close among the mountains. The men of Mawddwy were very fierce, and never scrupled to take anything they could set their hands on. They always had plenty of horses, so that they could ride away like the wind when chased. Rhys the Red had a horse named Lightning, and he was very fond of it.

" 'Never mind, my beauty,' he said one day, stroking his horse's splendid arched head and glossy neck, ' thou art swift as the eagle in its flight from Caer Eyri—bright as the lightning in the Pass of Glasslyn—firm as the rocks in wilds of Montgomery !'

"More than gold, more than maiden or wife, and, next to his own life, Rhys the Red loved his horse. In speed it surpassed the swiftest horse among the mountains, and it would venture where any other animal feared to stand.

"Rhys the Red had over five hundred men at his beck and call when the · law set a price on his head, and in less than a year the number had dwindled down to three hundred. One day he divided his company into three, and sent one to the west, one to the east, and one to the south, reserving the other part for himself and fifty men. Rhys and his men rode on into parts unknown to them, and, while wandering through some woods, the party came to be separated. By-and-bye, Rhys noticed that, while pondering deeply on the course he intended to pursue, he was left behind. At first he thought it was accidental, but at last, after shouting with might and main, he believed himself to be betrayed. He rode swiftly on, and soon heard the roaring of a torrent down below him. Then, looking back, he saw the king's men in full pursuit. If Rhys turned back he must fall into their hands—to ride on was to fall into danger unknown. But ride on he had to, because the English were chasing him. At last, after riding at the top of his speed, and outstripping the king's men, lo and behold, he reached the torrent that he had heard in the distance.

"Rhys the Red halted a minute or two to consider what was to be done. The king's men were behind, the yawning torrent before him. He must be taken, or leap the torrent!

"'My Lightning, my Lightning!' he said, stroking his trusty steed's head, 'fleet of foot as thou art, I like not to try thee here. But, O my life, my prize! thou must leap! 'Tis better to perish together in the torrent than to be taken!'

"The horse seemed to understand his master's wish; then, waiting as if to measure the distance, he leaped across the torrent and swiftly and safely reached the other side. The king's men held their breath, and then the leader cried out, 'Surely in the length and breadth of the land there is not a braver man than Rhys the Red!' And to this day the spot is known as the 'Robber's Leap.'"

Before the Merry-Man ceased, the wind began howling in the chimney, the waves roared, the rain was beating against the window panes, and twilight gloom proclaimed the near approach of night. For a short time the Merry-Man sat silently in the cheerful fire-light; but when the candles were lighted, he deserted the art of story - telling for that of antics, to the infinite pleasure of all beholders in the quaint old kitchen of the inn at Port Dinorwic.

He was the last of his kind, for the Welsh Merry-Man should not be confused with clowns and acrobats of to-day. In every sense he was a very simple, harmless, and popular maker of mirth, whose chief business was to relate laughable stories, with interludes of song, curious dances, grotesque grimaces, and extraordinary feats demonstrating muscular power.

The Merry-Man never wore powder, paint, or mottled garments. He was simply a relic of the Morris Dancers of old and wandering minstrels of the past.

The White Women of Lundy

LOOMING dim and mysteriously through shrouding mists of morning, the storm-beaten cliffs and wave-riven rocks of Lundy looked like grim and voiceless wardens of unrecorded romances and forgotten tragedies.

Scared with grisly seam and haggard cleft, the dark and barren granite ridges, hurled in wild disorder on the sparse shingle, caught the first red gleam of the summer daybreak. Above, on the bare and wind-blown heights now capped with cloud-reefs, all was cold and grey and unfriendly. Below, among the lesser cliffs, fantastic coves and shadowy grottoes, myriads of sea-birds whirled wildly, as though glad to welcome the return of sunrise. All the jagged ledges and jutting rocks were swarmed with them, and the morning air was filled with their wild and discordant screams.

In the words of an old chronicler, it is "so immured with rocks, and impaled with beetle-browed cliffs, that there is no entrance but for friends."

Drayton in his *Polyolbion* sings—

" England and Wales strive in this song,
   To whether Lundy doth belong ;
   When either's nymphs, to clear the doubt,
   By music mean to try it out
   This while in Sabrin's court, strong factions strangely
      grew
   Since Cornwall, for her own, and as her proper due,
   Claimed Lundy, which was said to *Cambria to belong*,
   Who oft had sought redress, for that her ancient wrong."

He then goes on—

" Of all the inlaid isles her sovereign Severn keeps,
   That bathe their amorous breasts within her secret deeps
   (To love her Bury much, and Scilly though she seem,
   The Flat-Holm, and the Steep as likewise to esteem),
   This noblest British nymph yet likes her Lundy best."

The decision appears in the next canto—

" In this song Severn gives doom
   What of her Lundy should become."

In conclusion, the poet sings—

" Then take my final doom, pronounced lastly—this,
   That Lundy like ally'd to Wales and England is."

Around the peninsula of Lametor and Rat Island, the silver green waves of the Atlantic rolled surging against the cliffs, and at their base the surf foamed and frothed ceaselessly.

The ruins of Marisco Castle looked gloomy and grand as the clouds lifted, and the first faint sunbeams worked curious traceries thereon.

It was a day to be remembered by the few islanders that remained.

Before the troubled times of the great Rebellion, and when it was almost deserted by its hereditary owners, Lundy was known as one of the very worst of pirates' nests.

It afterwards became the refuge for people during the civil wars. Echard, the old English historian, states that after Lord Say and Sele "had lived to see his fine ambition defeated by the supremacy of Cromwell, he sought a voluntary retreat, or rather imprisonment, in the isle of Lundy."

Later on, the island regained its old reputation as the headquarters of pirates and desperadoes, and a safe resort for criminals and adventurers of all nationalities.

In 1663, reports were sent to the Admiralty that "pirates and desperadoes" had "established themselves there," and that "one Captain Pronoville, a Frenchman, having grown desperate, had fixed himself at Lundy, and was doing great damage to merchants."

For three years Pronoville had been playing

havoc in the Golden Bay, as Barnstaple Bay was
called, because of the numberless prizes gained
there by pirates.

On this June day in 1666, when the Atlantic
rollers caught the first flush of sunrise, and over
the vast green water wastes the earliest golden
glory of the summer sunshine rippled in quiver-
ing radiance, two white-sailed skiffs, with sea-
birds wheeling in their wake, rounded Rat
Island and entered the roads.

Pronoville, the pirate, standing on the heights
like a bird of prey, sent down his minions to
demand the cause of the intrusion of the
strangers. Buccaneer as he was, he felt fearful
of spics—of other pirates coming to share the
island, and above all he was much afraid of his
powerful rivals the Dutch.

"It looks like the Dutch," said he, scanning
the skiffs.

Then he descended from the lordly heights
above the sea, and went down to the roads.

"Who may ye be?" thundered Pronoville to
the three men just landed.

"We be peaceable Welshmen, come over to
see some of our relatives that do live in the
island," said the spokesman of the party.

Pronoville had doubts, whereupon the Welshmen produced satisfactory proofs in support of
their statement, so they were allowed to pass

in peace to the Gannet's Coombe to their relatives, who gained their living as feather " pluckers."

The three men were the sons of the veritable master of the Mumbles (a suburb of Swansea) man-o'-war, which, he said, was armed with " three leatherin' guns and a handspik'."

They came to see and befriend their only sister Mary Marriner, formerly Llewellyn, who had recently been widowed and left in ill circumstances.

When the Welshmen reached Mary's home in Gannet Coombe, a thoroughly Celtic greeting took place.

It was " Oh dear, dear, an' here you be, come to see your poor sister; " and " Didn't I know it was you ? " and then in Welsh, " Look, look, my little children."

Then amid tears and sobs and smiles, the Welsh element subsided, and order once more resumed its sway. It was pleasant for Mary Marriner in Gannet Coombe, because her brothers had brought " plenty of money " and spent it freely.

In their rude manner all this " spendin' " was intended to assuage the soul agonies of the widow, and still the sorrows of the orphans. After a few days had passed, Pronoville was disposed to seek the society of these Welshmen, and, before the week was out, he spent the greater part of his time with them.

One day, while Pronoville and the Welshmen were regaling themselves with undiluted spirit in Gannet Coombe, the wary old sea-pirate suggested that the visitors should " have a try " at his own profitable profession.

" You'd make money ding-dong," said Pronoville, slapping one of the men on the shoulder.

" Don't know so much about that," said Jacob Llewellyn. " It would take a long time to learn, an' by the time I did know the way how, I'd be ready for my grave."

Pronoville laughingly scorned the idea.

" You're a young man yet," said he with a friendly poke.

" Not so young," said Jacob. " I'm on the wrong side of sixty now."

" Then *you* had better have a try at my game," to the other Welshman.

" Well," said Reuben Llewellyn, " it's uncommon kind of you to give us a chance, and, if my brother Pharaoh would join, I don't mind trying, an' see what'll come of it."

" What do you say, Pharaoh ? " asked Pronoville.

" I've a mind to try, but I'd like to take a few days to think over it," said Pharaoh.

" By all means," said Pronoville.

It was agreed that three days hence decision should be made. That night, in the Gannet Coombe, Jacob was by no means agreeable. He disliked the idea of Welshmen leaguing with wicked "sea-thieves and robbers," and went so far as to say that there never had been any Welsh pirates, or wild rovers and robbers Whereupon he was reminded of the Welsh buccaneers, who had scoured the seas, and scourged the merciless taskmasters of the far West.

"Let's turn buccaneers," said Reuben; "it's a fine game, Pharaoh."

"Ay, ay!" responded Pharaoh.

Mary Marriner, listening to this conversation, observed that although Jacob appeared to be opposed to the proposition, there was a curious twinkling in his eyes, and secret satisfaction with the course his brothers intended to pursue. And she moreover observed that, although Jacob fretted and fumed when any of the "pluckers" were present, he rubbed his hands and chuckled to himself when the brothers sat alone. The three days passed, and Pronoville came for the answer.

"Agreed," exclaimed Reuben and Pharaoh Llewellyn.

"What about yourself?" asked Pronoville, addressing Jacob.

"I'll have nothing to do with it; no, not I," said Jacob. "When they do begin their work I'll go back to Swansea."

"Work will begin next week," said Pronoville. "Time means money."

He rubbed his hands and chuckled gleefully.

Like the spider luring the fly, the old sea-rover loved to catch the unwary, and laid his plots accordingly. He saw that the Welshmen had money to spend, and, if anybody could get it out of them, he would. He wanted partners with money badly just now. "Trade had been dull," he told himself—not revealing the fact to his new partners—and he wanted more craft and crew. The Dutch were gradually becoming powerful rivals, and he feared they would take his "Golden Bay" prizes from him; and again, he wanted younger men to fill his place in a trustworthy manner when, work-weary, he might wish for rest and temporary leisure. Not that he—the intrepid sea-robber—ever intended retiring from business, not he!

> "The sea's my bonnie bride,
> And whatever may betide,
> I will never leave her side.
>   Never! Never! Ho! ho! ho!"

sang Pronoville.

New life and fire filled the Frenchman's heart,

and he went about ordering his men with the air and importance of a monarch who has augmented his army.

"It's a grand thing to be bold, fearless, intrepid, daring, and — honourable, isn't it, Pharaoh?" asked the pirate, sturdily beating his breast.

"That it is," responded Rueben.

"Ay, indeed," added Pharaoh.

But they did not see where the "honourable" came in.

"We begin with the tide on Monday," said Prouoville. "My plans are laid, and all will be ready for action by Sunday evening.

That night in the Gannet Coombe, Mary Marriner was sad and poor spirited. Her own brothers, sons of her own mother, were going to "bemean" themselves by "taking to" a nefarious trade. It was more than she cared to contemplate, and, before her brothers retired for the night, she gave them "a piece of her mind." Mary Marriner spoke warmly, as one who bitterly disliked even the very thought of it, and she concluded her attack by declaring her intention of packing up her "belongings," and quitting Lundy when Jacob returned.

"When are you going?" she asked Jacob.

"In a week or two," he replied.

"Are you going to stay here so long as that!" exclaimed Mary, almost screaming. " Will you look on at such dreadful wickednesses ? "

Mary was in a perfect rage.

Seeing this, Jacob whispered a few words in Welsh, which had the effect of instantly and completely subduing her.

With the tide on Monday, Pronoville, accompanied by his new partners Reuben and Pharaoh, commenced " business," and apparently with great success.   As trade increased, Pronoville grew lazy, and in course of time he drank heavier and oftener.   Sometimes he would remain for days carousing in his headquarters with boon companions, while Reuben and Pharaoh worked.   Jacob returned to Swansea, but Mary, after all, remained to look after her brothers.

Meanwhile, rumours floated among the islanders that somebody had seen a ghost flitting about the ruins of Marisco Castle, and strange rappings and noises were heard in different parts of the island.   As time passed the spirit rappings increased, and the ghost had taken a partner.

Pronoville did not believe a word of it.

There always were strange noises in Lundy, he said.   It was "the noisest hole in the world," and, " as for ghosts," he did not believe in such "old womanish inventions," they were not worth thinking about.

Pronoville continued to drink heavier, and the more he drank the worse his nerves grew.

" I'm getting shaky," he said to Reuben one September day, when, from the great sapphire rollers, the Atlantic sent the foam flying over the Templar Rock, and the storm-wind sent the salt-spray fleeting like mist over wide wastes of heather and countless hillocks of drift.

Confusion reigned supreme in Lundy.

The wind roared wildly in the Devil's Chimney; the tide seethed and whirled around the Cheeses; the long and heavy swells broke in furious cataracts on the Shutter Rock, and rolled huge boulders to and fro in the darkness of the caverns under the Devil's Limekiln.

Against the inky black sky innumerable white and grey winged sea-birds appeared in bold relief, as they soared aloft, and with wild notes and shrieks rejoiced in the storm, while the din of wave-warfare reverberated among the grim precipices that towered into the rain-drifts and clouds above.

In the lonely recesses of that wild and wave-washed island, fresh additions were already being made to the numerous relics of wrecks stored there, while the rain on land, and the storm at sea, boded further calamity.

Captain Pronoville and his French crews were holding revelry at the headquarters, while the tide rolled "mountains high" into Rattles Bay, and the relentless rain lashed the ruined towers of Marisco Castle. Although Pronoville found Reuben and Pharaoh and their money useful, he did not trust them so implicitly as his own dearly-loved Frenchmen, and, on the other hand, his Welsh allies shrank from the "foreign" orgies of the notorious pirate.

Reuben and Pharaoh returned to Gannet Coombe, there to wait until the storm passed. Mary Marriner catered for them in the generous and hospitable manner known to country folk in general, but to Welsh housewives in particular.

The storm lingered, and on the third day it increased almost to a hurricane.

One day during this period of storm, Pronoville experienced what he termed a "strange feeling," but, in truth, it was a fright.

Early in the afternoon, during a pause of the rain, the wily old sea rover crept up to his grey and weather-beaten outlook, Marisco Castle. There he remained until the gathering twilight warned him it was high time to return to Rattles Bay.

While looking out to the wild wave-distance, he

heard the sound of a wailing voice calling slowly in a long-drawn, husky tone—"Pro-no-ville."

Again it wailed, almost groaned, "Pro-no-ville!"

"It is my fancy," said Pronoville, "and perhaps the wind helps it."

He knew all his men, in fact all the inhabitants on the island called him captain. Not a person would venture to address him only by his surname.

But he disliked the wailing voice, and, putting his fingers in his ears, he swore loudly and strongly about the weather in general and the wind in particular.

Then he started to descend the stairs.

As he reached the top, which formed a sort of landing, he saw emerging from one of the rooms a gliding figure going ghostlike into an adjoining apartment.

Pronoville started back in terror. He had seen the ghost!

But he was not going to be "humbugged" he said, so, taking courage, he followed the figure, to find the room which he entered quite empty!

Then he descended the stairs, and before reaching the ancient portal, that voice, that blood-curdling wailing voice, called, "Pro-no-ville!" again, and yet again.

Like one soul-driven, Pronoville rushed away. His fingers were in his ears, and, as if to drown all recollection, he swore vehemently.

For some reason best known to himself, he turned to look back, and there, horror of horrors! standing in the ruined window of the room which Pronoville thought to be empty, was the ghost!

There it stood waving its long shadowy arms in the windy twilight, like a wraith of the mist, or a hag of the night.

Pronoville fled in terror, and his men down in Rattles Bay stared aghast to see their "intrepid" captain rushing amongst them as "if he had seen the ghost," they said.

Pale to the lips, scared and trembling from head to foot, the pirate entered the quarters, and none dared question him as to the cause of his commotion.

The storm continued with almost unabated fury, and Pronoville did not go to his outlook for nearly a week.

When next he visited the citadel, he saw the ghost, and heard the wailing voice as before. Worse still, the ghost glided after him, and he ran wherever he could, as if for dear life, down to Rattles Bay.

Three weeks passed, during which the wraith

continued to persecute the sea-rover, and, in due course, as the rumour had it, the ghost appeared with a partner.

Those—and they were few—who dared gaze at the ghosts, likened one of them to a tall, thin, and extremely shadowy person accompanied by a short, spare, and smaller figure.

Both were women, and both wore their long hair floating far down beyond their waists.

In due course the ghosts came to be called the "White Women," and they held their own, as though they had taken possession of the solitary and sea-girt Castle of Marisco.

Through the dreary and moonlight nights of grey and shivering October—through the dense fogs and rain-drifts of November—through the darkness and desolation of December, strange noises, mingled with unearthly wailings, were heard, and the ghosts maintained their sway.

In time the islanders came to be afraid to venture out once the brief daylight began to wane, while the "bold, fearless, intrepid, daring, —and honourable" Pronoville and his French crew fairly "shook in their shoes" with terror whenever they had to go to Marisco Castle, which was both store and ammunition room, as well as their "look out."

Only the sea birds—the gulls, the shoveler

ducks, the snow-buntings, and the "white-fronted geese"—were fearless. The peregrine falcon soared high and haughtily above the ghostly tracks, and the snow-white gannets remained loftily immovable and indifferent, as though leagued against wraiths and the spirit-world in general, and the "White Women" in particular.

Still the ghosts continued their mysterious walks abroad.

Even when the whirling snow flung its pure shroud over the lonely island, and the leaden sky looked down upon the steel-blue sea, those wraiths haunted the place.

Men grew fearful, women shuddered, and children crept into the corners when the first footfall of mysterious night—so like death—appeared.

Great grey waves thundered in Rattles Bay, and men shivered in the morning. Dense white mists crept through the desolate and lonely coombes, and the women sighed and looked scared in the twilight.

White foam-flakes were driven by the wind far inland, and the children cried in the starless and moonless nights.

Lundy was like No-Man's Land, where ghosts in passing greet one another on their way with the melancholy cry, "Whither—ay—whither?"

When the winds of March had passed, and April with her tears and smiles wandered along the earth, a surprise came to the island.

"I told you so," exclaimed Reuben.

"It's never her," said Pharaoh.

"What are you talking about?" asked Pronoville.

"Enough, I should think," said Pharaoh. "Don't you see in the offing the Mumbles man-o'-war?"

Pronoville swore.

"My father means friendly," said Reuben.

Pronoville, persecuted by the ghosts, was in "no mind" to be agreeable or to see strangers.

In came the Mumbles man-o'-war, with its "three leatherin' guns and a handspik'," and the master thereof landed.

He was warmly welcomed by his sons, who were overjoyed to see him.

Pronoville's men "took to him" at once.

Even Pronoville got to like him in a day or so.

Davy Prosser, one of the men of the Mumbles man-o'-war, was told of the ghost.

"I do know more about it than our cap'n," said he, in a confidential tone to Pronoville over their grog.

"Iss, indeed. Thirty years ago Admiral Nutt, the great buccaneer, was Lord of Lundy. 'Twas

Q

he did infest the Narrow Seas, and I was in one of the Government ' whelps' that was chasing him.   Old Nutt caught us, an' we, the crew of the *Little Sally,* was kept on Lundy for months."

" What then ?" asked Pronoville.

" We did see what the island people did call the ' White Women of Lundy.'   'Tis a bad sign when they do come, so we did hear then. When the ' White Women' do prowl about, it do mean coming dangers—loss, ruin, sickness, and sometimes—death ! "

The pirate shivered.

His luck seemed to have departed with the coming of the " White Women."

All his courage had long since forsaken him. He had grown strangely restless, moody, fearful, and tremulous, and worse so because of the deep draughts of ardent spirits quaffed to keep off their disembodied contemporaries.

The Mumbles man-o'-war came as a boon and a blessing to Pronoville.   He would be equal with those detested " White Women." They should not any longer be forewarners of danger, loss, ruin, sickness, and—he shuddered to think of it—perhaps death ! Life became insupportable, and the old pirate's nerves were hopelessly shattered.

In May he quitted Lundy for ever.

He sailed with his partners, Reuben, Pharaoh, their father, Davy Prosser, and Mary Marriner, in the Mumbles man-o'-war, bound for Swansea.

Before reaching Wales, Pronoville, seized by " a strange brain fever," died, raving in his death agony, " The White Women—the White Women —see, they're following us ! "

They buried him in the sapphire waves of Swansea Bay, and his body went to be the prey of those terrors of the sea to which he had committed so many unfortunate mortals.

Then, and not before, it was known in Lundy and elsewhere that the " White Women " were Reuben and Pharaoh Llewelyn, who for a heavy bribe, willingly offered by merchants and other sufferers by piracy, invented a ruse whereby to rid the island of the renowned and intrepid but wily Captain Pronoville.

His crew remained in Lundy, but their sway was of short duration, for on the 3rd of June 1667, the collector of Barnstaple wrote to the Board, " that some small Flushing privateers, which lie skulking under the island of Lundy, have taken six small barks coming from Ireland laden with bullocks, sheep, wool, and tallow ; " and a few days later, a report was sent to the Admiralty by John Man, " that French privateers, lying at Lundy Island . . . took a trow, kept the master, and sent the men ashore at

Barnstaple to procure money for the redemption of the vessel and lading, taking out of her a hundred sheep and other provisions for themselves." A later report states that "three privateers at Lundy put terror into all the vessels; much shooting had been heard for three or four days."

On the 21st of June very few of Pronoville's men remained, for the officer in charge of the district wrote to the Admiralty : " Lundy Island is very slenderly guarded, four or five men from a vessel riding on a cross wind crept over the gates, and went to the people's houses before they saw anybody. If the Dutch should take the island it would block up the Severn, and a dozen good men would secure it from the world."

The Mumbles man-o'-war's men lived to a good old age, and they never grew weary in telling the story of the "White Women of Lundy."

The Black Bride of Caerwen

THRICE had snow fallen and melted on Y Wydd-fa (Snowdon)—thrice had Summer the singer wandered through the woodlands of Carnarvon—thrice had autumn dyed the leaves in the dark ravines, and the fourth April, with tears and smiles, wended her pensive way among the primroses of Wales, yet Watkin Griffith of Caerwen had not returned.

In the hall of the ancient house, which once was a monastery, Rhys Griffith sat by the fireside, and waited and longed for Watkin, his rollicking and only son, to come home.

Day after day the old man gazed wistfully through the tall windows looking southward across the meadows and moorlands, or wandered restlessly through the house, as if strange voices called him from afar. Day after day his footsteps wearily echoed along the oaken floor, as he went to the spacious porch, there to look out with a long sad smile to the court-yard, along which his son with manful pride strode in the summers gone by.

There, on the pegs in the lofty hall, hung Watkin's powder-flask and gun, together with his hunting-crop and hat. There by the deep bay window, where he loved to sit in the summer evenings, was his son's favourite chair, now empty!

Looking out through that ancient window, towards the lofty summit of Snowdon, and the ravines and woodlands below, where the birds were building their nests, and nature rejoiced with the triumph of revival, a mist came before the old man's eyes, and he turned away with a sigh, and the murmur, " When will he come ?"

Every night as the clock struck seven, the Calvinistic minister of Salem—no matter what the weather might be—entered the great gateway, crossed the court-yard, and took his seat in the fireside of the settle. He is there to-night.

" And how are you ?" he asks in a cheery tone of voice, at which the old man's heart expands, as he answers, "The same as ever—waiting for our Watkin."

Then they gossip in the ruddy fire-glow, while the April twilight deepens without, and the early moonbeams stray in through the mullioned windows.

After a while Rhys Griffith returns to the one sad thought that haunts his mind.

"No news," he says wearily ; "no news."

The minister of Salem, striking the ashes out of his pipe, replies, "Just like youth ; and Watkin's young blood is fiery, like his father's before him."

At this the old man smiles, for he too had wandered "over the hills and far away" in his youth, and was ever restless and impatient at home.

Then taking a letter from his pocket, he reads word by word some of the letters received from Watkin, who had sailed the Western Seas in search of El Dorado.

Watkin and his party had sought it in the crowded towns and cities of the United States—in the hunting grounds of the Red Indians—in the treasure regions of Peru—in the plains of Mexico—in the cañons of California—but in vain—in vain !

And now, lured away to the East, they seek the charmed spot among the South African gold fields.

Full of adventures are the young man's epistles. Abroad, and free as the air he breathes, he writes of days of danger in the far West—of months among the Red Indians—of perils in Peru—of the heat of the Mexican plains—the grandeur of the cañons of California and Colorado, and lastly of strange experiences in Africa.

" Dear me, to be sure ! " exclaimed the minister of Salem.   " If we were young again, we'd like to be with him.   I daresay he's making money out there in South Africa, and some day he'll come home and settle down, and marry somebody."

That Somebody is spoken with a very large capital.

" Who's somebody ? " asks Rhys Griffith.

" Don't you know ? " asks the minister.

" There's no somebody for our Watkin, so long as he roams the world like this," says the old man.

" But he's left somebody behind him," says the minister.

" And who may that be ? " asks the old man sharply.

" Rachel Lloyd of the Shop," replies the minister.

" Rachel Lloyd of the Shop, indeed ! " says the old man, re-filling his pipe, " I daresay he's had more than one Rachel Lloyd by this time, and they're all forgotten now."

Months pass.   Every night at seven the minister comes to Caerwen—every night at nine he returns home.

A day comes, and with it a letter.

At seven o'clock the minister of Salem ascends the uplands to Caerwen.

September moonbeams play around the old house, and steal slowly into the woodlands, where the red and yellow leaves flutter down through the evening air, and the trees begin to lose their beauty.

The minister of Salem is greeted by the owner of Caerwen, with " I've had news."

The old man leans forward in his chair.

" Listen," he says, and the minister obeys.

" I skip some," says the old man, "and give you a wonderful piece of news."

He reads out. " You will be glad to know I've settled down at last——"

"Very good. Well done, Watkin !" interrupts the minister.

" Settled down at last," repeats Rhys Griffith, " and have got married to a beautiful African."

The minister of Salem grows pale in the face. He lifts his hands in horror.

"A beautiful African—African ? " queries the minister.

"There never was a good-looking, to say nothing of a beautiful African," says the old man. " As sure as I'm alive, I'm ashamed of our Watkin."

" To think of it !" says the minister in shrilly tones.

"Ay, indeed to goodness, to think I should live to see our Watkin marry a—black!"

"And does he say anything about coming home?" asks the minister.

"Iss indeed, worse luck, I could hide my head under a bushel for shame," says Rhys Griffith. "To think of our Watkin arming a black wife here by Snowdon!"

"What will the people say?" asks the minister.

"He'll be the talk of the county!" exclaims the old man.

"Of the principality," adds the minister. "Whoever heard of a Welshman, let alone a Griffith of Caerwen, marrying a black-a-moor!"

"She shan't live here," exclaims the old man, growing fiery, and bringing down his right fist with a ringing thud on the round table beside his chair.

"She shan't come to our chapel," says the minister, who is willing to go out to the heathen abroad, but unwilling to undertake the conversion of the heathen that is expected at Caerwen.

"He'll not have a penny of me," says the old man. "Every wife that has come to Caerwen for these three hundred years has been a credit to the house. There was our Watkin's mother—where could you see a nicer woman than she was—and my own old grandmother——

who looked better than her, I should like to know."

"One can't always go by looks," says the minister, thinking of his own better half, who was old, crabbed, and ugly!

"But to think that our Watkin should go and marry a—black!" continues the old man. "Bah! How could the boy go a-courtin' and—kiss her!" says the owner of Caerwen. "I was always against the Sassenach (Saxon), but I'd sooner see our Watkin marry an English woman than come back with a—black!"

"What has come over the boy?" queries the minister. "He was always taught in our school to look upon the blacks as heathens, an' if he did but remember the Scriptures that do say, 'How do the heathen rage,' he'd have been afraid of the black-a-moor's temper. Well, 'everybody's got their own liking,' as the old woman said when she kissed her black pig. But a black 'ooman—ugh!"

"Don't you mention a word to anybody," says the old man in a whisper, "and I won't; and we will wait and see what we can see, as the blind man says."

"*I* won't say a word," says the minister, as he bids his host "Ffarwel nawr" (good-bye now), and goes home.

That night the minister of Salem fails to

sleep. He tosses, and turns, and twists, much to the annoyance of his crabbed partner. In his dreams he sees "our Watkin" coming to the chapel door with his fat, black, African wife leaning upon his arm.

The minister of Salem believes the African woman to be fat and forty, and—black as ebony.

Then he—a Christian minister—refuses to allow the black woman to enter Salem. For which an angel rebukes him, and they wrestle. He awakes to hear his wife saying, "It's the first time you did ever rebuke *me*, Richard Williams, and I ken tell you, you shan't do it agen!"

"I did think I was wrestling with an angel," says the minister of Salem. "But, 'twas all—a dream!"

"Thank you kindly," says the irate Mrs. Williams. "You do strike *me*, and think you was hitting an angel, 'stead of which 'twas me, an' now you do say 'twas all—a dream! And pray, what may you have been wrestling with an angel for?"

The minister of Salem remains silent. To tell his wife would be to break his word with Rhys Griffith.

After breakfast the next morning the owner of Caerwen mounts his nag, and rides leisurely into the beautiful town of Carnarvon.

Through the soft haze of the lovely September morning Snowdon looks almost gloomily grand, purple mists girdling the peak, while below, far below, the quaint old town of Carnarvon is bathed in golden sunshine.

As Rhys Griffith rides along this morning, the "everlasting hills," that generally have a wonderful charm for him, are unrecognised. The glorious views, the silvery waters of the Seiont and the Menai Strait, are unnoticed— even the wayside children observe that the owner of Caerwen is unusually pre-occupied in thought as he rides by with only just a nod and not a word of greeting.

Into the town of Carnarvon he rides, with a friendly nod to one and another, then he alights at the door bearing the inscription "L. J. Pritchard, Lawyer." He ties the horse's reins to the garden railings, and slowly enters.

Llewellyn Pritchard warmly greets him.

The owner of Caerwen and the lawyer of Carnarvon were schoolboys and playmates in the long ago.

The lawyer sees that something troubles his old friend, but waits to hear the news. At last the truth is told.

"An African!" exclaims the lawyer. "An African! I can't believe it!"

"Read for yourself," says Rhys Griffith.

The lawyer does so.

"What a mistake," he says, shaking his hoary head.

"Something must be done," says the aged father in mournful tones.

"What can be done?" asks the lawyer, reading the letter again. "Watkin says he was married by the Wesleyan minister, and his marriage is legal, and cannot be dissolved. Perhaps she is a good woman after all. There are Christianised tribes in Africa, and — who knows—perhaps, she is a princess."

"Princess or no princess, she's an African, and I can't abide the blacks with their rolling eyes and big lips—Bah!" exclaims the owner of Caerwen.

"I am very much surprised — and deeply sorry," said the lawyer deliberately.

"And now I mean to cross our Watkin's name out of my will," says Rhys Griffith. "Caerwen is his by right of heirship, but the money I have made and saved I can do as I like with."

"Do nothing rash, Rhys," says the lawyer.

"No, no, Llewellyn. I've thought of it ever since the letter did come, and I've made up my mind to leave my money in another way. By this time next week have a draft ready, and I will come to hear you reading it."

Then Rhys Griffith gives the necessary directions.

The week passes, and once more the owner of Caerwen goes to Carnarvon, and arranges his will to his own liking.

Caerwen, and all the goods and chattels therein, are Watkin's by right, but the money made and saved is divided between Rhys Griffith's nearest relatives.

Months pass, and life goes on much the same among the mountains of North Wales.

March in lusty vigour sends its wild winds roaring around and under Snowdon, and they whistle loudly through the woodlands beside Caerwen.

The minister of Salem is seated opposite Rhys Griffith, who is saying, "Our Watkin is coming home. He will reach England in April, and will come here by the first of May. I shall never be able to lift my head once she's here."

"Better for him to have left her in Africa. He could have come over here for a few months, and gone back, and nobody would have been a bit the wiser," said the minister of Salem, "but now——"

"The truth must out, and we might as well let everybody know that she is a black," says Rhys Griffith.

"A black—princess shall we say?" asks the minister.

"No, no," says Rhys Griffith; "because perhaps she isn't and——oh! dear me, to think that our Watkin should marry a black!"

The owner of Caerwen wept.

"It'll bring my white hairs with sorrow to the grave!" he adds, drying his eyes.

And now the kindly and simple old men picture to themselves the African wife that "our Watkin" is bringing home.

Rhys Griffith in fancy sees a wild half-clothed savage with a snowy turban on her head, and a tiger skin for a robe, and rolling eyes, and big thick lips.

The minister sees a short and fat African, tricked up with European finery; a Paisley shawl resembling the one his wife wears on Sunday—a black silk dress that "will stand of itself," as the women say—a Tuscan bonnet with purple ribbons—massive rings in the ears, and a big jewelled one in her nose!

The news soon flies like wild-fire.

"Watkin Griffith is bringing home a black wife," rings along the country for miles.

Who ever heard of such a thing?

A Welshman married to a black!

"I'd have kept the black-a-moor in Africa," says one.

"Or have tried to whitewash her," remarks another.

"How can the Ethiopian change his skin?" murmurs the minister of Salem, with folded hands.

"I can scarcely bear it," says Rhys Griffith, restlessly pacing the great hall one day during the last week of April.

The blood in his veins now freezes, then burns. One moment an icy chill runs through his body, then fierce internal fires rage in his heart, and all the energy of his Celtic spirit revolts at the thought of "our Watkin's wretched marriage."

It is the last day of April.

Blossoms of pear and plum, of apple and cherry, fill the beautiful orchards, and on the garden walls of Caerwen the petals of the peach-bloom glow like fairy fires.

In all the hollows and sheltered places the primrose stars are shining, and the forget-me-nots look like the blue eyes of fairies by the riverside.

The crimson light in the western distance, burns like the camp-fire of the Sun, the wanderer—the nomad who will return to-morrow and fill the day with splendour.

"To-morrow!" exclaims the owner of Caerwen, with a shiver, as, after pacing the hall, he

R

resumes his seat, and waits the coming of his friend the minister.

"To-morrow!" sighs the minister of Salem, as he comes through the leafy cloisters of the woodlands.

"To-morrow! Iss indeed, to-morrow!" says the housekeeper of Caerwen, and the farm servants begin to grin, the girls giggle immoderately.

"A black-a-moor is coming to Caerwen," says one of the saucy lads.

"'Tis the end of the world is comin', I believe," says another.

The old men are smoking their long "churchwardens," and now and again they talk of "our Watkin."

"They must save for themselves," says Rhys Griffith. "I've altered the will. Our Watkin shall have his own, but the money made and saved by me shan't touch the fingers of the black!"

"All the neighbours are surprised," says the minister of Salem.

"You'll see she'll come to Salem," says Rhys Griffith. "I daresay she's converted. Our Watkin would never marry a heathen—I should think not."

"'Tis a godless age," says the minister. "Men and women would marry the Old Nick himself for money and worldly gain, I b'lieve."

" Ay, ay," is the response.

The cuckoo clock strikes nine, and the minister rises to go home.

" You'll be here to-morrow," nervously says Rhys Griffith. " I can't bear up alone."

" I'll be here," says his friend, sighing. " About what time ? "

" Read for yourself," says the owner of Caerwen, handing a letter to the minister.

The words run thus :—" We shall post from Carnarvon, and reach home about half-past seven o'clock in the evening."

" Just after my usual time for coming," says the minister, as with a heavy heart he says " Ffarwel nawr."

" Ffarwel for the last time," he says, jogging down hill. " I'll never go up there once the black woman comes. He " — meaning Rhys Griffith—" must come to see me."

It is May-day.

Away in the distance Snowdon looks bold and almost defiant, while sunshine and shadows meet and mingle in the magnificent lowlands of Carnarvonshire.

Early in the morning the inmates of Caerwen are astir. Preparations are being made for the reception of the bridegroom and bride.

Such a bride!

Heavy-voiced and sad, as one who has a leaden sorrow in his heart, the owner of Caerwen gives directions for the reception of the home-comers.

Now he paces the hall and the courtyard. How slowly he walks! The feet that would have fleeted swiftly to meet the coming of "our Watkin" move in a flagging way, and the eyes, instead of sparkling and beaming with joy at the return of the wayward wanderer, are dull, spiritless, and fixed on the road leading to Carnarvon.

It is six o'clock, and Rhys Griffith goes in to shiver and feel chill, or to burn with the burning of a fever. His pipe is laid aside, and, in his loneliness and sorrow, he strokes the old house-dog that is stretched across the hearth.

A few tears trickle from his eyes.

They are tears of joy and sorrow. Joy because "our Watkin" is coming home; sorrow because of the calamity in the person of a black bride.

In the remote district of Wales, the people have a deeply-rooted antipathy to marriages with the English, not to mention "foreigners." They like their sons and daughters to marry their own country folk, and it is considered lucky not to have to change the surname in marriage.

At seven o'clock the minister of Salem arrives.

For nearly half an hour the two old men sigh and groan, and conversation is conducted chiefly in monosyllables.

"It is a thousand pities that our Watkin ever went abroad," says Rhys Griffith.

"It is, indeed!" responds the minister. "But it can't be helped. 'What God has put together let no man put asunder.'"

He says this clasping his hands prayerfully.

"They come!" exclaims the housemaid, who has been doing duty as sentinel.

Rhys Griffith seizes his stick and stands firmly in the gathering shadows of the old hall.

The minister of Salem supports him.

"They're passing the church now," cries the housemaid.

"They'll soon be here," says the housekeeper from her position in the porch.

The clatter of horses' hoofs are heard in the great courtyard. There is the sound of many scampering feet, and the slamming of the carriage door, and "our Watkin" enters the porch.

"My father—where's my father?" he cries eagerly, as he greets the old housekeeper.

Rhys Griffith comes forward from the shadows and clasps his son in a close embrace. The minister of Salem does the same.

But the bride—what of the black bride?

The owner of Caerwen asks for her.

She comes, smiling and radiant, towards the old man. She comes—the African comes and places her small white hands in Rhys Griffith's broad palms, and then, child-like, she lifts her face up for a kiss as naturally as if the old man was in truth her own father.

"I can't understand," says Rhys Griffith, like one spell-bound, looking into the blue eyes of the lovely little lady before him.

"Neither do I," says the minister of Salem.

"What is it?" asks "our Watkin."

"I thought you married—you told me you had married an African," says Rhys.

"I thought the same," says the minister.

"So I have married an African," says Watkin. "Alice, my dearest, you are an African, are you not—a real born African?"

"Oh, yes," she answers. "I was born at the Cape. My father was born at the Cape too."

"And I made sure that our Watkin had married an African woman, an——" says Rhys.

"A black-a-moor," interrupts the minister unceremoniously.

"A black wife!" exclaims Watkin, bursting

into laughter. "Oh, Alice, Alice, the fun of it! They have been expecting to see a black!"

The bride and bridegroom laughed heartily.

And now, good but simple old men, in shame they look at each other, and when the first astonishment is over, they too laugh lustily.

All their fears are at an end. All the sorrow is supplanted by joy. For, instead of a black bride, a merry golden-haired and lovely new mistress has come to Caerwen.

It is the third day of May.

Like a sunbeam, Alice the bride flits about the house, to the delight of everybody.

Rhys Griffith rides in to Carnarvon to alter the will, "without knowing to anybody but the lawyer," as he says, and the new will is made wholly in favour of the heir of Caerwen.

"Our Watkin" has made what is called a good match. His wife is the daughter of an English merchant, whose father was the officer of an English regiment stationed at the Cape.

Years pass—Rhys Griffith is gathered to his forefathers. Watkin and Alice are surrounded by a troup of merry children, whose laughter makes the old hall ring when their father tells them the story of the black bride of Caerwen.

· · · · · · ·

Not even the ruins of Caerwen now remain, and the last of the race of Griffith died a bachelor, and was buried in Carnarvon church-yard.

Bound for Llandovery

ONE cold and rainy evening, in the autumn of 1546, three travellers bound for Llandovery lost their way, and when night-fall came they approached a lonely farm.

It was in a very desolate neighbourhood, and appeared to be the only house for many miles around.

"What are we to do?" asked one of the travellers, whose name was Roger.

"Beg shelter at this farm for the night," said Timothy.

"Or walk on, and try to find our way to Llandovery," said John.

"We can't do that," said Roger. "See, the night comes on apace, and it promises to be very dark. There will be no moon either."

"Let us knock at yonder door," said Timothy, who promptly suited the action to the word.

"We be three benighted travellers," said

Timothy to the good woman who answered the knock, "and we would fain have shelter and rest for the night."

"Can't have it here," said the dame snappishly.

"But we be three honest men, and not rogues," said Roger.

"And bound for Llandovery," added John.

"Then you'd best go to Llandovery," said the irate dame, slamming the door in the strangers' faces.

"What shall we do?" asked Roger.

"We can't go on, and 'tis too dark to turn back," remarked John.

"I see a way out of the difficulty," said Timothy. "Yonder is a cart-shed. Let us take shelter there."

They did so, and found sufficient straw to form a rough bed. But the men were both too tired and too hungry to sleep, so they lay awake.

In about an hour's time a lantern-light flitted across the yard, and presently the men heard three raps at the house door. From their position and proximity to the house, the men observed that the door was thrown wide open, and who should enter but the village priest.

"Welcome, Sir priest," said the dame blandly, and in silky tones.

"Welcome, my daughter," was the response.

Now it chanced that the kitchen window was only partially curtained, and Timothy, ever full of mischief, crept upon his tiptoes and peeped in.

What a feast was there!

The table fairly groaned with tempting viands. There were roast goose, partridges, a capon, rich puddings, and dainties of all sorts. To crown all, and in the midst of these good things, there stood a huge flagon filled to the brim with *cwrw da.*

It was very exasperating to see a feast within, while those poor travellers suffered from hunger and cold without.

Timothy felt quite angry; in fact, he had "half a mind" to rush in and make a raid upon the good things.

By-and-bye he observed that the dame of the house and the priest repaired to another apartment. Timothy told his companions that they had gone into the "dining-room," because he noticed the maid "carried the food after them."

"It is enough to make a man mad," said Roger, who was a noted eater.

"To think that *they* may 'eat, drink, and be merry,'" said John, "while we are left to die —so far as she cares—is, to say the least, vexatious."

In about fifteen minutes after the feast went into the apartment known as "the hall," rather than the dining-room, the good man of the house returned.

Before he could reach the door, Timothy stepped forward, followed by his companions.

"Good sir," said Timothy, "we be three travellers, and have lost our way to Llandovery, kindly give us shelter for the night."

"Whom do ye go to see at Llandovery?" asked the farmer.

Timothy gave the name of their friend.

"I know him well," said the farmer. "Come in, come in, all three of you. I would not have my friend and thine think I am 'short' to any benighted traveller."

The three men were most thankful, only Timothy winked when he saw that all traces of supper had been cleared from the kitchen. Still more surprised was he, on entering the dining-room or hall, to see the table cleared, and to find that the priest had made his exit.

All had been secreted when the farmer's footsteps were heard.

"Come around the fire," said the farmer kindly. "Thee'rt all cold, and 1 should say well-nigh famished."

The men confessed they were.

"Now, Betsy," said the farmer to his wife,

"let's have the best of what there is in the house."

"I've only got bread and cheese," said Betsy snappishly.

"Well, let's have that, and some *cwrw da*," said the farmer.

The three men were only too glad to have anything, and as their host was very generous with the ale, they consumed a considerable quantity.

After supper the farmer begged the men to draw around the fire.

The farmer then said he had seen some amusing tricks played in the neighbouring village, and that was the reason he came home so late.

"I know a trick or two also," said Timothy.

The farmer was "all alert."

"Let's have them," said he.

Timothy, in great solemnity, muttered "*Abracadabra*" thrice, and then said, "Shall I tell thee what is in this house that thou know'st not of?"

"Ay, ay," said the farmer.

"Well," said Timothy, "there's a fine fat goose in yonder cupboard."

He pointed to the cupboard on the right-hand side of the fireplace.

"And what else?" asked the farmer.

"Partridges," replied Timothy.

" What beside ? " asked the host.

" A fine fat capon."

" Anything else ? " asked the farmer.

" Yes : rich puddings and dainties of all sorts."

Betsy could not stand this, so she made her exit.

" Now, thee must prove thy words," said the farmer.

" Roger," said Timothy in a tone of authority, " get the goose out of yonder cupboard."

Roger did as he was bidden, and the other dainties were produced in quick succession, after which the company sat down and supped to their hearts' content.

While the host and his guests proceeded with their supper, the goodwife of the house fretted and fumed in the kitchen.

" What shall I do ? " she whispered to Jane the maid.

" About what ? "

" The priest, girl—the priest ! "

" Bother the priest ! " exclaimed the maid impatiently. " Why do you have him here at all ? You know the master objects."

" Because he is a Protestant—that's all, and I've been brought up in the faith of my fathers ! "

" Well," said Jane, " and where *is* the priest ? "

" In the cupboard on the left-hand side of the

chimneypiece, to be sure—where else could I thrust him at a moment's notice like that?" said the mistress.

"Among all them feathers?" exclaimed the maid. "Why the poor man will be stifled, as sure as I'm a livin' woman."

Jane worked upon the feelings of her mistress to such an extent, that the good wife of the house was in a fever of excitement.

"What if he should be stifled?" she murmured, and presently began to cry.

Meanwhile, the men in the hall were enjoying themselves finely.

Presently Timothy's mischief could no longer be restrained. He began to wonder where the priest could have been, as he thought, "stowed away." Soon afterwards he fancied he heard a movement in the cupboard beside which he sat.

"Mine host," said Timothy, "before retiring for the night, I would fain put a poker in the fire, and therewith warm a portion of my beer."

"Thee can'st put the poker and the shovel in the fire, if it doth please thee," said the farmer, who was astonished, almost dazed, at Timothy's "tricks."

When the poker was perfectly red-hot, Timothy quietly took it out, and slightly opening the left-hand cupboard, placed it therein. Immediately the company saw a great blaze, a cloud of feathers,

and out of the midst of all, the priest rushed like
a madman, yelling with might and main.

The farmer hastened after the retreating figure,
but the terror-stricken priest, half-suffocated, and
quaking with fear, ran out of the house as fast
as his legs could carry him.

Next day the three men proceeded on their
journey to Llandovery, and when they parted,
the farmer warmly thanked Timothy for his
" tricks."

Never again was the Church worthy seen in
the farm, and whenever the subject was mentioned, at home or abroad, Betsy always persisted
that the strange and " wicked " travellers had
conjured up " the fiend," although her husband
believed it to be the village priest.

'Twas in Beaumaris Bay

1758

THE King's Head was a wayside hostelry
when George the Second was king.
William, commonly called Billy Prosser,
was master and owner thereof, and also of three
schooners and a barque that plied up and down
channel with passengers and merchandise. The
hostelry was known as the King's Head. It
was a queer quaint place, well known to His
Majesty's naval officers, for though Billy frequently secretly dealt in contraband goods, he
had been a Jack Tar who had served his
monarch in many a battle. He had lost a
leg in the King's service, and was disabled for
future action. So he settled down at the
King's Head, and started a line of trading
ships, which proved of great service to Wales.

It was a week before Easter, the officers of

the *Stag* sat smoking and drinking grog—Billy knew so well how to mix grog!

Arnold St. John was not a heavy drinker, and while sipping his grog he looked out. Into the bay came a sloop. Presently all eyes were fixed on her. Telescopes were quickly uplifted. In came the sloop rapidly, and was soon riding at anchor in the bay. Later on the captain of the sloop came to the King's Head, and asked Prosser if he could accommodate two ladies and an old gentleman until the storm ceased. The captain was a Liverpool trader.

"They begged a passage up, an' I couldn't refuse."

"Certainly not," remarked Billy, drawing the captain aside. "Have they got money?"

"Plenty, my boy. He's a doctor—of laws, mind you—from somewhere in the Gower land."

"All right, run 'em in, my boy."

The officers of the *Stag* were on the alert for the visitors, who soon entered the best parlour of the King's Head. Billy, after the fashion of those days, explained who the visitors were, and then quitted the room.

"Most pleased to have the honour of meeting His Majesty's representatives," said courtly Dr. Gibbon of Rhossilly, "in the dim land of Gower." He was a descendant of the old Norman Gibbons, who had married and intermarried with the Welsh until they boasted of a long line of Celtic ancestry. "Gentlemen," added Dr. Gibbon, "allow me to introduce you to my wife and daughter."

Very soon the officers were doing their utmost to entertain the visitors.

The gloomy afternoon waned. "Whew!" whistled the wind around Beaumaris. "Hiss-hiss!" went the waters among the rocks of that wild Welsh coast. Darker grew the clouds and whiter gleamed the waves that rolled mountains high.

"It is a wild night," remarked Dr. Gibbon, when candles were brought in.

"Likely to continue wild, I fear," said Captain Vasey of the *Stag.* "I trust the weather will not inconvenience you, sir."

"Not in the least. We intended spending Easter in Liverpool on our way to Scotland, but having found better company, I shall gladly remain here." So the party settled down, determined that whether the storm passed or not, Easter would be spent at Prosser's.

"Do you play?" Arnold St. John was asking Miss Gibbon; "will you have a game of chess with me?"

"With pleasure," said Miss Gibbon.

By this time Dr. Gibbon was deep in politics

with the commander of the *Stag*, leaving one of the officers to entertain his wife, and Lieutenant St. John to amuse Miss Gibbon.

"In Beaumaris Bay," said St. John in a low tone to his companion. Miss Gibbon's eyelids drooped, and she blushed. "Isn't it strange?" continued St. John.

"It is," demurely remarked Miss Gibbon.

"Do you remember our last meeting here?"

"Do I! can you ask?" replied Miss Gibbon somewhat reproachfully. "But don't let my father know that we ever met before."

"Oh no," said St. John. "But he knows you were here last summer?"

"No; it was quite by accident that my cousin's ship put in to Beaumaris, and were it not for a threatening storm, I——"

"You would not have been in Beaumaris Bay, neither would I have known that you existed."

"Prosser does not recognise me," remarked Miss Gibbon.

"That's a comfort," said St. John. "Do you know I have often thought of coming down to Rhossilly, especially when we have passed your shores. You know why I wished to come; why——"

"Hush!" murmured his companion, "you will rouse suspicion."

"But I told you that when promotion came

all should be right for us. Now—well I mean to tell him. At least I'll do so before we part."

"St. John!"

"Ursula!"

"Your playing is excellent," said St. John with a smile, as Dr. Gibbon approached them.

"And yours is very clever," responded Ursula.

Did they mean the game of chess, or the game of playing at being strangers? Their smiles were too pleasant to be caused by a mere game of chess. Next day when they were sitting at dinner (people dined at two o'clock in those days), St. John proposed taking Miss Gibbon down to the shore for a walk. The wind had not ceased, but there was a lull in the rain storm. Though the waves were in riotous confusion, a walk along the shore would be invigorating, if not wholly pleasant. Dr. Gibbon readily granted the request, but Mrs. Gibbon demurred.

"It may be agreeable to a gentleman," she said, "hardly so for a lady. But of course you can please yourself, Ursula."

St. John noticed that a fiery light leaped in Ursula's dark eyes, and her lips quivered, but she remained silent. When dinner was over she quietly turned to St. John, and said, "I will join you in a few minutes.

The lieutenant was amazed at her self-possession, for he saw plainly that Mrs. Gibbon's words conveyed a desire to thwart Ursula's intentions. St. John's heart beat with rapture when Ursula joined him, and they both walked rapidly to the shore.

"What a relief, what a pleasure!" exclaimed Ursula, as the wind blew keenly against her face. Her eyes sparkled with delight.

"Mrs. Gibbon hates me to have one moment's joy," she added.

"Why do you always speak of her as Mrs. Gibbon?" asked St. John.

"Because she's not my mother. She's only father's wife, and—and——"

Ursula dropped her voice to a whisper, which the winds would have conveyed away had not St. John bowed his head so low, that his lips almost touched the girl's beautiful brow.

"I verily hate her," said Ursula.

So warmly did she express her dislike, that St. John, smiling, said, "If you can hate so well, tell me how strongly do you love?"

By this time they had turned the cliff point, and were quite out of sight of the King's Head.

In a moment Ursula was clasped in St. John's arms. " Darling, darling," he said, "tell me you love me. Tell me that after months of absence you haven't forgotten?"

" St. John, dear St. John," said Ursula, "I love you. You know I do. I never, never could forget *you*."

" Heaven be thanked, my darling," he said, kissing her again and again.

Presently they began to be aware that twilight was creeping apace, and a dense white fog came quietly rolling up the bay.

"Never mind, dear," said St. John. " I am with you. Besides which I must tell you something."

He took Ursula's arm under his, and commenced retracing their way to Prosser's.

"Ursula, dear," said St. John, "I am very poor, and couldn't marry for quite a year hence. Can you wait—will it weary you?"

" No," replied Ursula bravely.

" Promotion will come in a year's time, and then—then I can claim you," said St. John. "Meanwhile, may I tell your father?"

" Oh yes," replied Ursula. " But don't let father know we have ever met before."

So it was arranged, and during the next day Dr. Gibbon was consulted.

"I strongly object to my daughter marrying

anybody but a Welshman," said Dr. Gibbon. "We were originally Normans, but from the Conquest downward the Gibbons have not broken the record. And I much dislike—nay, I oppose my daughter—she shall not go out of the beaten track."

"I am of Welsh lineage too," said Arnold St. John.

"How so?" queried Dr. Gibbon sharply.

"I am one of the St. John's of Bletsoe—surely, sir, that is enough. Nearly all my ancestors were Welsh to the backbone."

This put the young man's proposal in a different light.

Dr. Gibbon then inquired into the young man's prospects, and after duly considering them, he said, "Come to me at the end of one year from this date, and if you are then both of the same mind, I will see what can be done. But do not live upon the least shadow of a hope. Until then, Ursula must be free."

Ursula and St. John were somewhat disappointed, but, after all, they came to the conclusion that Dr. Gibbon did so for the best.

"There is no need for a formal engagement," said Ursula on Easter Sunday, as St. John walked with her from morning service in the parish church.

"I knew that," said St. John, "but——"

"Surely you can trust me?" said Ursula, warmly.

"My darling, I never could doubt you."

Later on, towards twilight on Easter Sunday, they went down to the shore, and talked of the future.

"It won't seem long to me," said Ursula. "Even though we shall not meet, I shall always be thinking of you."

"Nothing shall ever come between us," said St. John, "I—I swear it!"

"And I will be true to my troth, yes, for ever!" said Ursula.

"For ever!" responded St. John.

"For ever!" shrieked the wind.

"Ever!" muttered the echoes among the distant caves fringing the lonely shore. The tide breaking beyond the bay sighed sadly, and the wave-wafted response of the Menai Strait came brokenly from the dim sea-distance.

1760

June revelled among the roses in the lovely land of Gower. Midsummer mists hung around the sheep-walks, and broad belts of sunshine fell across the Oxwich Salt Marshes.

On Worm's Head the sun's burning rays

withered up the grass and embrowned the pastures. Rhossilly's barometer, commonly called the Devil's Blow - Hole, was silent. June hushed the premonitor of storms, and not even an ominous sound broke the silence. Far away Carreg Cennin reared its head in the golden sunshine, and Rhossilly lay bathed in a flood of glorious light.

It was the last day for the Gibbons to remain at The Grange. The old home was in the hands of the money-lenders. Dr. Gibbon sat down and wept. His tears rolled to the · ground. The house held for centuries was no longer his own. If Ursula married the Welshman, who had gotten his gold in far-off climes, all would be right. But the lieutenant, the adventurer, as Dr. Gibbon called him, who had promised to claim Ursula, was an obstacle to all desires.

" He'll never turn up," said the doctor. " It's more than two years since we saw him. If he thought anything more about you he'd have been here before this."

" I still have hopes," said Ursula.

" You are a perfect fool !" exclaimed Mrs. Gibbon savagely. " Who but *you* would see your aged father turned out of his home when it is possible to save him ? "

" Marry Lloyd Pryce !" exclaimed the doctor

vehemently, adding somewhat proudly, "Any girl would willingly consent to become Lady Pryce. Marry Sir Lloyd—marry him and save me."

Dr. Gibbon fairly sobbed.

"I cannot," sighed Ursula.

"It will be the death of me to go hence—nay, it *shall* be. Do as you please, girl—marry Lloyd Pryce, or see a Gibbon buried on the cross roads, with a stake run through his corpse! My life is naught to me!"

Her father's agony was more than Ursula could endure. Where was St. John?—why, oh why did he tarry? Yet, if he came, could *he* save her father? In the hour of sorrow her heart failed her. Perhaps St. John had forgotten her; and if so—well, it mattered little who became her husband. She went out moaning into the sunshine. "St. John—St. John! why don't you come?" Slowly, as one in a dream, Ursula mechanically wandered along the sheep-walks towards Worms' Head. "Oh, my love, my love!" she cried, "why don't you come?—why have you broken your troth? —what shall I do without you? God give me strength to drain this cup of gall!"

"Miss Gibbon!" exclaimed somebody behind her.

"Sir Lloyd!" she responded.

Sir Lloyd Pryce was by no means an unpleasant man. His manners were those of a gentleman, and there was a sadness in his tone that won Ursula's pity.

"I am sorry to see you thus," he said. "You know what I told you a few days ago, dear? I am quite prepared to keep my part of the compact. Promise to be my wife, and I will rescue the old home from the money-lenders. And I love you, child—oh, so dearly! Heaven knows I speak truly, Ursula."

They were walking slowly along the sheep-walks where the June sunbeams glared mercilessly down upon the parched grass and sun-scorched ferns.

"One day more at Rhossilly," Ursula mentally uttered aloud. "My poor father—it will break his heart!" But mentally she pursued, "Oh! St. John—St. John! why do you tarry?"

Then she sank down upon one of the ridges and wept—wept bitterly.

Lloyd Pryce was deeply distressed.

He was by nature most gentle and refined, and a woman's grief always sorely touched him.

"Ursula," he urged, "child, I can't endure you to suffer. Will you not trust yourself to my keeping?"

"My life, perhaps," she said, "but not my love—never expect that."

"I do not ask it, but will try to win it—

try to merit it. Will you be my wife, Ursula? Tell me, dearest!"

Then, choking one deep agonising sob, she said, "To save my father, I will."

Lloyd Pryce gently drew her towards him, and fain would have pressed his lips to hers, but she quietly thrust his arms from around her and said, "Don't—you mustn't."

"As you wish, dear," said Pryce. "But I love you more than life, and I will do my utmost to make you happy."

Sir Lloyd Pryce knew nothing of Lieutenant St. John. Dr. Gibbon had kept that episode a profound secret.

So they walked homeward, Ursula wishing that the sun's fierce glances would wither her life, as it crushed out the existence of the ferns and grasses around her.

At The Grange gateway they met the doctor striding rapidly towards the village.

"Father!" she cried, seizing his arm.

There was a fierce unnatural light gleaming in his dark eyes as he angrily thrust her away from him.

"Get away. You are no longer my child!" he exclaimed. "A truly dutiful and unselfish daughter you are!"

"Father!" she gasped, "Sir Lloyd will tell you all. Spare me—spare me."

With that she darted indoors.

Sir Lloyd Pryce quickly informed Dr. Gibbon of the change in Ursula's plans, and before the day died, all arrangements were made for paying off all the debts and retaining the old home.

"I never can be sufficiently grateful to you," said Dr. Gibbon.

"It is for her sake," said Sir Lloyd, "I love her as I love my life."

He spoke the truth. From the first moment he met Ursula he was determined to try and win her. His countrywoman's youth and beauty had first attracted him, but her true worth he preferred above all.

Sir Lloyd Pryce was a merchant prince and slave-owner. Jamaica was his birth-place and home, but having, as his uncle's successor, become possessed of an additional fortune and the family title, he was obliged to return and settle, for a part of each year at least, upon the ancestral estates which were in North Wales.

In a few weeks' time Ursula became Lady Pryce, and the moment after writing her maiden signature for the last time she heard the bells ringing.

Ursula entered the carriage, put her fingers in her ears, and crouched back.

How those bells mocked her!

Every tone struck out the death knell of her heart.

"Untrue to your troth!" they seemed to shriek.

"False, fickle, fair, false!" they seemed to groan.

"Oh those bells—those cruel bells!" sobbed Ursula.

"For ever—for ever!" moaned the bells.

Clatter, clatter went the hoofs of the horses along the sun-parched highway, every hoof-beat causing Ursula's head to ache as though it were pierced with the sharp spikes of a thorny crown.

Crowds of villagers and visitors, even strangers who chanced to have business in the neighbour-hood, thronged the roadway leading to The Grange. Ursula shuddered as the carriage slackened its speed.

"Let the people see you," said Sir Lloyd. "They are longing to get a smile."

Ursula looked out. What did she see?

A vast crowd surging around the carriage. Yes, and a stalwart horseman standing beside his horse, which was reined up by the village inn.

Who could it be?

She had seen the face before. If only he would remove his slouched hat!

Taking a red rose from his coat, the horseman strode to the carriage, and tossed the flower lightly into Ursula's lap. This action remained unobserved by Sir Lloyd, who was giving directions to the postillions.

Ursula shuddered. She dared not look up. The horseman came to the carriage window, doffed his hat, and respectfully offered his congratulations to the bride.

"Too late," he whispered in a hoarse tone, reproachfully adding, "you might have waited!"

"Find out all," gasped Ursula. "Don't judge me harshly."

The horseman vanished. Later on he "found out all," and immediately quitted the village.

"St. John—St. John," sighed Ursula. "Oh, my love! my love! You were true to me, after all!"

1765

Sir Lloyd and Lady Pryce were staying at The Grange. Frequently since their marriage Sir Lloyd had gone away and left his wife to herself for many weeks. On one occasion he remained three months away, and once he went to Jamaica, staying there for more than three months. Ursula had no objection to his absences, but during the last two years of her life she

had tried to solve the reason of his flights.
Still she failed, utterly failed in her object,
and still her husband remained kind, loving,
and gentle to her. · Sir Lloyd was very quiet
and grave, the most suitable companion that
could be found for Dr. Gibbon. His utterance
was generally subdued, and his conversation
full of thought, yet his friends and his wife
owned to something about him which they
could not quite like—a something which in
an inexplicable way repelled them. He was
passionately fond of music. Ursula had a rich
thrilling voice, and often in the twilight Sir
Lloyd would have his wife sing to him, her
voice seeming to rise and fall like wind sighing
among snow-encumbered trees. It possessed a
poignant sweetness, and she sang the songs
in which his heart delighted with exquisite
expression. Those were happy hours to Sir
Lloyd—they were too precious, he said, because
they made the hours when he was away from
her too great a contrast.

"Oh, Ursula, come here," he said one December afternoon.

She had been singing to him in the twilight.
It was intensely cold, and the firelight shed a
witching glamour around Ursula Pryce's face
and figure. Slowly, but steadily, the snow-
flakes were falling on the frozen earth, and

T

ominous clouds fleeted across the waning crimson sunset.

"Ursula, dearest," said Sir Lloyd, looking lovingly at his young wife, who was gazing at the sea that always cruelly seemed to mock her broken troth.

"Yes," she replied calmly, not coldly.

"Ursula dearest," he continued, going to her, and clasping her in his arms.

"What is it?" she asked.

"I shall be obliged to go away to-morrow dear, and——"

"To-morrow?" she said.

There was a slight sound of fretful disappointment in her tone. Could it be possible, thought Sir Lloyd, that her feelings were changing, that his wife began to cherish, or ever so faintly to welcome, his love?

"At last! at last!" he uttered passionately, as he kissed her uplifted face.

Ursula was amazed.

"Darling—darling," said her husband. "It seems so strange to hear you express regret at my leaving. I have hungered for your love so long—so long. It seems so hard to have to go to-morrow—now that I have attained you. Ursula, I have won heaven, and you are its only angel for me. My precious wife, how I love you."

Ursula was surprised at her husband's outburst of feeling. Her manner mellowed to him, for though she had no love for him, his love of her was surely worthy respect. She knew he loved her deeply. Laying her hand gently on his arm she said, "Can't you defer going now?"

"Darling—darling, I wish to heaven I could, but I cannot. Business has to be accomplished. Ah, God! why can't it be deferred!"

Sir Lloyd clasped his wife closely in his arms and kissed her again and again. Then calmly he said, "My own precious wife, there are important matters to settle. I will return as soon as possible, but probably not before March."

"Going so suddenly," mused Ursula. Then she remembered that her husband always went away at a moment's notice.

"Never mind, dear. If I can possibly return before March I will," said Sir Lloyd.

In half-an-hour he was ready for the journey.

He would go to Swansea and there embark on board his own ship, the *Dominica*, for London.

"As we sail down channel," said Sir Lloyd, "I will keep a good look-out for you. If the weather permits, go to the top of Worms' Head and wave a white kerchief—will you, Ursula?"

"I will," she said.

"And I will wave mine in return," said Sir Lloyd. "Now, sweetheart, adieu, adieu!"

In deeply passionate tones he once more told her of his love, clasped her in a close embrace, and kissed her red lips again and again. He looked at her with hungry love, kissed her hand lightly, and departed.

As he walked out through the doorway he muttered, "Ah God! why can't it be deferred?—cursed fate that wrests me from her now, now of all times!"

Ursula and the servants distinctly heard his remark.

"He loves me deeply," said Ursula. "I must be a good wife to him, for the sake of his great love."

On the afternoon of her husband's departure it ceased snowing. Two days' subsequent frost had hardened the snow's surface, so that it was possible to walk with comfort.

Ursula started for a walk.

"Where are you going?" asked the doctor.

"To Worms' Head," she replied. "Lloyd and I are going to signal to each other."

"Oh, oh, I merely asked," said the doctor, delighted to find that, after all, the marriage had brought love.

Had it? Ursula could best answer that question.

Lady Pryce hurriedly wended her way along the sheep-walks, and soon gained a secluded and sheltered spot on Worms' Head. For six weeks, and ever since her arrival from North Wales, she had sought that nook almost daily at all hours. Sometimes it was night when she came, and only the glittering stars knew of her coming.

"Why did she come? Why—why?" asked the waves as they laughed down on the shore.

"Why—why?" screamed the sea-gulls as they sought their nests in the clefts of the terrible cliffs.

Dark clouds fleeted across the sky and promised more snow. The wind whistled and howled ominously through the caves along the shore, and Rhossilly's barometer roared.

Ursula drew her red-hooded cloak closely around her skirts and shivered. She stamped her feet to keep them warm.

Presently she was joined by a stalwart man— the horseman of her wedding day, the admiral of all her dreams.

"So he's gone again," said he. "Ursula, are you prepared for strange news?"

"Have you found out?"

"Yes."

"And who is it—what's the—the other wife's —the Jamaica wife's name?"

For Ursula had come to the belief that her husband had another wife out in Jamaica.

"Ah," said St. John, "you—both of us have judged him harshly. There isn't another wife at the bottom of it, after all. I discovered it most oddly. Think of it—I have been more than a year trying to ferret out his secret, and now only obtained it by sheer accident. Have you ever asked why he goes away from you?"

"No."

"Do you mean to tell me that he has never hinted why?"

"Certainly not."

"Well, Sir Lloyd Pryce is liable to temporary but terrible fits of insanity. When they approach he places himself under restraint. They occur about twice a year. He is quite sensitive of their approach, and prefers giving himself up to his doctors than alarm his friends. During his father's lifetime in Jamaica a private keeper used to attend him. Since his father's and uncle's death, Sir Lloyd has adopted a new plan."

"My husband a madman?" said Ursula, in an incredulous tone.

"Yes. Would you know where he is now?"

"Until I do—until I see him mad, I will not believe," said Ursula.

"You must leave all arrangements in my hands, or your father will be suspicious," said St. John. "A letter shall come asking you to join your husband in London. I will meet you at Swansea and accompany you to town. I shall still keep up my disguise. When can you go? Next week?"

"Not *next* week. That's too quick. What of the second week hence?"

"Very good," said St. John.

"There!" exclaimed Ursula—"There—there's the *Dominica*, I'm sure. See, he's waving his kerchief, St. John; please wave mine in return. I have no strength to do it."

St. John did as he was bidden.

"All the same," he said, "I don't believe it's the *Dominica*."

"Nonsense, it is," said Ursula. "Now go—St. John, go—or I shall get mad too."

"Meet me here to-morrow," he said.

"I will."

Ursula's heart throbbed wildly as she returned to The Grange. If her husband were really mad could she live with him any longer? Never! And yet—there, she must not indulge in a wild reverie. She was as firmly manacled by the bonds of wedlock as any living woman. Death alone could set her free. One afternoon, later on, Ursula went again to Worms' Head, there once more to meet St. John. This time she allowed him to clasp her in his arms, to kiss her once for the old love's sake. Just one dear delirious afternoon, after long years of pain, of heartache, of sorrow. St. John might have tempted her to forsake her husband, but he did not. He was too chivalrous for that. Yet, when she sought his help to find out the cause of her husband's absences, he willingly assisted. His love for her had never waned; hers for him had increased through the years. Yet never was there a more noble, honourable affection than that which existed between Ursula and St. John.

"Many men would ask you to forsake Sir Lloyd," said St. John, "but I could not. Such a sin would be monstrous. Darling—my lost love—you are Sir Lloyd's wife. Nothing but death must divide you both."

Then they parted.

"Good-bye, my love," said St. John, as he watched Ursula going down the ridges. "May Heaven protect her through the dreary and— perhaps dangerous future. It is well she should know, lest, in a sudden seizure, he might be tempted to harm her. Dr. Griffith was right. She ought to know the truth for her own safety's sake."

Ursula, after descending from Worms' Head

by the sheep-walks of old, paused where the road led to the village. "It's only four o'clock now," she said, looking at her watch. "A walk will do me good. I shall only be an hour later."

The rising breeze was life-giving, and it brought fresh vigour to the woman who breasted it.

Ursula walked on.

Not that she had pleasure in doing so, but because she was urged by a terrible unrest that would no longer let her remain in one place for any length of time.

Her husband a "madman!"

It seemed too terrible, but was there any truth in it? Perhaps it was only a *ruse* on St. John's part to get her away from her husband. Yet, so far, she never had reason to doubt St. John. At all events, she must be on her guard.

Suddenly a wild piercing cry, like that of an animal run to earth, only much more terrible, sent a horror through her blood and made her recoil. As she did so something darted at her, and a man's fingers gripped her throat.

"Let me go," she gasped, seizing the man's hands with a grip of iron.

"Never again!" yelled the man, whose arms she had seized.

What horror was before her!

Distorted as the face looked, she knew it to be her husband's.

She knew it was him, even though the new moonlight was pale, and the passion-filled face was only partially distinct in the weird twilight.

His face appeared terribly changed. The eyes seemed to protrude unnaturally from their sockets, and had in them a frenzy and terror pitiful to behold.

Ursula felt she must assert her self-control. Madmen's frenzies had been assuaged by strategy.

"Lloyd," she cried, "speak to me. Tell me why I see you thus?"

Sir Lloyd released his hold upon her throat.

"I am your wife," she said gently, soothingly.

For answer, he seized her in his arms, kissed her passionately, and fled.

She followed him swiftly, tearing her garments among the brambles as she crossed the lonely heath.

Through the weird light she ran breathlessly, though her husband was soon far ahead of her. A few seconds later and she lost sight of him. He had escaped her. Where was he hiding now?

Then she became afraid, and dreaded the snow-filled hollows on that lonely heath, lest her husband might once more wait for her among the brambles, only to spring upon her again,

and perhaps murder her! She paused to take
breath, and to consider what had better be done
under the circumstances.

Suddenly the click of a pistol rang through
the air, and before she could reach the hollow
where her husband had disappeared, three men
stood beside him as he lay prone on the snow.

"It's seldom he has such a bout as this,"
said one of the men, when Ursula came to the
spot where they stood; "and he's never run off
before."

"What is the matter?" asked Ursula.

"This gentleman (he's quiet now) met us in
Swansea, then escaped. He's been wandering
for a couple of days. We've found him here
at last, having tracked him all the way from
Swansea."

A gentleman rode up.

"I see you've found him," he said to the
men.

"Yes, sir; but he's quiet now. It's all over
with him."

"All over!" exclaimed Ursula. "What do
you mean?"

"That—that——"

"Speak out, man. Is the fit over?" asked
the gentleman. "Madam," he added, addressing Ursula, " this unfortunate baronet escaped
my care. He is subject to fits of temporary

insanity. This attack has been sharper than usual. Indeed, I fear it is not yet over, though the men assure me it is. This poor gentleman ought to live a life free from any excitement, either pleasant or otherwise."

" He is married," said Ursula, in a dazed way.

" Married ! " echoed the doctor.

" He is my husband," added Ursula. " Did he never tell you of his marriage ? "

" No ; it's the first time I've had him under my care," said the doctor. " I merely took charge of him for Dr. Griffith, who has attended him for years, but just now my friend is somewhat seriously indisposed."

" It's all up with him, sir," said the men.

The doctor went to the baronet, who still lay prostrate on the snow.

" He's shot himself," they said.

Ursula shuddered.

" My good madam," said the doctor. " All his wandering fits have come to an end. Sir Lloyd Pryce is dead—he has died by his own hand ! "

The click of the pistol that Ursula had heard a few minutes previously proclaimed her husband's death-warrant.

" God be thanked that he has not injured anybody else," said the doctor. " And to think he was married too—might have shot you, dear lady."

Ursula crept to her husband's side and kissed his forehead, while her tears fell heavily and fast upon the frozen snow. When least expected, death had divided them, and in the early days of her widowhood, Ursula felt deeply grieved that her handsome husband's history was so sad, and had such a tragic ending.

In a year and three months after Sir Lloyd Pryce's death, St. John and Ursula renewed the troth they had plighted in Beaumaris Bay.

The Scarlet Ribbon

"H—SH!" muttered Ditty Morgan, rocking herself before the fire.

"Why?" asked the slumberous girl sitting on the settle.

"'Teir nos ysprydion,'" murmured Ditty under her breath.

"'One of the three spirit nights,'" echoed Winnie.

"Tick!—tick!—tick!" went the eight-day clock, while every lattice rattled, and snow fell so heavily, that it promised to be deep for the New Year's Eve service.

"Why are you listening?" asked Winnie, starting. "It is only the gwynt traed y meirw!" (wind blowing over the feet of the corpses).

"Pw — no!" said Ditty solemnly, as she leaned her elbows on her knees, and buried her withered face between her hands.

"What is it then, boba?" (grandmother) asked Winnie.

"O anwyl! anwyl!" added Ditty, moaning and looking into the fire. " 'Twas the cyhyraeth. Didn't you hear it comin' with the wind?"

"No," responded Winnie.

"Whew! whew!" whistled the wind, responding to the roaring waves among the desolate cliffs and crags of Glamorganshire.

"There 'tis agen," sighed Ditty, " the cyhyraeth moanin' up an' down the road. We shall have sickness in the place, or some trouble."

"Boba!" exclaimed Winnie.

"Fy mlentyn, fy mlentyn bach!" (my child, my little child) replied Ditty, "I do never feel afeared of the Almighty's warnin'? Something will surely happen before long."

"You always tell us something will happen," remarked Winnie, " but nothing comes of it."

"Nothin'! what about years ago 'fore you was born?"

"What happened then?"

"Well, I was comin' home from chapel with your mother, an' I did see with my own eyes an angel going in front of us. 'Leave it pass,' ses I to your mother. 'What pass?' ses she. 'The angel,' ses I."

"Did mother see it?"

"I b'lieve so, only she wouldn't own to it."

"And then?"

"As I was tellin' you, the angel went in front

of us an' crossed the bridge. She had beautiful shinin' wings, an' was carryin' a babe in her arms. 'Look,' ses I to your mother, and 'fore we could turn, the angel went up an' opened our window, an' the next minit she did come out by the front door."

"What of that?" asked Winnie.

"Well, the angel didn't come out alone."

"Who came with her?"

"She was leadin' a young ooman out—'twas your own mother, an' 'fore the week's end, you was born, an' she was dead."

Winnie, shivering, crept closer to the fire. It was a relief to her to hear a distant voice singing one of the songs that used to be sung while ploughing with oxen in Wales.

"It's Llewellyn," said Ditty.

"Llewellyn, indeed!" exclaimed Winnie. "I'd know Llewellyn's voice a mile off," and tripping lightly to the door she sang a milking song.

"Well done, Winifred—well done!" shouted Ishmael Williams, the bard, as he paused to shake the snowflakes from his coat. "Where's your father?"

"Gone to chapel."

"Are you going too?" asked Ishmael.

"Yes," said Ditty, and presently the trio were trudging through deeply drifting snow to the service held on New Year's Eve, to watch the coming of another year. What a service! Simple yet grand, a service of song and thanksgiving in the cold loneliness of night and winter, in desolate, snow-bound Wales.

" H—sh !" cried Ditty, as her grand-daughter led her up to her own home, where refreshments would be ready for everybody.

" Why ?" asked Winnie.

" The cyhyraeth—the cyhyraeth !" cried Ditty.

Winnie paused and listened. The wind whistled through leafless trees ; wild waves roared, and the river rushed dark, almost black, between its margins of snow.

As a voice from the dead—a hollow sepulchral voice, came Ditty's half sobbing tones in broken accents—" The cyhyraeth moanin' on the shore do mean more corpses ; on land, fever or trouble—trouble to a many of us. H—sh ! there 'tis agen !"

" Whew ! wh—eh !" whistled the relentless wind.

.   .   .   .   .   .

" Dewi (David) Jones, perhaps you'll favour us with a song," said Isaac Morgan, the sexton, rapping the table with his unstrung bow.

" 'Pon my word, I did never try a song but two times in my life," was the reply.

" When did you try ?" asked the rector, seizing his flute.

U

"When Ned my brother was married, and when Job my cousin did come home from sea. No: I kent sing," said Dewi, mopping his face with a red kerchief, and looking sheepishly towards the table whereon Winnie placed glasses of metheglin and bowls of flummery for her father's guests. Observing Dewi's glance, Winnie offered him refreshment.

"Dewi bach," said Ishmael Williams, known among bards as "Eos Morganwg" (Nightingale of Glamorgan), "why, man alive, don't eat flummery before you sing."

"More you do fill me the better I ken sing," said Dewi, encouraged by Winnie's glances.

"Nobody can sing with a throatful," said Isaac Morgan.

"Come you," said Ditty, "don't you mind 'em. After a long ride, a drop o' meth will warm you a bit," so she poured out a glassful, and Dewi drank it at a draught.

"That's uncommon good," said he, mopping his face.

"Now then, now then," clamoured the increasing company.

"What is it to be?" asked the sexton.

"Well, to be shure—an' if I must sing I must. Now, what d'ye say to *Merch Megan?*"

"Dewi," exclaimed Ishmael Williams; "do you want us to lose our hearing?"

" I ken sing that better nor nothin'," persisted Dewi.

" But the song is not the right pitch for your voice," remarked the rector.

" Well, I ken sing it high—high up or low down, down in a whisper if you do like," said Dewi.

" You've a marvellously convenient voice," said Ishmael, " but, Dewi, my boy, if you sing that, you'll——"

" Show how anshient you be sometimes in tellin' of people who kent sing, an' never a word 'bout them as ken sing."

What did they know of his singing! Then to the accompaniment of the sexton's fiddle, the parson's flute, and the bard's harp, Dewi began. Leaning forward in his seat, he clasped the table with a clutch that seemed immovable. Loudly and powerfully he sang—his roar rattled the windows, and shook the rafters.

That this song should be followed by a hymn was by no means an unusual event, for Welsh gaiety is never unbridled, its gravity is seldom lugubrious.

" Will you give out a hymn?" asked the rector, addressing a dissenting farmer.

" If you will be good enough to join in, I will give out a hymn, an' help as far as I can," said the farmer, standing up and leaning his hands on the back of a neighbour's chair. "Next paage to the Kiver, common mater (metre)," said he, for the benefit of those who possessed hymn-books. Then he recited the whole hymn, and repeated the first verse a second time.

Lustily the thirty or more persons present sang the popular hymn, while the farmer swayed his body to and fro "like a sea-lion," as the sexton remarked. The hymn was re-demanded, then followed songs and sweet pennillions without number.

"Winifred," said the rector, "come here. It is your turn now."

Winnie was missing.

Not a few seconds previously she was among the girls, clustering around the three-legged oaken table.

"Winifred!" shouted Ishmael Williams, opening the kitchen door.

"Winifred!" cried the women from the porch.

"Winnie—Winnie Morgan!" shouted the girls, going out into the snowy roadway.

One of the girls lingering after the others beyond the gate uttered a cry of surprise.

"What is the matter—what is it?" asked her companions.

"The scarlet ribbon!"

How they fluttered around it.

To whom did it belong?

There was no time for guessing. Voices and revelry echoed through the midnight air, and presently the girls rushed into the house to escape the Mari Llwyd and its revellers.

No further heed was taken of Winnie's absence by the guests that night, only the rector going homeward through the churchyard fancied he saw her flitting down the riverside. Turning his lantern light across her path, he said, "Winifred Morgan, is it you? You here at this time of night, and alone?"

Quick as lightning the girl, without replying, darted past, leaving him to wonder if it could be Winifred at all. "It must be," he said, "and yet——" there was a rustling sound beside him, as half in fear, half in bewilderment, the rector hastened home, for the small hours of the morning were advancing, and as yet highwaymen and footpads had not ceased in the land.

.   .   .   .   .   .

Away, down through the churchyard, and into the lane went Winifred Morgan, never pausing a moment, but running breathlessly towards the hills. At every turn along the frozen ground treacherous snowdrifts impeded her movements, still she ran and soon reached a riverside hollow. Threading her way through a snowy thicket she entered a solitary cavern, where, in flickering torchlight, a crowd of people stood listening to a speaker who was just concluding his speech. His striking resemblance to Winifred could not fail to be noticed—the dark eyes and hair, the quick and active manner touched with *hauteur*, inherited from one of the princely tribes of Wales—revealed the kinship existing between Llewellyn Gwyn and Winifred Morgan.

"We are poor," exclaimed Llewellyn, "overworked, badly paid, our lives are altogether wretched; we have no representation, and are oppressed by privilege and the aristocracy. Who looks after us? So far as the State is concerned we are not looked after at all, but live neglected, despised, and crushed. The rights of man are denied us, the rights of labour are thwarted; we are bowed down with sorrow, but are we going to continue thus? Are we going to remain voiceless slaves?—a race of miserable creatures, afraid to enforce the rights of labour, or to demand the People's Charter? Why do the aristocracy and the officials oppose us? Why, lads? Because our Charter will give us better food and wages, lighter work and liberty! Listen, lads — you that can't read English, but can speak and understand a good deal—here are the six points of the People's

Charter. Manhood suffrage, vote by ballot, annual parliaments, abolition of the property qualification, payment of members, and the division of the country into equal electoral districts. We want a share of the law-making power; we want the middle and working classes represented; we want the People's Charter made law; and, my lads, we mean to have it. Come, my countrymen, be prompt in action, be determined, and we shall soon see the day when this mighty Charter will be part of our constitutional system! Lads, come up without delay, and sign the People's Charter!"

Loud applause followed the speech, and in less than ten minutes thirty Welshmen had enrolled their names or marks to the People's Charter.

Winnie eagerly listened and waited for the speaker to cease, then, stepping a pace forward, she whispered " Silence !"

In a moment the crowd became a mute group of downcast faces, over which slouching hats cast grim shadows. A moment later, extinguished torches smouldered on the ground, among snow-encumbered boughs and tangled brushwood that vainly struggled to surmount the deepening snow-drifts.

With song and merriment the Twelfth Night revellers and roysterers wended their way down hill, under the snow-crowned crags and beetling rocks fringing the riverside, and, as they passed, one of the cavern-hiders said, "It's only the Mari Llwyd."

Until the Mari Llwyd party were well out of sight and hearing, the cavern crowd remained silent, and were about to relight their torches, when Winnie said, "Idris, and sons of my countrymen and friends present—beware! Dewi Jones is in my father's house—he means no good. Go home while there is safety; I'll take care of the messages."

If the Chartists had dared, cheers would have echoed and re-echoed for Winnie, but silence and mystery attended these nocturnal meetings, and only a subdued murmur of emotional applause greeted the girl.

In the dark starless night the Chartists dispersed, and Winnie returned home to find the house unexpectedly quiet, and its door locked against her.

"This is Dewi's work," she muttered, "but I'm not afraid of *him*."

She rapped loudly, and soon obtained admission.

"Winifred!" angrily exclaimed her father, "where have you been?"

No reply.

"Answer!" he thundered.

Still she remained silent.

"This isn't the first time you've bin an' gone," continued her father. "To-night everybody was wonderin' where you was. Winifred, if you don't tell me where you've bin, and what you've bin doin' till this time o' mornin', I'll— I'll be the death of you!"

Winnie remained speechless.

"Won't you tell me?" shouted the angered sexton, dragging her to the settle.

He threw a brand on the smouldering fire, poked it, and a lurid flame leaped upward, lighting the room with its garish glow.

"Winifred," he said, looking steadily into her face, which was uplifted and pallid, "if you don't tell me what your night tricks an' the like be—if thou wilt not confess what do take thee out o' nights uncommon often of late, I'll— there, I'll——" The sexton was too exasperated to conclude that sentence, and Winifred remained unflinching while her father resumed speaking. "It's for no good whatever, an' if it had pleased the Lord to spare your poor mother to me, you'd no more be out of a night at all hours—— There, I'll tell Parson Llewellyn of thee. If there's one thing I kent abide, it's a ooman given to night tricks, for its a shure sign they be goin' to the pit as fast as Satan ken take 'em. Now then, maid, what 'ave you got to say for yourself?"

"Nothing," replied Winnie. "I have done no harm, and can come to no danger."

"No danger,' hissed a husky voice from the stairway.

Winifred started.

Even her father looked surprised, for he imagined and hoped that Dewi Jones was asleep. Fire-flames leaped and flung long shafts of light across dark shadows beside the settle. In that light stood Dewi Jones, who, in sinister tones, repeated—

"No danger in having dealings with Chartists, eh?"

"None whatever," said Winnie, confronting him.

"No danger meetin' Chartists, in carryin' messages to and fro between hot-headed demagogues like Llewellyn Gwyn and his crew!"

Isaac Morgan stepped a pace backward, still clasping Winnie's shoulder with a firm grip, under which the girl winced. He looked into her faced and asked, "Is he speaking truth? Art thou a friend of Chartists? Dost thou dabble thy fingers in that black puddle of iniquity?"

"The scarlet ribbon!" exclaimed Dewi. "See —she wears it!"

With a fierce gesture her father tore it from her breast.

"She made a banner for them," continued Dewi; "an' what's more, there's a song of hers sung by the Chartists."

"A song of Winnie's?" asked the sexton.

"Iss; 'The Lion of Freedom,'" replied Dewi. "These are the very words—

> 'The Lion of Freedom is come from his den,
> We'll rally around him again and again;
> We'll crown him with laurel our champion to be—
> O'Connor the patriot for sweet liberty!'"

Dewi Jones paused.

"Go on," said Winnie. "There are three more verses. You're a capital reciter."

"So thou art a Chartist!" murmured Isaac Morgan, in sad, subdued tones. "A dealer in devilry, riot, an' godless doin's. Gell, hast thou too renounced thy God to keep covenant with demons? Go,—to me thou art my daughter no longer, but Winifred Ddu now and for evermore!"

Dewi Jones watched her between the light and shadows as a lion watches prey.

"I have not renounced my God," said Winifred Morgan. "All Chartists are not unbelievers; Llewellyn is not, neither am I."

. . . . . .

It was twilight. Ditty crooned by the fireside : " I did know trouble was comin' to many of us. The cyhyraeth do never moan for nothin'; but O anwyl, anwyl, that I should have lived to see this day, an' Winnie a Chartist !"

"Times is bad, an' them Chartists do make a sight of damage an' havoc 'mong honest people who ought to be livin' quiet at home, instid of jauntin' 'bout the country," remarked Dewi Jones. "But don't you bother about Winnie— she's right anuff."

Winnie, singing a milking song, passed to the dairy.

" Come here, Winnie," shouted Dewi, and soon from the dairy Winnie came.

" Sit down here on the settle by me," said Dewi. " I do want to have a liddle talk with you."

" What is it ?" she asked.

" Where's Llewellyn Gwyn ?"

" I don't know," replied Winnie.

" Don't know where your lover is," said Dewi smoothly.

" My lover! My cousin, you mean," said Winnie.

" Iss, your lover. I do know all 'bout it. You did take a sight of trouble to throw me over for him."

" Throw *you* over ! Dewi Jones, I never

knew *you* to come a-courtin' *me!*" exclaimed Winnie.

"Never knew! Pw—, Winifred Morgan. You did know all along that I was for you, an' that your father'd never go agin the match."

Winifred laughed outright as Dewi continued :

"If you didn't understand me, twasn't my fault. Well now, Winnie, listen. There's the liddle farm at Gellygaer, an' properties down 'bout Aberavon, an' my mother's house to come after her in Llantrissant, an' then I was thinkin' we could go and live up in the hills. I got a tidy an' respectable general shop with the butcher's business up in Dinas, an'—pw—, gell ! you don't know half what I've got ready for you. It's only for you to say the word, an' we'll be one."

Ditty only half heard what was going on, and still sat crooning in the corner.

"Now or never !" said Dewi.

"I'm a Chartist," replied Winnie.

"Never mind," said Dewi ; "you wont be a Chartist when you're Mrs. Dewi Jones. Listen, gell."

He drew forth from his prodigious pocket an equally prodigious bag, and shook it before her. How the money jingled, rang, and danced in that wonderful bag !

"Let's have more light on the subject," said Dewi, and Ditty stirred the fire.

" Here ! " exclaimed Dewi, lifting the round oaken table nearer the glow. " Come here, Winnie, an' count the money. There's three hundred pounds in hard cash, an' more at home in the till ; an'—wait you a bit—I've a couple of notes or so 'bout me. Look here."

Dewi drew forth a roll of papers from an inner coat pocket, and placed them among the golden sovereigns that were heaped upon the table.

Winnie glanced down, peered at the notes— just a glance, no more ; before Dewi could stay her, she snatched one of the papers and threw it into the fire.

" There ! " she exclaimed ; " that's my answer to your love-making ! "

" Are you mad ? " asked Dewi. " It's fine work to take valuable papers an' throw them in the fire. Never mind, Winnie ; you an' I'll be married yet. When you're Mrs. Jones, you'll learn to respect them bits o' paper an' me too."

For a moment he paused and fumbled with other papers in his pocket, while Winnie stood speechless and triumphant before him. Dewi proceeded to examine the contents of all his pockets. " There's the lease, an' there's the will, an' there's the mortgage deed—but shure anuff I've left it upstairs. 'Tis a mistake to make love in the middle of business. Wait a minute, Winnie, an' I'll go an' look for it."

He darted away, and returned saying, "It must be here, for 'tisn't upstairs. P'rhaps 'tis with the notes. Fuming and fretting he re-examined the papers, and suddenly looking up, shouted, almost raved, "What 'ave you been an' done? — you've ruined me for life — you've—"

"What is it? what is it?" asked Isaac Morgan, coming from his workshop, and quaking with fear.

"The warrant—she's been an' destroyed the warrant," shouted Dewi.

"What warrant?" asked the sexton.

"The warrant for the arrest of Llewellyn Gwyn," said Dewi.

"Llewellyn Gwyn—what has he done?"

"Treason," hissed Dewi.

Winifred Morgan laughed.

"H—sh!" said Isaac Morgan angrily. "You may laugh if you like, but 'tis no laughing work. D'ye know what you've bin an done? The law will have a hold on you——"

"As soon as Dewi tells—Oh, I am ready for that," said Winnie merrily.

"You kent be my flesh an' blood," said Isaac Morgan tartly, as Winnie, turning to Dewi, remarked, "You're helpless now."

He began to rave at her.

"H—sh!" she said, "don't expose your loss. Take it quietly, bear up like a man, and all will come right in the end."

"Wait till mornin'," said Dewi, "we'll see then."

For in truth the man was too bewildered to know what to think, or tell the girl who had outwitted him.

.   .   .   .   .   .

Snow covered the Welsh mountains, and filled all sheltered nooks from deep dingles fringing the Severn Sea, to ravines penetrating the fastnesses bordering upon Breconshire. All the dim land was snow-bound, and the coaches failed to run. The earth was one vast waste of untarnished snow, hiding hedges and even thickets with its hard-frozen foldings. Frozen so hard was it that in most places, horses and foot-passengers could travel with tolerable ease and security, but all vehicular traffic had ceased. People complained about the weather just as they would if it had been a wet winter, or an unusually mild one. Snow was tiresome, but then, so would rains and floods have been, and a milder winter would have reaped a harvest of ingratitude, for which even swallows coming earlier could not atone.

It was a winter of unusual severity and

distress; grumbling and discontent had set their cruel fangs upon the class described by the French as *Prolétaire*, and there seemed to be no antidote for the poisonous virus, which, going down deeper and deeper, threatened to seize hearts, and thwart their better feelings.

Fierce, fitful flames of Chartism leaped and throbbed among the populace, gaining fresh vigour here and there, penetrating remote parts of Wales, bringing votaries from nearly every town, village, and hamlet in the principality. Men of education, ability, and eloquence, impassioned poets and bards, quickly gained hearers, and were surrounded by throngs of earnest and devout fanatics, all enthusiasm, yet thoroughly sincere. Feargus O'Connor, the renowned and once dreaded leader of Chartism, hatched plans and concocted schemes which were amplified or simplified as occasion or locality demanded, while leaders and sub-leaders led little groups of Chartists from out-of-the-way villages and towns; and later on, when agitation had assumed a more active form, the schemes which began with Birmingham demonstrations and Leicester meetings ended in Newport riots. Even now, though the influence of Chartism has passed away, and people are enjoying three gained points of the People's Charter, many are living to tell of thrills that ran through their hearts when

x

Chartist secret meetings had not developed into riots; long before Frost, Jones, and Williams paid penalty to the law, which afterwards gave them their vote by ballot, manhood suffrage, and the abolition of the property qualification.

Llewellyn Gwyn was shepherd of a little Western Wales fold of Chartists, members living between Cardiff and Swansea, not higher among the mountains than Dinas, nor nearer Monmouthshire than Caerphilly. He had been scouring the villages for many weeks, steadily gaining converts, while, wherever he went, people soon flocked around him. He could sway them with his eloquence, his strong biblical quotations smote their souls, causing hearers to sigh, sob, and weep, as though their hearts were broken. In his speech people discovered omens of doom, and could hear the rattle of eternal chains. Suddenly his mood would change. Freedom from shackles, pardon, prosperity, and heaven were offered, lifting listeners to heights of happiness until they would break forth into feelings of joy, gratitude, and unutterable emotion.

.　　　.　　　.　　　.　　　.　　　.

Just six weeks after Dewi Jones entered the lists of Cupid, he made up his mind to "turn Chartist," for he declared "'Prhaps Winnie will come to in a bit, an' if I was a Chartist 'tis like anuff my three hundred pound will weigh 'gainst Llewellyn in the end."

Isaac Morgan could not forgive Winnie, though he suppressed his feelings for the sake of "peace in the house," "but," he added, "I do fear bad will come of it, an' if so, it must rest on their own shoulders."

"H—sh!" murmured Ditty under her breath. "The cyhyraeth——"

"Whew! wh—ew!" whistled the wind.

"Moanin' on the shore it do mean corpses—on land fever, trouble—trouble to many of us. H—sh! there 'tis agen!"

Llewellyn Gwyn and Ishmael Williams entered the house.

"You here, Dewi!" said Ishmael. "Why, old man, people won't know you when you go back."

"What about the business up at Dinas?" asked Llewellyn.

"Leave off chaffin' me, both of you. If you did know what did bring me down here in such weathers you'd respect me."

"Dewi," exclaimed Llewellyn, "you came here to arrest me; can I ever respect you again?"

"Not if I was to sign my name to that there paper I did show you last night?"

"Oh, oh!" said Ishmael Williams, "if this is

the way you are going on, the quicker I get away the better." Calling Llewellyn aside, he added, "You had better go in for hiding now for the good of your country. Spies are abroad."

"Where ?"

"At present about five miles off. There is no time to be lost. Make your way to Llantrissant, and I'll follow."

"Disguise yourself," suggested Dewi, "or you'll be overtaken."

"Right !" exclaimed Ishmael. "Winnie to the rescue."

It was but a moment's work to find apparel.

"They'll think it's me," said Winnie, "only just lower your voice."

"Don't talk of lowerin' his voice," said Dewi; "you ken talk loud anuff when you do say 'No' to a respectable man's offer of marriage."

Fully equipped for his night journey Llewellyn Gwyn came out from the little parlour.

"Well, to be shure, what a diff'rance," exclaimed Isaac Morgan.

"How like Winnie !" said Ishmael.

"Good anto me well, if I was to meet you sudden round a corner I'd believe you was Winnie herself," said Dewi. "Winifred Morgan, my anwyl !"

"Winnie," said Llewellyn, "take care of yourself. I'll return when all is safe; they won't remain here long—perhaps only pass, and not even search here."

"Don't be rash," replied Winnie, uplifting a warning finger.

Llewellyn was accompanied through and for a short distance beyond the town by Isaac Morgan, Ishmael Williams, and Dewi Jones, who said, "We'll go just for to make 'em b'lieve 'tis Winnie."

They had been gone but ten minutes when a secret messenger came, saying, "Tell Llewellyn they're come, an' will be down here in a twinkling."

"He's gone—he's safe," said Winnie, who bolted and barred the door against intruders. "Before Llewellen can reach Llantrissant he'll be caught," sighed Winnie, sitting down to think how she could best help her cousin and lover. There was little time for escape, yet if she could only plan a ruse to thwart their movements for one brief day !

"H—sh !" moaned Ditty, "the cyhyraeth— there 'tis agen. On land it do mean trouble— trouble to a many of us ?"

And the wintry wind whistled, blowing over the feet of the corpses in the churchyard, where the sorrows of generations were recorded on grey melancholy stones and crowded tablets fixed against the outer walls of the quaint

and lonely church beside the snow-swollen river,
flowing dark, deep, and swiftly between its
margins of snow.

.   .   .   .

" Llewellyn Gwyn is taken!" was the cry,
and all who had flocked to his fold were saddened
and distressed.   He was overtaken a mile or so
beyond the town, and arrested for having frequently held illegal meetings, inciting persons to
discontent and dissatisfaction with the Government, and charged with conspiracy and dis-
obedience to all law and order.   The scarlet
ribbon was in his buttonhole, and upon his
person several treasonable documents were
found.   For a night he was detained in the old
town, whence he started for Llantrissant, and
next morning the constable and his companions
took him to Cardiff.   Proceeding along the high
road, with its picturesque surroundings, the constable and party, with the prisoner, passed
through the quaint villages of Bonvilstone and
St. Nicholas, and on to the lofty hill known as
the Tumble, overlooking a vale almost unequalled
for beauty in Glamorgan.   Southward the Severn
Sea glittered and gleamed in the morning sunshine ; eastward Cardiff looked grey and cold ; to
the north Llantrissant, cradled among its hills,
nestled, as it were, under a coverlet of snow,
while far away and beyond it, range after range

of snowy mountains loomed gloomily grand from among leaden clouds that promised more snow.

These men coming up from the west—fearing Llewellyn Gwyn's presence in Cardiff would rouse people—took all necessary precautions during his transit, yet on reaching the river Taff he was recognised by a great crowd.

"Llewellyn Gwyn!" shouted the people. "Speak to us."

"I dare not," he cried, "seeing that my speech is watched."

The sound of his voice, though he spoke quietly, caused a wild wave of enthusiasm to pass over the multitude, and affairs began to look somewhat menacing.

"Be careful," whispered the constable.

"You need not warn me," replied Llewellyn. "All I can safely tell you is this: Welshmen and women, whatever you do, stick to your Charter!"

Deafening cheers and applause greeted Llewellyn's words, and followed him as he proceeded to prison.

Cardiff magistrates were inclined to be very lenient. So far, they saw little harm in the "hot-headed demagogue." Perhaps he had spoken unwisely, but there was only a frail charge against him. Still investigation was necessary, and Llewellyn remanded, had to

return to prison for a week—yet longer. Three
weeks elapsed, and during that period the case
assumed a formidable aspect. Several charges
were brought against him, and eventually the
prisoner was committed for trial at the next
assizes. He was asked if he desired to make
any statement previous to his return to prison,
and, if so, to be careful.

For a moment there was profound silence in
court. Everybody expected a speech. Instead
of which, Llewellyn stood up, and fixing his
eyes upon the presiding magistrate, said, "I am
not guilty of the charges brought against me.
Further, you are committing the——"

Dewi Jones' voice, from the far end of the
court, shouted, "Wrong person!"

What a scene in court! People gazed and
rubbed their eyes—even the constable who
made the arrest looked dazed. The magistrates
were puzzled. What could it all mean? Dewi
Jones was called forward.

"Do you know this man?" asked the magistrates. "If he is not Llewellyn Gywn, who
is he?"

"Andeed shure," replied Dewi, after being
sworn as a witness, "you may as well ask, for
my own eyes deceived me; an' to tell you the
truth plump an' plain, 'tis Winnie, Winifred
Morgan, fy'ngariad anwyl?"

Winnie's gravity broke down, the gravity of the court was upset, while Dewi added, "If your honours ken keep her in prison a spell till she do come to, an' promise to be Mrs. Jones, I'd thenk you kindly, but if you kent make it convenient I——"

"Well done, old man," shouted somebody.

"Silence in the court!" bawled the clerk.

"If this is true," said the presiding magistrate, who feared a plot in the case, "we cannot release the person until further proof of identity is forthcoming."

"Good anto me well; to think they won't b'lieve my word on oath that 'tis Winnie," said Dewi Jones.

"Man alive," said Ishmael Williams, "they don't know *you*."

"Is that it? An' I could 'ave taken my oath that everybody from Dinas to Swansea did know Dewi Jones of the Shop. An' I be a constable too!"

"H—sh!" said Ishmael. "Don't mention that fact. It would take the gilt off the gingerbread."

There was very little time lost in identifying Winnie. Ishmael Williams, Isaac Morgan, and a host of others came forward to testify that the prisoner was not Llewellyn Gwyn.

Winnie retired, and soon reappeared dressed

in her own garments, but still wearing the scarlet ribbon.

"Are you a Chartist?" asked the magistrate, glancing at the ribbon.

"I am," replied Winnie, "but I do not make speeches," whereupon the people who imagined her to be Llewellyn Gwyn, cheered lustily, remembering her speech on entering Cardiff.

"David Jones, stand forward," continued the magistrate.

Dewi obeyed. He doffed his hat, and as Ishmael Williams remarked, "revealed the anshient anshientness of his noble brow."

"If you wish to win this girl for your wife, you can do no better than turn Chartist," said the magistrate, laughing; "but I'm afraid you'll find many rivals."

"Thenk you kindly, sur, but now Llewellyn is gone, I've got hopes she'll come to. I ken bide a bit an' see how the tide'll turn."

.   .   .   .   .   .

"How did you manage it?" asked Ishmael Williams, as he accompanied Winnie home.

"By putting on Llewellyn's clothes and going down the road. I knew they would take me— we are so much alike."

"I do see how *you* ken keep a secret an' no

mistake," said Dewi. " 'Tis plain anuff you was born to be Mrs. Dewi Jones."

.   .   .   .   .   .

" Perhaps the cyhyraeth prophesied the death and burial of quaint old Welsh customs ; legends are becoming hoary, angels have not been seen in the land since Ditty saw one, and here we are loyal Chartists, welcoming Her Majesty's Jubilee," said Ishmael Williams.

"We'll keep Nos dydd Galan (New Year's Eve) at home this year," said Llewellyn Gwyn.

"And make-believe we are down in dear old Wales again," adds Winifred Gwyn.

The prosperous London merchant and his wife, surrounded by numerous children and grandchildren, are welcoming their Welsh friend and guest in old Welsh fashion. Though Dewi Jones is gone over to the majority—though the sexton's fiddle and the parson's flute have long been laid aside, the bard's harp is tuneful as ever, but as Eos Morganwg declares, "We are beginning to feel the anshient anshientness that comes with silvery hair and failing powers."

The Legend of Rhitta the Giant

(Translated from the Welsh by the late Taliesin Williams, son of Iolo Morganwg.)

"THERE were two kings formerly in Britain, named Nynniaw and Peibiaw. As these two ranged the fields one starlight night, 'See,' said Nynniaw, 'what a beautiful and extensive field I possess!'

"'Where is it?' said Peibiaw.

"'The whole firmament,' said Nynniaw, 'far as vision can extend.'

"'And dost thou see,' said Peibiaw, 'what countless herds and flocks of cattle and sheep I have depasturing thy field?'

"'Where are they?' said Nynniaw.

"'Why the whole host of stars which thou seest,' said Peibiaw, 'and each of golden effulgence; with the moon for their shepherdess to superintend their wanderings.'

" 'They shall *not* graze in *my* pasture,' said Nynniaw.

" 'They *shall*,' said Peibiaw.

" 'They shall *not*,' said one.

" 'They *shall*,' said the other repeatedly, in banded contradiction, until at last it arose to wild contention between them, and from contention it came to furious war, until the armies and subjects of both were nearly annihilated in the desolation.

" Rhitta the Giant, King of Wales, hearing of the carnage committed by these two maniac kings, determined on hostility against them; and, having previously consulted the laws and his people, he arose and marched against them, because they had, as stated, followed the courses of depopulation and devastation, under the suggestions of phrenzy. He vanquished them, and then cut off their beards. But, when the other sovereigns included in the twenty-eight kings of the island of Britain heard these things, they combined all their legions to revenge the degradation committed on the two disbearded kings, and made a fierce onset on Rhitta the Giant and his forces. And furiously bold was the engagement. But Rhitta the Giant won the day.

" 'This is *my* extensive field,' said he. And he then immediately disbearded the other kings.

"When the kings of the surrounding countries heard of the disgrace inflicted on all these disbearded kings, they armed themselves against Rhitta the Giant and his men, and tremendous was the conflict. But Rhitta the Giant achieved a most decisive victory, and then exclaimed, 'This is *my* immense field.' And at once the kings were disbearded by him and his men.

"Then, pointing to the irrational monarchs, 'These,' said he, 'are the animals that grazed in *my* field; but I have driven them out— they shall not longer depasture there.' After that he took up all the beards, and made out of them a mantle for himself, that extended from head to heel, and Rhitta was twice as large as any other person ever seen."

In a note to this legend the late Taliesin Williams says:—"It is a feature strongly in favour of the antiquity of Welsh literature, that most of the prominent characters found in old English and French romances and ballads are borrowed from it. Even the seats of Government, under the British princes, previous to the Saxon dominion, such as Carlisle, Caerlleon, &c., are selected as scenes of action. King Arthur, Queen Guenever (Gwenhwyfar), Sir Kay (Caihir), Glaskerion (Glas-Geraint), or

Ceraint fardd Glas, or Gadair (Ceraint the Blue Bard of the Chair), Mordred (Medrod), and many others, figure in frequent recurrence in these compositions."

The Legend of Rhitta Gawr appears in Percy's *Reliques of Ancient English Poetry*, under the title of " King Ryence's Challenge." It was sung before Queen Elizabeth, at the grand entertainment at Kenilworth Castle in 1575. In a letter describing these festivities, it is thus mentioned :—" A minstrell came forth with a sollem song, warranted for story out of K. Arthur's Acts, whereof I gatt a copy, and it is this :—' So it fell out on a Pentecost,' &c. After the song the narrative proceeds :—" At this the minstrell made a pause, and a curtezy for Primus Passus. More of the song is thear, but I gatt it not."

The story in Morte Arthur, whence it is taken, runs as follows :—" Came a messenger hastily from King Ryence, of North Wales, saying, that King Ryence had discomfited and overcome eleven kings, and everiche of them did him homage, and that was this :—they gave him their beards cleane flayne off. Wherefore the messenger came for King Arthur's beard ; for King Ryence had purfeled a mantell with kings beards, and there lacked for one a place of the mantell, wherefore he sent for his beard, or else he would enter into his lands, and

brenn and slay, and never leave till he have thy
head and thy beard. Well, said Arthur, thou hast
said thy message, which is the most villainous
and lewdst message that ever man heard sent
to a king. Also thou mayest see my beard is
full young yet for to make a purfell of, but
tell thou the king that—or it be long he shall
do me homage on both knees, or else he shall
leese his head."

In some of the old Welsh MSS. it is stated
that "Rhitta Gawr struck the ground with his
foot till the earth trembled! till the skies
trembled! till the stars trembled! till the
tremor ran through all the worlds unto the
uttermost depths."

Mantles appear to have taken a prominent
place in Welsh romance. The old ballad of
"The Boy and the Mantle," in Percy's *Reliques*,
is based on Welsh romance, although the com-
piler of that work says:—"The incidents of
the 'Mantle and the Knife' have not, that I
can recollect, been borrowed from any other
writer."

Among the "Thirteen Treasures of the Island
of Britain," was the "Mantle of Tegaw Eurfron
(Beauty of the Golden Breast), that covered a
chaste woman, but would not an unchaste one;
that would cover a truth-teller, but not a
liar."

Lady Jane of Sutton

A STORY OF THE ANCIENT STRADLING FAMILY

T is a lonely spot.

There, in the midst of swampy land, where hillocks of stunted grass and patches of broad water-flags abound, daffodils bloom in the early spring days, and the flowers of the marsh-marigold gleam serenely under the changeful sky of April.

There, when autumn mists and vapours steal solemnly along the earth, the will-o'-the-wisp or jack-o'-lantern performs its wildest antics and dances, and hovers deceptively over every sedgy hollow.

Through the centre of that marsh-land the rains of winter form pools, and trickling streamlets, and quagmires, but in summer it is dry and parched.

On the borders of this marsh or swamp stands Sutton, now a farm-house.

Even in the present day, so strongly marked are the traces of its ancient importance that it makes it a place of dreams, in which the mind can wander back through long and hoary centuries, and live for a season among the people of the far past.

Quaint windows, great heavy and massive doors and doorways, a broad open staircase, antique hall and curious entrance—all testify to its former importance as a Manor House.

It was formerly the property of the Stradlings of St. Donats, and there, as a rule, either the second son or the dowager retired when the new heir succeeded to the estates.

In the days of Sir Harry Stradling—before that unfortunate baronet fell into the hands of Colyn Dolphyn—Sutton was occupied by Lady Jane, the mother of Sir Harry.

Lady Jane was the daughter of Henry Beaufort, who afterwards became a Cardinal, and she was also the widow of Sir Edward Stradling, who, says the ancient chronicle, "took a journey to Jerusalem, and there was made a knight according to the order of the Holy Sepulchre. On his return he brought with him from Italy a man of skilful hands in stone-carving, who made the ornamental columns that we see even to this day facing us in the walls of the Castle of St. Donats."

Sutton was one of the manors sold to pay the ransom to Colyn Dolphyn for Sir Harry Stradling.

Early in the last century common report declared Lady Jane to have been so enraged at the sale thereof that she died an " unnatural death."

Where, how, or when the lady died, the old women could not tell. It was only rumoured that the Lady of Sutton wandered about, especially when the wind was high or when the autumn mists enveloped the swamp. Then, of course, she always carried a lantern in her hand to guide her homeward over the morass.

One October evening, in the year 1739, when the air was chill and a dreary breeze crept sluggishly in the highway, two men came along the road about a mile distant from Sutton. They were bound from Wick to Llandow. After the fashion of those days conversation turned to ghosts and the laying thereof.

" I'll never believe all the stories told about ghosts and haunted houses," said the younger of the two men, and the off-shoot of generations of farmer folk.

" If you'd ever known *one* you'd believe in all of them," said the stranger.

" Did you ever see one ? " asked the young man.

" Did I ? " reiterated his companion in a somewhat sneerful tone.

" Ah ! " remarked the stranger, " so you want to know more about ghosts, even if you don't believe in them ! "

They were now ascending rising ground that led under a thicket where firs abounded.

October was scattering its coinage of gold and bronze leaves upon the sodden earth, and the brambles were bright with their banners of crimson and amber. Even the fading ferns were momentarily gaining fresh life from the kisses of the October sunset, and, as the odours of decay were borne upon the autumnal air, there was a weirdness in the subtle smell thereof. The young man felt that mystery clung around the fir branches, and the old man felt that stern realities are sometimes more strange than fictions.

As they went deeper into the fir shadows the young man renewed his questions.

" Tell me—have you ever seen a ghost ? "

" I have," replied the old man.

" Where—when ? "

" In Sutton, on September the twenty-seventh of last year, 1738."

" Tell me all about it," said the youth.

" Well—to begin at the beginning—I never before believed in ghosts. Now don't interrupt, or I'll not tell you a word. You must let me tell my own story in my own way—or not at all. In January 1738, I was sent to St. Donats Castle on an errand for a distinguished archæologist. Antiquarian research is my profession— if it may be so termed—and this new excursion had considerable attraction for me, and for more reasons than one. Strange to say, my name is Stradling. I was born in Coombe Hawey, over in Somerset—and this much I know, that I am one of the direct descendants of the Stradlings of St. Donats. If you doubt it, read Mr. Pepys, and you'll find the truth. I cannot tell you how glad I was to be bound on a mission of archæological research to the place where long generations of my ancestors had dwelt. My work would most likely occupy nine or ten months, and, as my patron was a very wealthy man, there was no reason why I should be in haste, I am only a humble researcher among all sorts of antiquities, but I love my work, though I am as poor as a church mouse. I thought the journey from Cardiff to St. Donats could not be pleasant, because I heard the roads were infested with highwaymen and footpads. Besides which —being a man well read in quaint lore, and capable of ferreting out the secrets of stone walls and faded parchment—I had upon my person several ancient documents, and sufficient money to keep me for at least three months. Still, you see I had the spirit of a real old Stradling. Don't I look like one? Here I am, six feet in my stockings, and strong and broad to boot. Not one of your flattened and lean-looking gentlemen, that dejectedly and persistently droop like fallen reeds against each other in our mediæval family pictures, nor yet like those prayerful folk who wandered up and down the long corridor of the castle in melancholy Indian rank and file. I am, as you see, a stalwart Briton, ready to fight any new Colyn Dolphyn that might masquerade his piratical ancestor's pranks. And it always occurred to me that if my respected ancestor Sir Harry Stradling, had possessed more 'gumption,' he'd not have been carried off by a sea-thief. But it isn't for me to talk of other people's shortcomings. I've always had more than enough of my own.

"It was late in January, and as the evening was gloomy I much longed to get to the end of my journey. The gentleman who arranged this work for me had been in communication with Sir Thomas Stradling—then in France—and the result was, I had to board and lodge in the castle.

"Before I reached my destination, a clinging mist began to creep along the roads and a thick sea fog came up channel. A chilling rain fol-

lowed, and as we approached St. Donats the
wind arose. I was somewhat awed by the soli-
tude of the place. Everywhere the great trees
waved their branches, stretching them forth like
restless spirit-arms, now extended down to earth,
then uplifted heavenward. At times the wind
sobbed mournfully in the hollows, or shrieked
like a sin-burdened soul fleeting away to its
doom. Away below the cliffs, the sea grieved
among the wave-worn crags and rocks, and from
the Nash Sands came muttered prophecies of
doom. Miserable enough it must have been to
those acquainted with, and had friends in the
locality, but still more weird was it to a stranger
in a strange land.

"I was glad when my guide declared we were
nearing the castle, which in a few minutes we
did, my advent being announced by a wild gust
of wind that caused the old oaken doors to slam
violently. The servants of St. Donats gave me
a very hearty welcome, and I as truly welcomed
the light and warmth of the spacious hearth. I
sat talking with the good folks till long after
midnight, and then, wearied out, I went to bed.
The next morning was one of the wildest I had
ever seen. All along the rock-bound coast the
waves ran in tempestuous fury, and a long line
of surf fringed the shore far above high-water
mark. Early in the forenoon I went to work

exploring the ancient domain. Now I tried to ferret out a peculiar piece of masonry, or endeavoured to discover the secret of some quaint old gargoyle, then I sought to learn the mysteries of the ancient Watch Tower. Those occupations kept me at work, with intervals of rest, until the month of September. On the first day of that month I went to Sutton, there to inspect some ancient masonry. I slept there the night, and all next day went through the various rooms. Towards the evening of the twenty-seventh I was in what they called the 'withdrawing-room,' which looked out into the garden. The lurid sunset touched everything with its crimson light. Deeply impressed by the beautiful sunset, I lingered at the window and looked out. Evening darkened into twilight, and the pale crescent moon gleamed coldly from the rainy sky. By-and-by I became aware of a rustling sound in the room, but I took no heed of it, and when again I heard the noise I attributed it to the wing-flapping of bats, or to the restlessness of owls among the ivy. Presently I heard the sound again, but this time it was more distinct. I looked across the room, which was growing dark with sombre shadows. There was little to be seen—only the least faint daylight falling softly upon the oaken floor, and the shadows growing darker as they crept away into far corners. Again I heard the noise, and once more I looked across the room, but without avail. The noise became more distinct as daylight waned, and at last I began to learn what the sound resembled. Of all things in the world it fell on my ears like the trailing of silken robes—soft in sound, yet rustling. Presently I began to feel that somebody or something was entering the room. I felt the more certain of this when I heard a tapping noise along the floor. Tap, tap, tap, went the sound as the rustling garments appeared to be trailing nearer. I confess to a feeling of surprise and considerable but subdued terror as the tapping increased. At last the weird sounds became distinct, though by no means loud. Then the tapping and the rustling came quite close to me. I could easily define the noises—high heels, silken robes.

"'How curious,' I muttered audibly. Then I looked around. As I did so I caught sight of a long, trailing object in the twilight. My first idea was to peep through the window, but some unseen power appeared to pinion me helplessly beside the casement. In fact, I was impelled by some strange force to remain where I was, and to wait or even to abide by whatever consequences might follow. I soon became aware that a somewhat stately figure was slowly crossing the room, and in a few minutes I could see that it was robed in a trailing gown of some dark colour, if not black. I obtained only a side-view of the figure. The face was averted. There was a stately grace about the form, to which I already attributed the supernatural.

"'It must be a family ghost,' I muttered. 'If so, I shall be glad to make its acquaintance.' You are astonished, young man, at my composure. Well, I had been used to wanderings in strange places and among strange people. I had seen halls that were reported to be haunted, and if ever a ghost had visited the earth I felt that I would be quite as ready to bring my antiquarian abilities to bear upon it as upon illegible legends and secret-keeping stones. At last I felt compelled to speak. The silence, the suspense were unbearable. 'Who are you?—where did you come from?—whither are you going?' I asked in quick succession, but I failed to gain a reply, and, as I spoke, the figure vanished. A few minutes later I heard the sounds of tapping footsteps and the rustling robes dying in the distance of the corridor, whither I followed them. But now all was silent—not a sound to be heard but the owls hooting and the loud flapping of bats' wings in the night-air. That night and for several more I kept my counsel, fearing to be made the victim of laughter.

"In the course of a few days I once more saw the apparition, and then I asked the inmates about it.

"'You've seen her,' said my host.

"'Then she's well known,' I remarked.

"'Yes; it's Lady Jane's ghost. She always appears before a death in the family. And now there'll be no rest till the person is dead.'

"'Dear me,' I remarked, smiling. 'Then let us hope the individual, whoever he or she may be, will soon depart this life, for our sakes at least.'

"My remark was received by my host with a shake of the head, which denoted disapproval at my seeming levity. We were sitting on the quaint oaken settle before the fire. Right across the kitchen long dark shadows fell, while smaller and more grotesque shadows crowded around the ancient furniture. Towards these the fire-light danced and leaped in maddened ecstasy. All the shadows grew smaller as the fire-flames grew fiercer, and by-and-by the fire-glow filled the room with its rich warm radiance. On the hearth three fine hounds lay basking in the warm fire-glow. Dreaming perhaps of some happy hunting grounds, or the ardour of an exciting chase, the hounds sniffed and snorted, and restlessly turned from side to side.

"'As a rule, when Lady Jane's ghost appears,

said my host, 'the hounds get restless, and some of them begin howling.'

"Even as he spoke, the dogs in the distant kennel began baying to the rising moon, and at length we could hear the hounds howling far away.

"My host shuddered and spoke in whispers. I was mute with astonishment—so weird were the sounds, and so ghostlike were the responsive howlings of other dogs in the village close by.

"'Lady Jane's abroad, sure anuff,' said the dairymaid, coming in. 'Did you hear the dogs, master?'

"'Yes,' said he somewhat curtly, and in a tone that silenced the maid.

"'Do you believe in this ghost?' I asked.

"'I do,' was the reply. 'I've always known deaths to follow Lady Jane's visits.'

"'Have you ever seen her?' I asked.

"'Yes, yes,' said my companion, in a somewhat pained and impatient tone of voice.

"His manner forbade further questioning, and I went out into the courtyard with the intention of taking a short walk. Second thoughts caused me to go and occupy myself in making additions to the daily report upon my antiquarian research. So I returned and went to one of the upper rooms.

"It was the twenty-seventh day of September.

I noticed that, simply because I had to head my diary with the date. I had been writing for more than an hour, when I was slightly startled by the sound of footsteps on the stairway. I went and looked down, but could not see anything. So I resumed my writing, and continued without interruption for nearly an hour. I looked around, and there, close beside my chair, stood the stately figure of Lady Jane. Her face was pale but comely, her features were finely shaped, and her manner was at once graceful and commanding.

"Some irresistible impulse led me to say, 'What are your desires—what are your commands?'

"Then I heard a whispered, but audible, 'Follow me,' and I followed.

"Lady Jane quickly descended the stairs, and I walked swiftly after her. On, on went Lady Jane, through several corridors and chambers, until we came to the top of the oaken staircase. On and out went my ghostly leader, and her occult influence compelled me to follow her footsteps. By this time I was perfectly calm and self-possessed. There was nothing to fear. Surely the phantom lady could not harm me, I had no dread of that. While mentally musing in this fashion, I became aware that Lady Jane was emerging from a back door on to the swamp. Then she quickened her pace, until I found that it was almost impossible to keep up with her.

"On, on, we went to the very far verge of the swampy land, upon which the autumnal moonlight gleamed sadly.

"'There!' exclaimed Lady Jane with a sigh, as she raised a warning finger, and pointed to a field beyond the morass. Then, in the twinkling of an eye, she vanished. I was alone. Alone in the midst of a desolate swamp, with only owls, night-hawks, and the bewildering will-o'-the-wisp for companions. The phantom had befooled me, and led me on for no purpose. Yet, I strode on into the field indicated by Lady Jane. As I did so, I saw two men meeting. The appearance of one was familiar to me. Presently, he turned round and confronted me. Great heavens! It was my kinsman Sir Thomas Stradling, second and only surviving son of the last Sir Edward Stradling! He pressed both his hands to his heart, while from a distance his companion looked—as I thought—heartlessly on.

"'Sir Thomas!' I cried, 'how came you here? I thought you were in France?' As I did so, I heard him exclaim in tones of suppressed anguish, these words, 'Too late—too late—but God bless you, my kinsman!' And

then he vanished. I was stunned. Clearly I
had seen my kinsman's spirit. I strode back
to Sutton, but, before I reached the great
entrance, I fell face foremost on the pathway.
I remember nothing more until I found myself
lying on the settle beside the fire. My host
declared he had found me prostrate on the
pathway. I had evidently stumbled, he said,
and there, in an unconscious condition, I was
found when he returned from Llandow. He
thought I had suffered from some kind of fit.
I never told him of my adventure, but allowed
everybody to take it for granted that a 'kind
of fit' was the cause of my bruised and black-
ened eye.

"Six weeks later the news reached St. Donats
that my kinsman, Sir Thomas Stradling, was
killed 'in a duel' at Montpelier in France, on
the 27th of September 1738.

"Lady Jane's visitation was truly an omen
to me of death, and I had seen the spirit of
Sir Thomas as it passed away from earth.

"Before Christmas I left St. Donats Castle,
only to return just now to complete a few un-
finished matters, and I shall have to remain
in Sutton for about a week before my departure
for Coombe Hawey."

On reaching Sutton the men parted company,
the younger man going onward to Llandow.

"Good-bye," said the young farmer. "I hope *I* shall never see the ghost of Lady Jane."

"I think you never will," responded the stranger, "seeing that quite recently, some godly men undertook to lay the ghost of the Lady of Sutton."

"For the King, or for Owen Glendower?"

1401

DARK, and gloomy, and frowning looked the castle and fortress of Dinas Bran. Moonbeams that glittered down in the valley failed to touch the ancient stronghold, where shadows lurked, and crows congregated, and moody-minded warriors waited the commands of their chieftain.

Down below, in the beautiful Vale of Llangollen, early summer roses shed their sweet wild petals among the tangles and thickets, and dew-drops sparkled upon the dying and dead May-blossoms, that drooped like melting snow-flakes in all the sheltered hollows.

Up above, among the grim grey rocks and crags around the wind-blown summit of the mighty mountain, a tall and stately man paced restlessly to and fro.

z

His men watched him with keen interest.

Too well they knew what troubled him—too well they understood the conflict that was going on in his mind.

Yet they did not blame him.

Mightier men than Howel Vychan had bowed down to Owen Glendower, who, in Sycharth, lived and reigned as the virtual if not the nominal King of Wales.

Howel, the last of the Vychans, or Vaughans of Dinas Bran, felt that he owed a debt of honour to Wales and the Welsh.

His ancestor, Gruffydd ap Madoc, retreated to Dinas Bran from the rage of his countrymen. Gruffydd caused the Welsh to rise in arms against him because of his marrying with Emma, the daughter of James, Lord Audley, who instigated him to side with Edward the First against his native sovereign and the princes of Wales.

From that time the Welsh had never trusted the owners of Dinas Bran.

Gruffydd ap Madoc had little rest in his almost inaccessible retreat. In a short time he became a weary, dispirited, remorseful, and conscience-stricken man, who eventually died of a broken heart because of his faithlessness to Wales.

His descendants in another branch took up

their residence at Dinas Bran, and firmly held the great British stronghold against Wales, and in favour of the English king.

Howell Vychan was the first to exhibit any feelings against the rights of ancient usage.

His heart was for Wales and freedom, but so far his sword had been for the King of England.

Sorrowful feelings overwhelmed his soul as he restlessly paced the narrow terrace of sward under the castle walls.

Down below all was peaceful.

In the vale he knew the nightingales were trilling mystic roundelays to the rising moon that crowned the eastern hills with splendour, while its radiance guarded the sacred Dee as with a shield of burnished silver.

Up above all was uncertain.

In the castle he knew his men openly were for the King of England, but he thought that of late many of them were secretly for Owen Glendower.

His thoughts perplexed him sorely, and, after pacing for some time alone up and down under the castle walls, he called his domestic bard to him.

· "Llew," he shouted, and forthwith a man old enough to be his own father approached. "Llew," he said, "I would consult with thee. Thou know'st or canst divine what is passing in my mind."

"I know," replied Llew.

"My mind wavers between two opinions. Sometimes, as of old, I lean towards the king, and yet—I confess my heart goes with Glendower. And ever and anon the question arises, Should I, a Welshman, and above all, a Vychan, stand by the King of England, or go forth and fight with Owen? My men appear to be for the English, but——"

"Secretly they are for Glendower," interrupted Llew.

"Dost thou in truth think so?" asked Howell eagerly.

"Shall I tell thee what hath passed within thy halls during the last few months? Shall I deliver over the secrets of others to thy keeping?"

"Ay!" exclaimed Howel.

"Let us wander downward to the mountain hollow where the first faint moonbeams creep, and the long crag shadows fall brokenly into the place of concealment," said the bard. "There shall we be safe from intrusion—safe from listening ears and spying eyes."

"I will do as thou dost wish," said Howell passively, for he loved Llew the hoary-haired bard.

In silence they descended the tortuous way from Castell Dinas Bran to the friendly hollow where silvery moonbeams strayed, and long shadows fell from the overhanging crags and rocks.

The warrior, fully clad in armour, looked a dark and sombre figure in the moonlight, that was pale and faint up there on the mountain heights. Llew, fully robed in the white and flowing robes of his office, looked like one of the Druids of old. His waving and silvery hair floated over his shoulders, and his long beard fell below his waist.

In a mossy corner of the hollow, a grey rock formed a pleasant and secluded seat, and there the men rested for consultation.

Howel Vychan was the first to break the silence.

" What hath passed in my halls of late—and what secrets have others from me ? "

There was a slight haughtiness in his tone, but Llew was accustomed to it, and merely said, " I will tell thee all. Since the early part of this year strange noises have been heard, and sundry tappings and rappings have disturbed the men in the armoury."

Howel Vychan knit his brows. He, too, had heard strange noises, and had been disturbed by curious tappings and rappings. But he kept his counsel.

" Further," continued Llew, " in rainy twilights of January, when the cloud-rack hung heavily over Dinas Bran, and the rifts were few, and the wind groaned hoarsely around the stronghold, a stranger, or spiritual visitor and not a mortal, was frequently seen to enter the castle and never went out."

" What dost thou mean ? " asked Howel.

" I mean this," said Llew.   " In the dusk of a day, when the wind howled among the mountains, and the rain beat mercilessly upon the stronghold, and the frightened crows in black and whirling crowds made unending noise and cawings over the towers, a stranger strode under the great gateway.   Without let or leave he entered the banqueting hall, and, as one accustomed to the castle, he crossed direct to the armoury, and there put off his visor and his armour.

Howel Vychan sighed.   He, too, had seen the stranger, and had watched him in the armoury.

" What next ? " asked Howell, still keeping his own secret.

" He never hath been seen to go out," said Llew.   " Thy men like not to tell thee, but they have confided in me."

" Did they give thee any word as to who the stranger might be ? " asked Howel.

" They did," replied Llew.   " Rhys, thy oldest man, said the stranger was the spirit-form of Gruffydd ap Madoc come up from his grave."

"Gruffydd ap Madoc?" questioned Howell.

"The same," replied Llew.

"How could Rhys know Gruffydd ap Madoc, who hath been dead over a hundred years?" asked Howel.

"By hearsay. My grandfather knew him well, and used to describe him, and the grandmother of Rhys was Gruffydd ap Madoc's cousin. Gruffydd was of medium height, thick set and muscular. His hair and eyes were as black as the raven's wing. His wife was small, fair, blue-eyed and English.

Llew paused, as if in contemplation.

"What more?" asked Howel earnestly.

Llew lowered his voice as though he feared the breeze of summer might overhear him, as he said, "Rhys told me that he made up his mind to speak to the stranger. One night, when an unusually severe storm raged, and Dinas Bran was enfolded in clouds, the stranger entered. In the banqueting hall the dim light of the log-fire glowed red upon the walls. The sleuth-hounds whined in their dreams, and the watch-dogs slept and snorted in the comforting warmth. Across the fire-glow that fell broadly from the hearth towards the centre of the room, the stranger went and stood for a moment where dark shadows congregated under the western wall. Crouching among the shadows in the hall, Rhys closely watched the stranger, who appeared to be quite at home. And, as Rhys looked, he saw the stranger going forward towards the hearth, where he seemed to be rubbing his hands and examining his sword. When Rhys stole quietly into the armoury, and crept to the far end thereof, and waited results, soon after, with slow and measured steps, the stranger entered, and in one corner he cast off his visor and his armour. Taking courage, Rhys said reverently, as one who wished not to vex the visitor, 'In the name of the Holy Mother, who art thou, and what dost thou want?' Gravely, and in deep-voiced tones, the stranger replied, 'I was Gruffydd ap Madoc, but now I am a restless wandering spirit from the regions of the unknown.' Then there was silence. 'In the name of the blessed Virgin Mary, what dost thou want?' asked Rhys. In a hoarse and far-off voice he answered, 'I want rest, right, and restitution. Rest will not come until the Vychans make restitution of their aid and force for Wales and the Welsh.' With that he vanished."

"Did Rhys ever see him again, or accost him?" asked Howel.

"He saw him again, and sees him now." replied Llew, "but he never accosts him."

"It is strange," said Howel to himself more than to Llew.

" It is," responded the bard.

" What is the meaning of the stranger's words ? " asked Howel.

" That is plain to see," said Llew. " The stranger cannot rest until the Vychans of Dinas Bran lend their aid and forces for the honour and freedom of Wales."

" In short," said Howel, " it means that I, the last of my race, must take a position for——"

" For the king, or Glendower — and that speedily," interrupted Llew.

The bard knew his words had gone home to Howel's heart like a sword-thrust, and, knowing it, he suggested that they should return to the castle.

In moody, almost gloomy silence, the two men returned to the stronghold.

Howel retired to a distant room, but the bard remained in the banqueting hall.

The last of the Vychans felt uneasy.

To break faith with the English king was to obliterate all the old usages of the family since the days of Edward the First. To go forth as a partisan of Glendower, was to step from a pinnacle of pride and ancient lineage to the feet of a Welsh gentleman, who, after all, was regarded as more or less of a rebel.

In the midst of his musing, Howel heard the voice of Llew, and, brokenly, from the distance, came the words of an ode by Iolo Goch.

Rich and sonorous was the recitation, forceful and persuasive were the words. First he lauded Owen's home in Sycharth. He described the " timber house " upon " four wooden columns," that raised his " mansion to the clouds," and, what was then most unusual, the dwelling had " smoke-ejecting chimneys " and " neatly glazed windows." In the words of an English translator—

> " All houses are in this compressed—
>   An orchard's near it of the best ;
>   Also a park, where, void of fear,
>   Feed antler'd herds of fallow deer, . . .
>   Of goodly steeds a countless host.
>   Meads where for hay the clover grows,
>   Corn-fields which hedges trim enclose ;
>   A mill, a rushing brook upon,
>   And pigeon-tower framed of stone ;
>   A fish-pond, deep and dark to see,
>   To cast nets in when need there be. . . .
>   Of various plumage birds abound,
>   Herons and peacocks haunt around.
>   What luxury doth this hall adorn,
>   Showing of cost a sovereign scorn. . . .
>   His mansion is the minstrels' home,
>   You'll find them there whene'er you come. . .
>   His bairns approach me pair by pair,
>   Oh what a nest of chieftains fair ! . . .
>   Here difficult it is to catch
>   A sight of either bolt or latch ; . . .
>   And ne'er shall thirst or hunger rude
>   In Sycharth venture to intrude ! "

Then he recited snatches of Iolo Goch's ode to Glendower as "crowned King of Wales."

In the words of the English translator they run thus—

> "All praise to him who forth doth stand
> To 'venge his injured native land ! . . .
> In him are blended portents three,
> Their glories blended sung shall be .
> There's Owen, meteor of the glen,
> The head of princely generous men ;
> Owain, the lord of trenchant steel,
> Who makes the hostile squadrons reel ;
> Owain, besides, of warlike look,
> A conqueror who no stay will brook. . .
> The scourger of the flattering race
> For them a dagger has his face ;
> Each traitor false he loves to smite,
> A lion is he for deeds of might. . . .
> Hail to the valley's belted king !
> Hail to the widely conquering—
> The liberal, hospitable, kind,
> Trusty and keen as steel refined ! . . .
> Of Horsa's seed on hill and plain,
> Four hundred thousand he has slain. . . .
> Hail to this partisan of war,
> This bursting meteor flaming far !"

A long pause succeeded the recitation, and Howel heard his men-at-arms begging Llew to sing a song.

"What shall I sing ?" asked the bard.

"A song of thine own," clamoured the men.

Llew pondered awhile.

Then he said, " We all remember ill-starred Hoel ap Einion."

They did.

Hoel ap Einion, a young bard, fell in love with the celebrated Welsh beauty, proud My-vanwy Vychan, who in 1380 lived at Dinas Bran. She was a cousin of Howel Vychan, present lord of the stronghold.   Many still remembered that the beautiful and haughty Myvanwy disdainfully treated the bard, who eventually died broken-hearted.   Two of the old melodies of Wales were known as "Ffarwel Ednyfed Vychan," and " Castell Towyn."   Both were in commemoration of Hoel's death.

" My heart aches when I think of Hoel," said Llew tenderly, as he dashed a few tears from his eyes, and in memory of him, I have composed my song called ' Ffarwel Myvanwy Vychan.' "

The men-at-arms were touched.

They remembered Myvanwy at Dinas Bran, and too well they knew that her disdain caused the death of Hoel ap Einion.

Llew took his harp, and after an appropriate prelude he sang—

> " ' Ffarwel, Myvanwy Vychan ! '   Dear
>   The flowers are slowly dying,
> And in the autumn of the year
>   Like lost hopes they are lying.

And this is what I sing all day—
'My heart is sad and lonely ;
The joys of life have passed away,
You come in visions only !'

"'Ffarwel, Myvanwy Vychan !' Now
The rime of winter chills me ;
The snows are falling on my brow,
And thy cold slighting kills me.
And this is what I sing all day—
'My heart is sad and lonely ;
The joys of life have passed away,
You smile in visions only !'

"'Ffarwel, Myvanwy Vychan !' Time
Will heal my heart of sorrow ;
But when age brings its silver rime
Love's light you fain would borrow.
And you will sigh through many a day—
'My heart is sad and lonely ;
But Hoel, he has passed away,
He comes in visions only !'

" In tangles of the sweet wild rose
The bard has found his guerdon,
There death has given him sweet repose,
And eased him of love's burden.
His voice is silent, and his lay
Of life both sad and lonely,
Like summer flowers has passed away,
He lives in memory only !"

Tears followed the song, and silence deep and
profound fell upon all present.

The men's emotions were roused, and even the stern soldiers sympathised with the unfortunate bard, whose farewell to his ladye-love had been tenderly sung by the renowned poet of Dinas Bran.

During the singing of the song, Howel ap Vychan had been a moody listener, and in the silence that followed, he went without thinking into the armoury.

Had he for a moment thought of the stranger, he would have retired to rest—if repose he could expect to get when his brain throbbed and his heart ached in an agony of great unrest.

Seated on one of the carved oaken benches of that period, Howel paused to think over the struggle that racked his mind, and made thought like a whirlwind for wildness.

He stayed there so long, that when he looked out into the night, the full moon was high in the heavens.   As he prepared to retire, the sound of footsteps coming from the banqueting-room, through the corridor leading to the armoury, arrested his attention.

At first he thought it might be one of his retainers, but when the great and massive oaken door of the armoury swung open, he saw it was the stranger.

Howel trembled with fear, and sank down upon the bench again.

He thought to address the stranger, but was tongue-tied by dread.

Indescribable horror made him shake from head to foot as he watched the stranger removing his visor and his sword, and then setting aside his armour.

There was no necessity for Howel Vychan to speak.

Slowly, deliberately, and with a stately step, the stranger advanced a pace or two towards the lord of Dinas Bran.

Howel Vychan felt as though the hand of death was upon him, and that the fatal and last grip of life almost relinquished his hold.

"Give me rest!" exclaimed the stranger. "Give me peace. There is no rest—no peace—even in the grave!"

The voice sounded as though it came from the depths of a cavern.

Howel Vychan shook like an aspen leaf.

"It is in thy power to give both," continued the stranger, "and both rest and peace I must and will have."

The stranger's tones were decisive.

Then Howel Vychan mustered up courage to speak, although his words were tremulous with fear.

"What would'st thou have me to do?" he asked hoarsely.

"Fight with the Welsh for Wales and freedom," said the stranger.

A long pause followed, during which the stranger paced the armoury as if waiting for a definite answer.

Howel Vychan's will struggled with his weakness for the mastery. Was he to battle against his will, and in the end allow his weakness to overcome and keep him pledged to stand by the King of England, while Wales, dear Wales, fought for freedom?"

Then he said to himself, "The time has come. It must be one thing or the other, and which is it to be—for the king, or for Glendower?"

"Answer!" exclaimed the stranger in an almost angry tone, at the same time lifting high above his head a sword, the blade of which glittered unnaturally in the uncertain moonlight.

It appeared as if the stranger had read Howel's inmost thoughts.

The uplifted sword, the stern command, awed Howel, who slowly and deliberately responded, "It shall be for Glendower and Wales."

"Dost thou faithfully promise?" asked the stranger.

"I faithfully promise," responded Howel earnestly.

"When thou dost fulfil thy promise, I will

rest in peace, and trouble thy household no longer," said the stranger.

When Howel dared to glance upward he found that the stranger had vanished, and the door of the armoury was shut.

Early next morning Howel requested Llew to see that all his men were assembled in the great courtyard before the hour of noon.

The men wondered what was going to happen. Had King Henry the Fourth sent for his powerful ally Howel Vychan?

Not a man could tell.

Did Llew know why they were thus mustered together?

The bard had not the least knowledge of his lord's intentions.

Just before the hour of noon Howel Vychan, clad in full armour, strode manfully into the presence of his men.

In a few words he told them of his altered feelings—how he felt that it was his duty to aid in the protection of Wales and the Welsh against the King of England, and how Llew was to go to Sycharth forthwith and inform Glendower of his intentions.

"Now," exclaimed Howel Vychan, "I must know which it is to be with you—for Wales or England. Those who wish to remain loyal to the King of England can peaceably quit

2 A

Castell Dinas Bran during the day.   Those who
are willing to stand by me, and join Glendower,
will remain here.   Question them, Llew."

The bard ascended the horse-block, and in clear,
stentorian voice cried out, " Answer now.   Which
is it to be—for the king, or for Owen Glendower?"

As one man all the warriors replied, " For
Howel Vychan and Owen Glendower!"

Loud cheers rang around Dinas Bran, and the
echoes thereof descended into the mountain hollows far below.

In the afternoon Llew departed for Sycharth,
and two days afterwards, he returned with the
request that Howel Vychan would visit the leader
of the revolt.

Three days later Howel Vychan was enrolled
in the list of Owen Glendower's supporters.   The
lord of Dinas Bran was, in a remote way, a rela-
tive of Owen Glendower.

Of the great Welsh leader, Hollinshed's Chronicles contain the following particulars, which
may be interesting to those who are unacquainted
with the stern opponent of King Henry the
Fourth :—" This Owen Glendower was son to
an esquire of Wales named Griffith Wichan
(Gruffydd Vychan); he dwelled in the parish
of Conwaie (Corwen), within the county of
Merioneth, in North Wales, in a place called
Glendourdwie, which is as much as to say in

English, as the valley by the side of the water of Dee, by occasion whereof he was surnamed Glindour Dew."

According to Hollinshed, "In 1402 Owen Glendower (with his Welshmen) fought with the Lord Grey of Ruthin, coming forth to defend his possessions, which the same Owen wasted and destroyed; and as the fortune of that day's work fell out, the Lord Grey was taken prisoner, and many of his men were slain. This hap lifted the Welshmen into high pride, and increased marvellously their wicked and presumptuous attempts."

Soon after this Edmund Mortimer, Earl of March, was defeated, and afterwards became Owen's ally.

Hollinshed then quaintly states: " About the mid of August, the king, to chastise the presumptuous attempts of the Welshmen, went with a great power of men into Wales, to pursue the Welsh captain, Owen Glendower, but, in fact, lost his labour; for Owen conveyed himself out of the way into his known lurking places, and (as was thought), through art magic, he caused such foul weather of winds, tempest, rain, snow, and hail to be raised for the annoyance of the king's army, that the like had not been heard of."

In the Chronicles of Adam of Usk—who

studied law in London with Owen Glendower,
and afterwards entering the Church, went on a
pilgrimage to Rome—Owen is styled "Oenus,
dominus de Glendordee." Adam of Usk says
about the defeat and capture of Lord Grey de
Ruthin :—"At so great a blow thus given by
Owen to the English rule, when I think thereon
my heart trembles. For, begirt by 30,000 men,
who issued from their lairs throughout Wales
and its marches, he overthrew the castles, among
which were Usk, Caerleon, and Newport, and
fired the towns. In short, like a second Assy-
rian, the rod of God's anger, he did deeds of
unheard-of tyranny with fire and sword. These
things I heard of at Rome."

In other parts of the "Chronicon Adæ," it
is stated that Henry the Fourth intended sup-
pressing the Welsh language altogether, and
that in the deadly campaign of 1401, more
than a thousand children were carried off into
English bondage.

After many brilliant victories, Glendower in
1402 held his celebrated assembly in the old
dwelling still known as the Parliament House,
in the Eastern Street, Machynlleth, and there
the great leader of Welsh insurrection was
crowned King of Wales.

Owen was then accompanied by the venerable bard Iolo Goch, who saw in his hero the

fulfilment of an old prophecy, in which it stated that a prince of the race of Cadwaladr should rule the Britons after emancipating them from Saxon thraldom.

In that assembly Dafydd Gam, the Fluellin of Shakespeare, endeavoured to assassinate Owen, but was frustrated. For this offence, Gam was seized and sent to a prison among the mountains above Sycharth.

Later on Owen, passing through Breconshire, totally destroyed Gam's house called Cyringwen, situated near the river Honddu.

In the autumn of 1403 Owen Glendower went to South Wales, and foremost in the battles was Howel Vychan. Cardiff, Swansea, Coity, Penmark, Llandaff, and Caerleon suffered badly from the ravages of the war. The siege of Coity was very serious. That castle was then in the possession of Alexander Berkrolles, the surviving representative of the "fighting Turbervilles." Tidings of this reached the king, who ordered his sons, Prince Henry and "Lord Thomas," to raise the siege of Coity. On the thirteenth of November the king issued mandates to the sheriffs of Warwick, Worcester, Gloucester, and other counties to provide a contingent each of twenty men-at-arms, and two hundred archers to join the army of his sons.

On March the eleventh, 1405, the celebrated

battle of Grosmont was fought. It was one of the most disastrous events in the whole of Owen's campaign. Between 800 and 1000 brave men were slain, and most of them were rebels of Glamorgan and Brecon. Owen was not present at Grosmont, but the reverse caused him to assemble all his remaining strength as soon as possible to try and atone for the loss.

This brings again to the front the brave and sturdy Howel ap Vychan, the lord of Dinas Bran.

March 15, 1405.

Swiftly through the afternoon air arrows darted in every direction, and a wild wind, blowing downward from the Breconshire mountains, fanned the faces of the warriors, who were hot and feverish with the terrible exertion caused by the fray.

"The day waxes," exclaimed Owen Glendower, still bravely standing in the front, "and I fear me the enemy will overcome."

"Press on!" shouted Howel Vychan, quitting Glendower's side for a moment to give directions to the men-at-arms, who were heroically struggling for the mastery.

During the morning the wind arose to a gale, in the afternoon its strength waned, and towards sunset scarcely a breeze could be felt.

To spare the English reader, the name of the locality is here once given, and need not be repeated. It is known in Welsh history as Mynyddypwllmelyn, in Breconshire.

Hard and fast in the ruddy sunset, Owen Glendower and his men attacked the king's army.

Now and again Howel Vychan turned to urge his comrades.

"On—Welshmen, on !" he cried, and with renewed inspiration the men-at-arms and the archers pressed forward.

It was a wild scene of disorder.

The king's army was very powerful, and as time passed, Owen Glendower and his supporters felt that the chances were going against them.

When the sunset deepened into night the truth was known.

Owen Glendower had lost—Henry the Fourth had won.

Grand, heroic, serene under defeat, Owen Glendower, leaning on his sword, paused for a while to look upon the scene and the loss of his latest hopes.

"Undone !" cried the great leader of insurrection to Howel Vychan.

"Alas !" replied Howel, "we were too weak. And yet—our men were brave !"

Owen Glendower sighed.

There in the shadows, his brother Tudor was numbered among the slain.

Just a pace beyond, Owen's son stood among the prisoners.

Fifteen hundred of Glendower's men were taken prisoners or slain.

It was a scene to make even the intrepid Welsh leader quail.

With a great sob, and a mighty sigh, Owen Glendower, turning to Howel Vychan, exclaimed, " It is craven-hearted to say so, but we must flee ! There is no help for us. Perhaps— but who can tell ?—in a distant day we shall arise with renewed strength and fight again for home, for Wales, and freedom ! "

Howel Vychan could only grasp his friend by the hand and say—" Whither thou goest will I go. I follow wherever thou would'st lead."

As the twilight deepened into night, Owen Glendower, accompanied by Howel Vychan and a few trusty and faithful followers, hastened from the scene of action.

In the first of the dark days, the party remained as outcasts in Glamorganshire. They had to shelter in caves, in secluded woodlands, and other hiding-places. The Dinas Rock in the Neath Valley, is pointed out by tradition as one of his hiding-places.

Then came the saddest part of all.

Deserted by everybody excepting Howel Vychan and a few other friends, Owen Glendower wandered among desolate neighbourhoods in order to secrete himself from the king.

Now he paused among the wild wastes of Plinlimmon, then he sought sanctuary among the rocks of Moel Hebog, and in time he reached a cave on the Merionethshire coast, about one mile north from the river Dysynny. That cavern has ever since been known as Ogof Owain or Owain's Cave.

It was evening.

On the white-crested waves of Cardigan Bay, the last flush of the crimson sunset cast rosy flecks, that contrasted vividly with the dark silver-green depths of the waters.

White-winged birds circled under the clear blue sky, and wheeled in the wake of the porpoises that sported themselves out at sea.

In Owain's Cave the shadows were dark, gloomy, and foreboding.

Three men alone were there.

Owen—worn with sorrow and broken-hearted —had lived to see his beloved Sycharth a fire-scathed ruin, and all his possessions seized by the king, and Howel Vychan survived to lament the loss of Dinas Bran.

After days of fasting and exposure to the

winds and weather, the brave Howel was seized by a fever, and there, in the loneliness of Owain's Cave, he lay prone and helpless under the care of his friend, the great but defeated Welsh leader, and a trusty man named Hugh.

"I fear he cannot survive," said Hugh, as the tears rolled down his deeply-furrowed face.

"Alas! and he hath been faithful unto death," sighed Owen. "Many a time when the sword hath been nigh to my heart, Howel hath averted it. Many a night when provision was short, Howell hath gone without to give unto me. Many a day when my lips were parched, and my tongue clave to the roof of my mouth, Howel hath foregone a much-needed draught of cooling water to give unto me!"

Glendower and Hugh sobbed together and aloud.

"What is it? make speed!" cried Howel in his quick and impatient Welsh way.

Glendower and Hugh tried to soothe him.

"I will fight," exclaimed Howel. "I will fight to the last. On men—on—press forward . . . For home—for Wales—for freedom!"

Then he sank back exhausted.

Just as the first faint rays of the rising moon glimmered across the waves of Cardigan Bay, and the shadows were growing deeper and darker in Owain's Cave, Howel Vychan once more stirred in his feverish slumbers.

"On Welshmen—on!" he cried. Press forward!
. . . Now—now . . . The fight is fought . . .
The battle is won ! . . . Not for the King . . .
For home . . . for Wales . . . and for . . .
Glendower !"

Then, like a tired child, with a deep and weary
sigh, he sank back upon his rude resting place,
and died.

There, in loneliness and sorrow, Owen Glendower wept as only a brave and strong man
can weep, while Hugh mournfully and tenderly
performed the last kindly offices for their dead
comrade.

"He is gone!" sighed Glendower. "And with
him go my long last hopes."

And once more he wept aloud.

In the golden radiance of the rising moon, in
sight and sound of the sea, the mortal remains
of the faithful Welshman were buried.

There ever the great sea sobs in winter, and the
autumn winds chaunt their saddest requiems.
There the song birds sing in the long summer
days, while the dirge of the wavelets sounds like
mysterious music ; and there, until "there shall
be no more sea," the silver sands will conceal
all that remains of the brave and faithful Howel
Vychan of Dinas Bran.

Pip, Flush, and Flanders

IP is an old house standing on the left-hand side of the rugged road leading seaward.

Flush stands exactly on the opposite side of the roadway.

Flanders is a hundred yards beyond its neighbours, and it has the advantage of being on sloping ground directly facing the morning sunshine.

Flush and Flanders only retain their ancient names. Pip is now known as the White House.

In the days of old, the three dwellings were only known as Pip, Flush, and Flanders.

Even the most rare and antique MSS. and documents bearing upon the subject, fail to clear up the meaning of the word Pip. Some have said it means Peep, other authorities regard it as Pip, which term the Welsh even now apply to anything small, such as a " pip of cheese," or a " pip," meaning a little piece of butter.

Flush was an abbreviation of Flushing, in Holland, and Flanders was so named after that province in Belgium.

The three houses were originally occupied by the Flemings.

These were the Flemings who emigrated to England, after the disastrous floods that inundated their own low-lying country in the twelfth century. Some of the Flemings settled at, and gave a name to, the village called Flemingstone, in Glamorgan, and quite likely the owners of Pip, Flush, and Flanders were offshoots of those families.

As time rolled on the property passed into other hands, and with the exception of the name in one or two families, not a trace of the ancient Flemings remained.

Vestiges of their art survived them for many centuries, but in time the weavers became extinct in this part of Wales.

In the seventeenth century, when witches were as plentiful as blackberries, and genuine wizards were few, an ancient dame, who bore the reputation of being conversant with the "black art," lived in a cottage known as the thirteenth century Monastery Gate-house.

All the good people dwelling in the neighbourhood were afraid of the old woman, who by common report was said to plague the three

Flemish houses more than any other in the
town. Some declared it was because Rachel
Flemynge bore in her blood traces of those old
settlers, whose descendants wasted their patri-
mony, and brought the reputed witch's great-
grandfather to beggary.

The inhabitants of the town were ashamed of
Rachel Flemynge.

Llaniltyd Vawr—or the " Sacred place of Iltyd
the Great," as it is translated into English,
although in the present day it is only known
as Llantwit Major—was always an eminently
respectable town. Somebody—English, of course
—slightingly described it as a "large village or
dilapidated town," and the people rose up in
arms. That the town of St. Iltutus, the site of
the fifth century and first Christian college in
Britain, the place sanctified by the footsteps of
St. Paul the Apostle, should be spoken of irre-
verently was, and is, more than the inhabitants
respectively of the past or present could or can
endure.

Pilgrims, students, and antiquarian nomads
of old—tourists and archæological societies of
to-day—and visitors from all parts of the world
even in these last years of a busy century—came
and come simply to inspect the antiquities of the
place. These include ecclesiastical structures and
domestic architecture of the twelfth, thirteenth,

and fifteenth centuries, while the great age of
the Llantwit crosses puzzles even the most
learned antiquarians, who contradict each other
with amazing pertinacity, and come to endless
squabbles on the subject.

To return to the three ancient houses.

In the year 1668 Pip was occupied by Edward
·Vanne, a descendant of the Vannes of the old
Manor Place at Llantwit. Flush was the residence of James Adam, the ancestor of whom is
thus described in Leland's Itinerary: "A little
from the Ripe is Castleton, a Manor Place on
a Hille ascending . . . it longged to one Hugh
Adam, a man of mene Landes. . . ." Flanders
was the abode of the widow and only son of
of Thomas Giles, and of his ancestor Leland
gives the following account :—"Half a mile by
the West Ripe standeth a Pile or Manor Place
called Gilestown and Village of the same
Name. . . . One Giles, a gentleman of an
ancient House yet having a Hundreth Markes
of Lande by the Yere, is Lorde of it."

. . . . . .

Towards sunset, on the eve of the 1st of
May 1668, those who still were accustomed to
kindle the Beal, Baal, or Beltane fire, in honour
of Beli, the Emperor of the Sun, repaired to the
great British encampment known as the Castle
Ditches, overlooking Colhugh Point, the rocks

of which stretch forth hungrily into the Severn Sea.

One of the men who helped in the work was a dreamy individual, who either rejoiced or lamented in being gifted with second sight.

Stephen Gamage, as he collected driftwood on the solitary shore, looked westward towards the sunset. His thoughts reverted to druidical lore, and the ancient days when the Druids paid adoration to Dwyvan and Dwyvach, the only survivors of the apocryphal Deluge; to Hu Gadarn, "who first showed the race of the Cymry the method of cultivating the ground;" to Ceridwen and her mystic cauldron, to Gwyn ap Nudd, master of the great Unknown, and to Beli, the Monarch of the Sun.

He pictured to himself the long-bearded Druids clothed in snowy vestments, and followed by the Roman warriors with their short and sharp two-edged swords and glittering helmets. In imagination, he heard the mingled sounds of wretched groans, shouts of rage, and the dull awful noise of bardic bodies hurled over precipices and rocks. Fancy led, he thought that the black staves of an ancient landing place or stage were the remains of Roman soldiers, who in ages gone were turned into stone for having persecuted the Druids. In his days, as in ours, those hardy wooden staves standing in the teeth of the storms, were known by some as the " Roman soldiers," by others as the " Black Men."

Stephen's thoughts went back to still more remote ages, of which he had heard much, and, in an imperfect way, had read a little ; of days when, in Wales, as an old chronicler records, " Dark forests of spruce and pine frowned on the mountains, save where the peaks were so elevated that they wore all winter long a mantle of snow. Savage and desolate heaths were spread out here, undulating and richly-clothed prairies there. The beaver constructed his dams across the streams ; the tail-less hare of Siberia sported over the plains ; the Lithuanian bison and the forest ox . . . fed in countless herds. Deer of incredible stretch of antlers were in the wastes ; the reindeer, the Artic elephant . . . the Siberian rhinoceros . . . roamed through the country in the winter time. Horses like those of the Tartarian steppes, foxes and wolves, wild boars and bears, shared with them the possession of the soil. . . . With every advancing summer came droves of migratory animals from the South, amongst which the lion, a kind of leopard now unknown, and hyænas . . . bore the sway."

Stephen was aroused from his reverie by Richard Flemynge, brother to Rachel, the re-

2 B

puted witch, who said abruptly, "Thee dost see,
or pretend to see, the future. Now, dost thou
know what manner of death I myself shalt die?"

"I do," replied Stephen.

"What is it?" asked Richard.

"A death that thou and thy people would
think the least likely," replied Stephen.

Richard Flemynge endeavoured to get Stephen
Gamage to explain his meaning, but the man
would not.

Then they toiled upward along the heights to
the British encampment.

In those days the steep eastern hill above
Colhugh was almost covered with dense thickets
of hazel, through which winding pathways led
to the summit. Among the deep entrenchments
where the blackberry brambles fell in long trails,
the may-blossoms looked like snow upon the
thorn bushes, and the fresh green leaves of the
hazels appeared like emeralds in the glow of
sunset.

On the summit of the hill, between the entrenchments and the western cliff-line, there is a
broad plateau of grass, and in the centre thereof
the people prepared the Beltane fire.

Tow and tar-smeared faggots were highly
piled together, and surrounded by dry driftwood, of which willing hands brought a large
store.

Then the people waited, gazing eagerly as the sun, like a ball of liquid fire, sank behind the western hills.

Slowly, like weary pilgrims, the last rays of the setting sun descended into the horizon, and as the carmine light faded among the distant cloud-folds, Stephen Gamage lighted the Beltane fire. Almost simultaneously, on each neighbouring eminence and promontory along the Severn Sea, on the heights of Porlock and the Quantock ranges on the English side, and on every high hill throughout Wales, Beltane fires burned and blazed in the waning daylight.

Just before twilight deepened into night, and as the May moon arose slowly from the east, those who congregated around the Beltane fire commenced dancing and singing wild roundelays. Old and young alike joined in the remnants of those mysterious rites and orgies with which the ancient Britons propitiated the sun.

In the seventeenth century these festivities consisted chiefly of weird songs and morris dances, and orgies more or less ludicrous and grotesque.

When the revelry was in its zenith, a dark, thin, and small figure ascended the ridges and approached the crowd.

It was Rachel Flemynge, the reputed witch.

At her coming those who saw her instantly turned the thumbs of each hand inward, and closed their fingers firmly upon them. Rachel, muttering and shrugging her shoulders, hurried towards the fire. As she passed on, the crowd made way for her, so that their garments should not touch hers.

In the strange and weird light of the Beltane fire, those who stood nearest the blaze appeared to be magnified, and the most marked figure in the multitude was that of Rachel Flemynge.

She was a small, thin woman, whose features still bore many traces of former beauty, though the nose and chin were pointed, and promised to draw nearer with age. Her eyes were bright and sparkling, and her movements were still active, although she was sixty. In her hands she held a stick, which she carried more to help her over the rugged heights and rough roads than for the support of age.

As she approached the fire some of the men started suddenly from her.

"Ye needn't draw back as if a snake had stung the lot of you," said Rachel sharply, as she went forward, and, taking up a large stick, poked the Beltane fire therewith.

Suddenly, from the centre of the pyre, the flames shot upward, and a shower of sparks fell like hail upon the multitude. In a moment dancing and song ceased, and the people stood spellbound, as a dark column of smoke ascended to the sky, where the May moon, veiled by soft evening mists, shone in chastened splendour.

Another shower of sparks fell among the crowd, and then half-a-dozen men rushed towards Rachel Flemynge.

"Burn her !" shouted the multitude. "Burn her for a witch !"

The people crowded around her, and two of the men seized the unfortunate woman, who was powerless in their grasp.

"Scratch her !" cried some of the women. "Get a few drops of the beldame's blood."

"Ay !" almost yelled the youths as in one voice; "a few drops of her black blood would be a boon."

"And stop her baneful workings," shouted the old men.

It was a wild and startling scene.

Dense clouds of smoke darkened the air, and bright sparks of fire fell in almost ceaseless showers of mingled red and yellow colours.

In the midst of the confusion the crowd surged hither and thither. Now the people swayed around Rachel Flemynge, then they surged in dangerous proximity to the Beltane fire. Yells, hisses, and hootings rang through the evening air, and as the multitude clamoured around the woman, every voice was raised against her.

"Burn her! Burn her for a witch!" was the cry.

At that moment, slowly, but determinedly, Stephen Gamage pushed his way through the crowd.

"Let the woman alone!" he exclaimed, and the men instantly relinquished their hold of Rachel Flemynge.

"Let her alone!" he repeated in a stentorian voice, before which all the people present quailed.

"She but thrust a log into the fire, and thereby, with spirited touch, did what those of old would have done had they been in her place. It is considered ill-luck to let the Beltane fire smoulder or go out. Rachel Flemynge, I beseech thee, follow me."

Rachel obeyed, and the crowd parting, made a pathway for the reputed witch and her protector Stephen Gamage.

Wending their way downward from the Castle Ditches, Rachel and Stephen were soon concealed from sight by the hazels that filled the ridges sloping towards the meadows.

Meanwhile, the people resumed their dances and singing, and some of the rougher classes indulged in strange but harmless buffoonery.

It was midnight before the crowd dispersed, and wearied out, went homeward.

Soon afterwards, Stephen Gamage returned to watch with the others, and replenish the Beltane fire, which was not allowed to expire.

"Why dost thou always take the part of the witch?" asked one of the company, addressing Stephen.

"Because I think her wrongly and shamefully treated," replied Stephen.

"And partly because thou'rt something like kin of hers," remarked Richard Flemynge.

"How so?" questioned a neighbour.

"The people call Rachel a witch, and all of us know that Stephen is a man of second sight," responded Richard.

"True, true," said the company in a chorus.

"It is not because of that," said Stephen decidedly. "How would ye all like your women-kind served so? We are all sons of mothers; some of ye are husbands of wives and brothers of good sisters. Would we like them to be hustled and held in inhuman grip, and well-nigh thrust living into the Beltane fire?"

Stephen spoke almost savagely as he knit his bushy brows, and tightly compressed his lips.

In silence, the other men stirred and replenished the fire, and then stretched their bodies forth on the grass, therefrom to see that the embers should not expire.

While the moon was still in its zenith, the watchers fell soundly asleep, and Stephen Gamage was left to keep his vigil alone.

He sauntered away from the verge of the lofty cliffs wherefrom he could gaze downward to and across the Severn Sea, and at the same time watch the Beltane fire.

In the soft haze of night and moonlight, Stephen became, as was his wont, dreamy and thoughtful. Fancy portrayed the past, when Druids wandered on new-moon nights through the groves of oak, or went in search of the healing and magical vervain, or dewy selago, and the three-leaved samolus, or paused to plant and transplant roots and herbs, together with seeds sown when the moon was on the increase.

He thought of dim, mysterious nights, when the air was heavy with the breath of battle, and the Druids invoked Taranis in the grim shadows that surrounded rude and primitive altars. His mind reverted to frosty nights in winter when the stars glittered in the dark blue heavens, and the Druids, Bards, and Ovates, with priestly pomp and ceremony, went forth to cut down the sacred mistletoe, the juice of which was supposed to cure the most deadly wound of spear or arrow. Then he recalled what he had read about the strange ceremonies and rites in connection with the anguinium or serpent's egg, which, according to tradition, protected the finder from danger, and in some instances from death.

Sometimes he paused in his reverie to replenish the Beltane fire, or to gaze dreamily at the moon as it went slowly westward.

To him there were magic and witchery in the scene, as the setting moon dropped like a silver ball behind the dark western hills, and the pale, tremulous light of morning made a rift in the eastern cloud-folds.

Stephen Gamage, the man of second sight, standing on the verge of the grey cliffs overlooking the grey sea, recited to himself the "Druid's Dirge" and the "Bard's Lament."

PART I.

THE DIRGE.

"It is too late! for twilight's solemn splendour
　　Is waning, and the moments in their flight,
Like weary warriors, full sadly render
　　Their numbers to the roll-call of the night.

It is too late! My soul is weary, yearning
　　For the grey gleam of dawn upon the rills;
It is too late! behold the gloom is turning
　　To golden sunrise on the morning hills.

My soul is sad! a gentle sound of sighing
　　Tells me the world is lost—the fight unwon;
Yet death upon his way here to me winging,
　　Catches a sweet smile from the rising sun.

My soul is sad ! How many hours beside ye
I have gone forth, but now must go alone,
With none to utter welcome, none to guide me
Through the dark star-ways to a realm unknown.

So ends my life ! From thee and all I sever
In anguish *too* sublime for earthly plaint.
So ends my life ! Alone, now and for ever !
Farewell ! The world recedes ! My soul grows faint !"

Part II.

THE LAMENT.

" Long years, ay many, we have roam'd beside him,
O'er ways and paths that we anew must tread,
And though wide realms of mystery divide him
Now from our sight, we cannot deem him dead !
We held him in our arms while life was failing,
In close embrace, and watch'd his fluttering breath,
While the dim moonbeams in the west were paling,
And day-dawn veiled the awful calm of death !
In morning light we saw then and for ever,
The grandeur of his spirit and its power,
E'en as his mortal vestment seem'd to sever,
We saw the immortal bursting into flower !"

When Stephen concluded the recitation of these
lines, he covered his face with his hands and
wept aloud.

As he looked up, the East was glowing with
rose-colour and gold, and the king-like sun
arose in all his splendour as a triumphant

and victorious warrior, who had vanquished the monarch Night and his minions.

With the first gleam of sunshine the Beltane fire expired, and soon afterwards only a heap of smouldering embers remained to mark the place where, with strange orgies, grotesque dances, and wild songs, the people had celebrated the eve of the first of May.

Stephen Gamage roused the sleepers, and could not refrain from taunting them as to the manner in which they had fulfilled the vigil.

Descending from the Castle Ditches, the company entered the meadows, and were going homeward, when they suddenly encountered a bevy of merry maidens gaily trooping seaward, apparently in quest of something.

"What do they seek?" queried one of the Beltane fire watchers.

"Dost thou not know what their quest is?" asked Stephen Gamage.

"How should I? 'Tis not long since I came to these parts," was the retort.

"Then know, once and for all," replied Stephen, "that these fair maidens are come in quest of May dew. 'Tis said that the dew collected on the first morning of May is a greater beautifier than all the dew of the month, although dew at any time, especially in the spring and summer solstices, is wonderfully efficacious in clearing the skin of all imperfections, especially of freckles. Besides which, it makes the skin smooth and fair."

"Thou should'st write a 'Book of Beauty,'" said one of the girls, overhearing him.

"Or else give directions for a small fee, after the fashion of the leech," remarked another.

"Thy skin is fair for a Welshman, Stephen. P'rhaps thee dost use May dew, and can personally testify as to its virtue," joked one of the men.

"My skin is fair, because, on my mother's side, I claim descent from the Scotch, while my brown hair is obtained from my father's people, who were all dark, and, in some cases, swarthy."

Thus talking and musing, the men went to their homes, where generous repasts waited their coming.

Meanwhile the maidens bathed their faces freely in the May dew, which was allowed to dry on the skin instead of being washed off.

The troop of merry girls had another object in view, in sauntering through the meadows early on that beautiful May morning. It was an old woman's story, that if a maiden took a piece of the charred wood remaining after the Beltane fire, and set it under her pillow at night, she would see her future husband, either in a vision or in a dream.

Therefore, when the May dew had dried upon the faces of the maidens, they ascended the Castle Ditches, and from around the still smouldering Beltane fire, each one gathered a piece of charred wood, and therewith returned home. Upon reaching the town, they parted, but not before each maiden had faithfully promised to relate the result of the mystic vision or dream of May.

PIP.

In one of the upper rooms of the house, over which a vine cast its traceries of pale green leaves and curling tendrils, Dorothy Vanne was busy at work preparing a wonderful skin lotion, and on the table before her was the following written recipe :—

Of elder-flower water brewed last year, .	3 parts.
May dew, ...	1 part.
Of water in which bruised almonds hath been steeped for six days	1 part.
Rose water, ...	1 part.

As Dorothy carefully amalgamated these ingredients in a large white ware bowl, she thought deeply of Owen Giles of Flanders.

Unfortunately, many maidens shared her sentiments.

Owen Giles was a finely built man, standing

about six feet without his shoes. He was fair-haired, and grey-eyed, and, above all, his gay and lively gallantry were almost a proverb in the neighbourhood. He, a childless widower, lived alone with his widowed mother.

Dorothy Vanne was a dark-eyed brunette beauty, whose pride and hauteur were matters of remark. But her friends and partisans excused her pride, on the ground that her ancestors were formerly owners of a dwelling then known as the Manor, the ruins of which are still called the Old Place. Fallen fortunes during the Civil War had brought her father to Pip, which, though a house of some importance, was, after all, not quite the residence for " one of the Vannes."

When Dorothy had prepared the lotion for which Stephen Gamage had given her the recipe, she lingered looking out into the moonlight of the first of May. Her desires and hopes were satisfied, when downward from the town on his way home came Owen Giles of Flanders.

He saw the beauty, and gaily doffed his hat, and waved his hand in passing.

Before retiring to rest that night, Dorothy carefully took the piece of charred wood she had secured from the Beltane fire, and placed it ·in a soft white kerchief which was duly concealed under her pillow. That night, each girl of the merry May-dew seekers did the same, with the exception of the kerchief, which the other maidens regarded as detrimental to the spell.

Dorothy fell asleep long before the May moon reached the zenith, and, in her dreams, she found herself in a pleasant park where deer abounded, and elms and chestnuts made pleasant shade. Yet, in all her wanderings, her one trouble was, that Owen Giles came not. She waited for him where the leaves of the chestnut-trees fluttering cast lightly-flecked shadows upon the whispering and quaking grasses, and she lingered until twilight came, but without avail. Then the dream scene changed, and Dorothy was on a lonely heath, far from any human habitation, and there she was met by Stephen Gamage, the man of second sight.

When Dorothy awoke she fairly sobbed, because Stephen Gamage, instead of Owen Giles, was the man of her dreams.

The morning of the second of May was an eventful one for the occupants of Pip.

Three of the cows refused to yield milk; the cream could not be churned, and all the contents of the dairy utensils had turned quite sour!

Dorothy herself, somewhat soured in temper, because of the unpleasant dream, and the man of second sight appearing therein, readily with others declared that Rachel Flemynge had bewitched the household.

Flush.

At sunrise on the second of May, Marjorie Adam awoke after the most pleasant dream she could possibly wish to have, simply because the hero was Owen Giles.

Marjorie went about her work with right good-will after breakfast. She sorted the linen, scattering between the folds thereof sprigs of fragrant lavender, then she set the huge chest in order, and afterwards, singing merrily, went to the kitchen to help her mother in matters of housewifery.

On reaching the domestic department Marjorie observed that the maids were silent, and the mistress looked as though something had fretted her.

"What is the matter?" asked Marjorie, ceasing her song. "Has the bell of St. Iltutus been stolen, or has it rained black rain?"

"Neither," said her mother fretfully. "But all the milk in the dairy has turned sour, and the cream refuses to churn. What we shall do, *I* don't know."

Marjorie did not wholly doubt her mother, and yet she could not quite believe that matters were so much awry. But when she saw for herself that the milk was curdled, and the cream refused to be churned, she exclaimed,

"This is Rachel Flemynge's work." In which supposition the inmates of Flush agreed.

FLANDERS.

Madam Giles, standing in the sloping garden, looked down through the closely clipped archway of arbutus and sweet-scented bay, and called her son to her side.

"What means all this commotion down at Pip and Flush?" she asked. "Our neighbours yonder are running hither and thither like people bewitched."

"And so in truth, they are," replied Owen, who related the experiences of the respective households.

"The milk in our dairy is not curdled," said Madam Giles, "and the churning was accomplished before breakfast."

"Do you know why?" asked Owen.

"Nay," replied his mother.

"Nicholas our ploughman, remembering the tricks of witches about the 1st of May, set small twigs of mountain-ash here and there around our premises. He says, as we all know, that the smallest twig of mountain-ash crossing the path of a witch will stop her career, no matter how wild she may be going."

Even as Owen Giles spoke, Rachel Flemynge,

2 C

curtseying, opened the gate, and ascended the pathway.

"What hast thou been doing?" asked Madam Giles sternly.

"Nothing, madam, nothing," replied Rachel, trembling and wincing under the old lady's glances.

"Dost thou call it 'nothing' to curdle the milk in the dairies of thy neighbours and betters, and to prevent the cream being churned?"

"It is not my work, madam," said Rachel, nervously clasping her hands. "Is the milk in Flanders curdled, and doth the cream refuse to churn?"

"Nay," replied Madam Giles, "and in good sooth there is a cause for the exemption. Nicholas our ploughman used his arts magic against the witch."

Owen smiled, and turned gaily away on his heel.

Rachel Flemynge looked very grave.

"Thou know'st thou'rt guilty," said madam, looking piercingly into Rachel's eyes when the women were alone.

"I speak truly, Madam Giles," said Rachel, "when I say that I did not, and know not how to curdle milk, or to prevent any one churning."

Madam Giles was angry, and expressed it by striking the path with her gold-headed stick.

For years the lady of Flanders had tried to induce Rachel Flemynge to confess to her knowledge of witchcraft, but had always failed.

"Why then doth the reputation of witchcraft cling to thee, and not to me?" asked madam, in a penetrating tone.

"Madam Giles," said Rachel seriously, "I know no more of witchcraft than of any other art or craft. As to the bad reputation clinging to me, it came in this wise. Many years ago I foretold the manner of death of one of the Flemynges of Flemyngstone. I was then a maid in Flemyngstone Court, and I practised the art of fortune telling and palmistry for simple amusement. Somehow or other I got into the habit of foretelling coming events. In a later generation they will call that foresight, and the power of judging from causes of the present the results of the future. Fate hath gifted me thus, and can I help it?"

Madam Giles, after pondering awhile, said, "It may be that thou art gifted with a strange art, but there is no need to exercise an evil gift. Why dost thou do so?"

"I seldom do," replied Rachel. Then, lowering her voice, she added, "I augment my poor pittance by telling fortunes for silly maidens; by selling charms, and reading the lines of the hand, but I do no harm."

"No harm, indeed!" reiterated madam. "I call it vast harm to delude maidens and make them believe all sorts and conditions of nonsense. Why not give up thy evil work?"

"Because I would starve. It is hard even now for a poor lone widow to get in these bad times a bare crust. What with losses by the great civil wars, and the fines to be paid, the county gentlefolks have little to give, and what is more, most of them have discharged many servants, and do with less workpeople than formerly. I used to get three, or even six days work a-week, when first I was widowed, but latterly I only got one or two out of the seven days, and of late I have not got one single hour, let alone a day."

"I know the times are bad, but they do not make a legitimate excuse for evil practices," said Madam Giles, adding, "Thou dost know the end of the sinner?"

"As described by other sinners," replied Rachel quickly and sharply.

"Dost add irreverence to thy other heinous offences?" exclaimed madam sternly.

"Nay, madam, nay," said Rachel. "But time and fate, and human kind, have embittered my soul, so that generally the little life that is left in me is like wormwood and gall."

"In the depths of my heart, I pity thee, Rachel Flemynge, but bad as thou art, even now it is not too late for repentance. They would receive thee into Galilee, if I favourably mentioned thy name," said Madam Giles.

"Into Galilee!" exclaimed Rachel. "There will I never submit to go. Why, madam, if I went there, I would at once openly confess and proclaim myself to be a wicked woman, and a witch also! Galilee will never see me!"

"Then thou must remain past redemption," said madam gravely.

"Ay! Perhaps so," responded Rachel.

The term Galilee was applied to that part of the parish church which was set at the service of the excommunicated. There, clothed in sackcloth and ashes, the offender was allowed to stand and hear the services, and afterwards pray for absolution, but, to gain complete forgiveness, he was obliged to humiliate himself on three different occasions. Then, as a rule, in Lent he was shriven, and duly received by the priest, after which he was reinstated among the worshippers in the church.

The Galilee of Llantwit Major parish church is, even in the present day, in a fair state of preservation, although time has rendered it roofless.

"Dost thou clearly understand what I say?" asked Madam Giles.

"That I do," replied Rachel. "Thou say'st

I must remain past redemption unless I consent to enter Galilee, and that I will never do. Why should I, madam?"

"To rid thy name of the stain and taint of witchcraft," replied Madam Giles.

"Could the priest, or any mortal, rid me of either?" asked Rachel.

"The priest, as agent of the Most High, could do so, and the world would thus believe thee to be absolved. Otherwise thou must remain content to bear the opprobrious cognomen of witch," said Madam Giles.

"So be it," said Rachel. "I had rather falsely bear the reputation of being a witch, than enter into Galilee. But I am detaining madam. The morning passes, and I must be gone."

Then, curtseying deeply, Rachel turned to depart.

"Stay," said madam in a kindly voice, "go around to the kitchen. Bad as thou art, thou shalt have a basketful of scraps at least."

Rachel did as she was bidden, and Madam Giles filled the basket with contents better and more than mere scraps, after which the old woman thankfully went her way.

Going homeward through the fields behind Flanders, Rachel encountered several maidens, who, doubtless knowing the old woman had been to see Madam Giles, had waited her coming.

"Here, Rachel," said one of the sauciest maidens, "I thought if we each obtained a piece of charred wood from the embers of the Beltane fire, and placed it under our pillows, the husband to be would appear in a vision or dream of the night."

"It comes to pass thus sometimes," said Rachel. "I don't always place faith in that act. What did'st thou see in thy dream?"

"Oh!" exclaimed the merry maiden, "I saw a horrid little old man with hair quite white, and he leaned upon a staff and leered at me most provokingly. Besides which he had a great bag full—of bones, I expect. From that I suppose I am to marry a beggar or a sexton."

"Nay," replied Rachel. "Let me see thy hand."

The girl laughingly revealed her left palm.

"Thou'lt marry a man many years older than thee. And he will be exceedingly rich. He was the man of thy dream," said Rachel.

"Oh! oh!" shouted the other girls, laughing heartily. "A rich old man! Fie for shame! Thou'rt a money hunter!"

"What did'st thou dream?" asked Rachel, addressing Dorothy Vanne.

"Nothing particular," said the proud beauty, with a toss of her head.

"Not of Owen Giles?" queried one of the girls saucily.

"The man of Flanders is nothing whatever to me," said Dorothy.

"Since when?" asked one.

"What a change!" remarked another.

"No change at all," said Dorothy. "I don't care a rap for Owen Giles!" But, although she sharply snapped her fingers, burning blushes fleeted over her cheeks, and her dark eyes sparkled wonderfully.

"What did'st thou dream?" asked Rachel. "*I* have a right to know."

"Well, there's no harm telling, since 'tis certain I shall never marry the man of my dream. I saw Stephen Gamage."

"Stephen Gamage!" exclaimed one of the girls.

"The man of second sight!" said another.

"That was not a bad omen," remarked Rachel. "It is good to dream of a man gifted with second sight. It means a romantic courtship, and possibly a strange and lofty marriage."

"There now," said one of the girls. "Perhaps thou shalt marry a fine lord and be a grand lady —far grander than to be mistress of Flanders."

"It may be so," said Dorothy. "Perhaps I shall have grandeur without happiness."

There was a slightly sneerful tone in her voice, and the maidens believed she could only gain happiness with Owen Giles.

"Thou art very quiet," remarked Rachel to Marjorie Adam. "What was thy dream?"

Marjorie hesitated.

She did not like to relate her dream because of Dorothy Vanne.

Seeing her reluctant to tell, the girls beseeched her.

"Thou must let us know," they cried. "We all have promised, and will not let thee be an exception."

Blushing deeply, even to the roots of her hair, Marjorie Adam said, "The man of my dream was——"

"Speak out," interrupted the girls, almost in one voice.

"Owen Giles," said Marjorie; then she hid her face in her hands.

"Tall and stately Owen Giles of Flanders," said Rachel slowly.

"Owen Giles will never marry again while his mother lives," exclaimed Dorothy Vanne, with a toss of her head, "and Madam Giles is only sixty this year. So anybody who waits for him will wait till their hair turns grey."

Then she tripped gaily homewards through the fields.

"She's jealous," said the girls to Marjorie, who, in reply, remarked, "That is why I liked not to tell, but all urged me."

"Ay," said Rachel, "a promise is a promise, and all agreed to abide by it."   .

Rachel Flemynge, after bidding her auditors a pleasant "good morning," proceeded to the gate-house, and the maidens fluttered like white doves towards the sea, singing as they went one of the songs of the period.   In sweet and perfect unison the maidens sang—

"The fairest hopes fulfilment find
          In May! in May'
All clouds and gloom are left behind
          In May! in May!
The hours are bright, the days are long,
And gladness comes with love and song
          In May! in May'

O maidens all, 'tis sweet to live
          In May! in May!
For love its rarest tokens give
          In May! in May'
And life is like a blissful dream,
When song-birds sing and sunbeams gleam
          In May! in May!

In all the years that are in store,
          Our fairest May
Will live in memory evermore!
And when the flowers and white thorns bloom,
In dreams will come, through care and gloom,
The voice that thrill'd, the words that brought
Love's magic spell to us unsought,
          In May! in May!"

The Monastery Gate-House.

If Rachel Flemynge hoped to be alone on the eve of All Saints she was disappointed.

Several visitors came to see her, and the herb concoctions with which she had busied herself during the afternoon were set aside for " customers."

A dense and dripping fog came ghostlike through the long meadows and ascended the hills. With its filmy warp and woof it encircled the fifth century university town, and totally obliterated the distance.

In the fog, the ancient monastery gate-house looked like a sentinel guarding the mysteries of the past. There, hoary with age, that last remnant of the thirteenth-century monastic buildings stood in the seventeenth century, and there it still stands in the present day. It is now in a condition of semi-decadence, uninhabited, but still fairly preserved with its outside stairway, and porch now covered with ivy. Down below the hill on which the gate-house stands is the church dedicated to St. Iltutus. In the churchyard are the celebrated crosses, some of which are supposed to have been erected so early as the fifth century.

Beyond the church, and in the centre of

the town, stands the hall of justice, with its gilded weathercock and ancient bell bearing the motto—

"Ora pro nobis sancte Iltute."

Beside the Town Hall, quaint and antique Tudor-built houses appear with their curious doorways and windows, and even in the present day numerous traces of its former importance are to be found in the fifth century university town of Llantwit Major, where, in the winter nights, the curfew bell has been rung from the days of the Norman Conqueror until the present year of grace.

Just as the curfew proclaimed the hour of eight, in the year 1668, Stephen Gamage passed through the churchyard and ascended the steep and rugged roadway leading to the gate-house.

When he rapped at the door, Rachel Flemynge immediately responded.

"Hast thou had any callers this evening?" asked Stephen Gamage, taking the fireside corner of one of the worm-eaten oaken settles.

"A few, but not so many as last year," replied Rachel. "The fog is bad, times are poor, and money is scarce."

Then they talked the general town gossip, in the midst of which somebody knocked at the door.

"Come in," said Rachel without moving, and Owen Giles entered.

" Good night to you," said Owen.

Rachel and Stephen simultaneously returned the greeting.

"I have come up to question thee," said Owen, addressing Rachel.

" What about ?" she asked.

"The horses in the stables refuse to move ; the cattle have not touched or tasted food for forty-eight hours, and one of the farm-boys has slept for twenty-four hours without waking," said Owen.

" And that is brought home to my doors, I suppose," said Rachel bitterly. "It is of course my fault. Dost thou believe so ?"

"I do not," said Owen. " But strange things have occurred of late, and there appears to be no explanation, even if thou can'st supply remedies. My mother begs thee to come home with me at once."

" On the supposition that only a witch can heal the effects of witchcraft," said Stephen mirthfully.

Rachel readily accompanied Owen Giles to Flanders, although the fog was dense, and the November night air was raw and chill.

Madam Giles waited for them in the kitchen.

" What hast thee been doing ?" she asked of Rachel.

"I have done naught," replied Rachel.

"In May last I spoke seriously to thee, but all to no purpose," said madam severely, "and now the twigs of the mountain-ash have failed to prove preventatives against thy witchcraft. Go now and treat the victims of thy art."

Rachel obeyed, and before she quitted Flanders the horses moved, the cattle began to eat, and the farm-boy, at the old woman's touch, quickly awoke.

Owen Giles accompanied Rachel home, and paused a moment at the door of the gate-house.

"Come in with me," said Rachel.

"Not again," replied Owen.

"Hast thou ever tried thy luck, or had thy fate revealed?" asked Rachel.

"Nay," replied Owen.

"Come in, then, and have one or the other," said Rachel. "None but Stephen Gamage shall hear or know of it."

Owen, by no means reluctant, entered.

"This is one of the three spirit-nights," remarked Rachel, as she poked the fire.

"I know," replied Owen, slightly shivering.

Rachel, observing this, begged him to draw nearer the fire, then she proceeded to read the lines upon his hand.

"The line of fortune promises some fame, but not great riches," said Rachel. "Thy fate will be fortunate, but some trouble precedes success.

Thou wilt be lured by beauty, and sometimes by pleasure of short duration, but thou wilt be gifted with prudence and wisdom, and will be happy again in thy later affections."

"Shall I marry again?" asked Owen.

"The woman that is to be thy second wife must first be married to another man. When she is widowed, and thou art in thy prime, the marriage will take place," said Rachel.

"Better twice than never," remarked Stephen.

Owen laughed.

While Rachel entertained Owen Giles in the monastery gate-house, merry parties of youths and maidens in Pip and Flush were burning nuts upon the hearths, or trying to snatch apples floating in tubs of water, or using every art to bite the apple instead of the end of tallow suspended by a cord from the rafters. Some of the girls, more venturesome than the others, tried the knife and sheath spell. In the *History of Llangynwyd*, by Mr. T. C. Evans, better known in Wales as "Cadrawd," this curious and ancient spell is thus described :—" If the operator was a girl she was to place a knife, stuck on end, in the corner of the leek-bed in the garden, retaining the sheath in her hand, on a dark night, and after ten o'clock, in absolute secrecy, she was then to walk backwards around the bed, carrying the sheath in her right hand. She was on no account to look behind her, and was to be very careful not to stumble. If her destiny was to be matrimony, her lover's shade would appear, take out the knife from the earth, and place it in the sheath. It is said that a young girl, on one occasion, in performing this trick, was beset by two shades at once. The consequence was that she became the victim of the wicked wiles of one of them, and eventually the wife of the other."

All the arts and practices recommended by Rachel, the witch, or by Stephen, the man of second sight, were tried to the utmost, and towards midnight, a crowd of boys went to peep through the keyhole of the church door to see the spiritual forms of those who were to depart this life during the ensuing year.

Some maidens following the ancient custom, ate apples while dressing their hair, in the hope that their future husbands would come and look over their shoulders, and into their mirrors (if they had any) before which they stood.

More than one girl set her body linen on a chair before the fire, and seated herself in a quiet corner, where, seeing and yet not being seen, she might watch the lover that was to come and turn the garment.

But not one of the girls ventured to place a piece of charred wood from the Beltane fire under their pillows again, since the report had gone forth, that when, in the May time, they did so, some witchery and mischief were connected therewith, else how was it that the milk in the dairies curdled and the cream refused to churn?

All the parish revolted against the use of the charred wood, which had been destroyed by common consent and fire before the Town Hall.

Love philtres and charms were the order of that eve of All Saints, and "first foot of winter," and late hours, even in the best regulated houses, were the rule in the whole district.

.   .   .   .   .   .

Fourteen days later Rachel Flemynge was arrested for witchcraft.

The accuser was Madam Giles of Flanders, and the offence was that Rachel Flemynge had, in the presence of Edward Vanne of Pip, James Adam of Flush, Owen Giles of Flanders, and John Turberville, declared she could fly. What was more daring, in Madam Giles' opinion, the witch assured them she was able to fly without the aid of wings, which even the smallest bird would have found impossible.

It was a great day when "Rachel was put on her trial."

People came long distances to attend the trial, and men, women, youths, and maidens congregated around the Town Hall long before the hour appointed for the assembly of the court.

2 D

Sir Thomas Stradling, of St. Donats Castle, was to judge the case, and, accompanied by several local magnates, he took his seat.

Witnesses were called upon both sides, and Madam Giles appeared in person.

When all the evidence had been obtained, Sir Thomas Stradling called out, " Rachel Flemynge, stand forth," and the reputed witch promptly obeyed.

"Thou hast declared to these witnesses that thou canst fly, and they believe it is impossible for thee to do so. Now I ask thee, on thy oath, and before these thy neighbours—canst thou fly ? "

"I said so, sir," replied Rachel, curtseying low.

"Then do so as soon as thou dost like," said Sir Thomas Stradling. "There is no law against flying. I therefore dismiss the case with costs."

All present were surprised, but Madam Giles was angry, and went home in hot haste.

"I never could have believed it, never," she exclaimed to her son. "A Stradling leagued with a witch ! He may be a patron of witch-craft, or even a wizard himself."

"Mother !" exclaimed Owen Giles.

"Yes; I blush to think that my countryman, Sir Thomas Stradling, Colonel of Infantry to King Charles the Second, should release a witch, who plays meg's diversions with all the parish, and confesses that she can fly, when anybody with sense knows such a statement to be preposterous," said Madam Giles.

"Sir Thomas always discountenances the mischievous and often fatal practice of trying persons for the offence of witchcraft," remarked Owen.

"Rachel will come to a bad end, mark my words!" exclaimed Madam Giles.

"Never fear," said Owen. "Rachel can mind herself, I'll warrant."

1678

Ten years had flown since the memorable May time, when the maidens of Pip and Flush had "tried their fortune" by means of the charred wood from the Beltane fire. Two years after Rachel's trial, Marjorie Adam left Wales as the wife of Captain Meredith, an English officer in King Charles the Second's Guards. Soon afterwards, Dorothy Vanne was married to one of the Stradlings, and went to the Devonshire estate of Coombe Hawey.

Captain Meredith died in 1676, and Marjorie returned to live with her parents. She had but one child, a daughter, who soon found her way to Flanders, where she was petted and spoiled by stately Owen Giles.

It was the eve of May 1678.

As of old, those who were accustomed to kindle the Beal or Beltane fire, went to the Castle Ditches. There the people as usual congregated, and sang and danced as in the days gone by.

In the twilight of that day Marjorie Meredith thought of her May dream ten years before. Her marriage, entered upon to please her parents, had been loveless. Still in her mind, and always in her reverie of the past, stately Owen Giles took the place of honour.

Musing in this manner, just where the grey wavelets of the Severn Sea came rippling over the yellow sands, Marjorie Meredith was not aware of the approach of a second or third person. One was Owen Giles, the other was Dorothy Meredith.

The merry laughter of her little daughter disturbed Marjorie in her reverie, and she got up from the rock on which she was seated to greet Owen Giles.

Looking up, she was almost awed by his stately stature, but she readily entered into conversation with him, and they soon wended their way homeward.

As they went along the meadows, just as of old, a group of merry maidens came singing the customary song of May, which, with others, she sang in the long ago. The song thrilled her heart, and every word seemed to sink into her soul. She thought of her "fairest" May, and only wished that her hopes could find fulfilment in the month of blossoms, or, for the matter of that, any other time, provided it would be soon —yes soon, very soon.

Owen Giles, observing that Marjorie was in a thoughtful mood, talked with Dorothy, and paused now and again to reach branches thick with May-blossoms for the child.

That night, when the people who took part in the Beltane festivities reached the highest point of excitement, and the dancers, hand in hand, went almost madly around the fire, Rachel Flemynge darted through the crowd as of old, and with her staff stirred the driftwood.

In a harsh croaking voice she sang—

"Through good and evil, through weal and woe,
    From life to death we all must go."

Then seizing a burning brand she held it aloft, and swayed it to and fro in the sight of the frightened multitude.

Mothers and maidens screamed with terror; men and youths looked amazed at the witch, who appeared to have taken leave of her senses.

While the vast crowd stood speechless and spellbound, Richard Flemynge excitedly pushed his way towards Rachel, and endeavoured to take the brand from his sister's hand.

With almost supernatural strength Rachel, still brandishing the faggot, fiercely thrust her brother from her side. What happened next everybody witnessed, but not a person could tell how the disaster came about.

As the terror-stricken people gazed speechlessly at the witch, Richard Flemynge was seen to sway to and fro like one drunken; then he staggered face forward into the midst of the Beltane fire, and there was no help for him!

Human hands failed to save him, and the crowd turned helplessly away from the sickening sight of flames fed by mortal agony.

In the commotion and subsequent astonishment Rachel Flemynge disappeared.

"She did the deed!" cried one in the crowd. "The witch thrust her brother into the Beltane fire."

"Stay!" shouted Stephen Gamage. "I foretold his death."

"Ay! ay!" responded several men, as in one breath; "we remember."

"What didst thou say?" demanded the others simultaneously.

"That he would die a death which he and his people deemed the least likely. I meant he would be accidentally burnt alive," said Stephen.

The crowd fairly groaned.

Then those who were malignant towards Rachel grew excited, and the spokesman of the party shouted, "She did it! The witch is guilty! She thrust her brother into the fire, and she shall suffer for it! An eye for an eye—a tooth for a tooth!"

With that, the infuriated multitude, whom no human force or persuasion could stay, rushed downwards from the Castle Ditches and hastened to the monastery gate-house, hoping to find and secure Rachel, but she was not there.

Scared by the terrible fate of her brother, and knowing that her enemies would accuse her of murder, Rachel escaped the town, but ultimately, lack of funds, and, most of all, exposure, hindered her progress, so that one day she was discovered in the woodlands around Llantrythid and brought home to Llantwit and to justice.

All the old schemes against her for witchcraft were set aside, in the new and more feasible charge against her. She was tried and found guilty of "a most unnatural and inhuman form of murder, fratricidal," and the reputed witch was sentenced to be "burned alive."

Accordingly a stake was erected near the ancient town cross, and thereto Rachel was led for execution.

On one side of her stood Edward Vanne of Pip, on the other was James Adam of Flush, both of whom were among the jurors.

Sir Thomas Stradling purposely absented himself from both the trial and the execution, and his place, as judge, was filled by Richard Basset of Beaupré.

"May I speak?" asked Rachel calmly when she approached the stake.

"Thou may'st," said the judge compassionately, as he silenced the mob that hissed and yelled unmercifully.

Rachel Flemynge folded her hands and looked prayerfully to the sky. Her poor pale face was painfully attenuated, her once bright eyes were tear-dimmed and deeply sunken in their sockets, her thin and wasted body was shattered by imprisonment and lack of nutriment, and her parched lips quivered with heart agony and strong emotion.

Clearly, and in distinct tones, Rachel Flemynge addressed the multitude—

"In the sight of heaven, and in hearing of my fellow-mortals, I solemnly declare that I am innocent of the crime with which I have been charged and proclaimed guilty. But I would say one word to those among whom I have lived a long life-time—'*Let him who is without sin cast the first stone*'"

She paused, and the multitude hissed and hooted amid cries of "Away with her !"— "Despatch the Witch !".—"Burning is too good for her !"

"Silence !" sternly commanded the judge, adding, "Let the woman have opportunity of speech for the last time." Then he directed Rachel to continue.

"I go," she said, "the last of the Flemynges, to the regions of the Unknown ; but before I depart, I prophesy that the last of the Vannes, and the last of the Adams, stand beside me. Their names shall die in the dust, and their gravestones shall be pavement for men's feet. I go — the innocent, the persecuted — to my martyrdom, not as a saint, but as a mortal condemned by sinners, and as a woman to whom fate hath been cruelly harsh. Farewell ! I forgive you all ! Now *' let him who is without sin cast the first stone.'* "

Vanne of Pip and Adam of Flush drew back a pace.

The men around the stake quailed. The crowd remained silent.

"Before I go hence, I would fain have a sip of water," said Rachel humbly.

For a moment there was no response, but while Rachel looked sadly yet eagerly around, Owen Giles pressed through the crowd, and with his own hand gave the poor woman a cup of cold water. It was little to give, but given freely and in deepest sympathy.

"A dying woman's blessings on thee and thine for ever," said Rachel, when her fevered thirst was slaked. "The name of Giles shall survive through long centuries when other names have passed away."

In the brief silence that followed, the men around the stake were busily engaged in disentangling the ropes that were to bind the victim for the burning.

Once more Rachel Flemynge lifted up her voice, and as the scalding tears fell like rain upon her pallid cheeks, she cried aloud, "*Let him who is without sin cast the first stone!*"

Then, trembling with emotion, and staggering backward, Rachel fell into the outstretched arms of stately Owen Giles.

"She is dead!" cried Owen Giles, in a hoarse but subdued tone, as he directed one of the bystanders to stretch his mantle upon the road beside the cross, and they laid Rachel Flemynge's body thereon.

No need now of ropes wherewith to bind the poor frail remnant of mortality ; no need now of tow, and hemp, and tarred faggots, for the burning; no need now of tinder and spark, or flame of fire.

Death in sinless sympathy had " *cast the first stone !* "

.   .   .   .   .   .

Quaint and quiet, in the midst of their old-time gardens, Pip, Flush, and Flanders still stand, but the Vannes and the Adams are gone, and their gravestones have become " pavements for men's feet."

But the name of the seventeenth century owner of Flanders, by the union of Owen Giles, widower, with Marjorie Meredith, widow, descended through long generations, and still survives in the surrounding country, although it has become extinct in Llantwit Major, formerly known as Old Llaniltyd Vawr, or the " Sacred Place of Iltyd the Great."

INDEX

Printed by BALLANTYNE, HANSON & CO., *Edinburgh and London*

Lightning Source UK Ltd.
Milton Keynes UK
173605UK00005B/41/P